Basic Trial Advocacy

Basic Trial Advocacy

Peter L. Murray

Robert Braucher Visiting Professor of Law from Practice
Edward L. Johnston Lecturer of Law
Harvard Law School

Tower Publishing
Original Copyright © 1995
Formerly published by Aspen Law & Business and by Little Brown & Company
Reprinted in 2003 by Maine Law Book Company
Reprinted in 2010 by Tower Publishing

This publication is designed to provide accurate and authoritative information in regard to the subject matter covered. It is sold with the understanding that the author/publisher is not engaged in rendering legal services. If legal advice or other expert assistance is required, the services of a competent professional should be sought.

Library of Congress Catalog Card No. 94-79042

ISBN (current 2010): 978-1-932056-96-9
(previous ISBN# 0-9747944-0-6 or 0-978-0-974794-40-2)

6 7 8 9 0

CCP
Published by Tower Publishing
588 Saco Rd, Standish, ME 04084
1-800-969-8693
www.TowerPub.com

Printed in the United States of America.

Summary of Contents

Contents

Preface

It used to be said that trial lawyers are born, not made. According to the traditional wisdom, the ability to make successful trial presentations is the result of natural talent rather than of any sort of educational process. You either have it or you don't.

In recent years the work of the National Institute of Trial Advocacy (NITA) and of trial advocacy teachers in law schools, law firms, and continuing legal education programs has demonstrated that trial advocacy can be taught. Trial lawyers can be made as well as born.

In any class or program in which trial advocacy is taught, some of the students seem to possess a natural aptitude that enables them to acquire trial skills with little apparent effort. Teaching these students is a heady and sometimes awe-inspiring experience. However, one can get the feeling that these students would become great trial lawyers even without deliberate instruction.

The real rewards in trial advocacy teaching come from those students who do not exhibit great natural talent, at least at the start. The discovery of the last twenty years is that, with sound training and some real-life practice, many such students can become competent, confident trial advocates. The trial advocacy teacher's most touching moments come not when a "natural" stars in a mock trial. The best times are when a person who is not apparently blessed with great natural ability uses the tools of the trial lawyer to put on a really sound case in court. Effective teaching and learning make such development possible.

This book is the result of over fifteen years of active teaching of trial advocacy, largely at Harvard Law School, but also at the University of Maine School of Law and in various NITA, law firm, and pro bono educational programs for both law students and young lawyers. This book reflects the author's conviction that understanding why trial lawyers do what they do will vastly increase the ability of the student to learn. It is not enough to learn by doing and watching what others do. The best education comes when the student acquires some understanding of "why."

Although trial advocacy literature has focused increasingly on the why's of trial techniques, our understanding of the multifaceted process of case presentation has been in almost constant expansion over the past twenty years. This book records the author's version of the present state of the art. We can be confident that as further attention is focused on in-court case presentation, our understanding of the art and science of the work of trial lawyers will continue to expand.

This text is designed for use in law school trial advocacy or trial practice courses. It is also written to be useful to inexperienced lawyers in connection with firm-sponsored or independent trial advocacy training. The order of the chapters more or less follows the author's model of topical development within a trial practice program. It is not intended to be prescriptive, however. The chapters will stand on their own if assigned in a different order.

Many trial advocacy teachers and seasoned practitioners will find pertinent topics that are missing from this text. Some subjects, such as jury selection and pretrial discovery, have been omitted in the interest of focusing on the presentation process during the trial itself. In many cases the coverage of different trial functions is limited. The effort has been to focus on the very basics and try to impart a good understanding at an elementary level.

The author hopes that this text will increase the slope of the learning curve and help bring competence and confidence in real-life experience. Systematic understanding of the trial advocacy process will enable the new lawyer better to apply the experience and observations that are available to develop the skills of trial practice. Finally, understanding more of how the process works helps develop ways in which it can be improved for the benefit of all.

Peter L. Murray

October 1994

Acknowledgments

The experience and wisdom of many judges, lawyers, and teachers of trial advocacy underlie what has been set forth in this volume. In earlier days the young trial lawyers' only source of learning other than their own haphazard experience was the practical teaching of mentors in the law who took the time and trouble to pass on their wisdom and the results of their experience. As this book goes to press, the author wishes to acknowledge with gratitude the learning and understanding generously imparted by such legal mentors as the late U.S. District Judge Edward T. Gignoux, the late Chief Justice Robert B. Williamson, retired Chief Justice Vincent L. McKusick, Ralph I. Lancaster, Esq., and the late Professor Richard H. Field.

The author is also grateful for the example and encouragement of U.S. District Judge (then Professor) Robert E. Keeton as an early leader in effective law school teaching of trial advocacy. Over the years, the author's understanding of trial advocacy and the content of this book have benefited greatly from fellow trial advocacy teachers such as U.S. District Judge William J. Young, Maurice Nessen, Rudolph Pierce, Professor Charles Nesson, and retired U.S. District Judge David Nelson. Current colleagues who have encouraged and commented helpfully on this work include Professor Charles Ogletree, Judge Steven Plotkin, Professors Judy Potter and Michael Mullane, and many of the regular and adjunct teachers in the Harvard Trial Advocacy Workshop, where earlier versions of this book were used prior to publication. The author wishes particularly to thank Judges Donald Alexander, Maine Superior Court, and Robert Morrill, New Hampshire Superior Court, for their careful reading and detailed comments on the last version of the manuscript.

The author appreciates the enthusiastic and thoughtful collaboration in concept and planning from Little, Brown editors Carol

McGeehan, Elizabeth Kenny, and Carolyn O'Sullivan, and the tactful, competent, and thorough text editing of manuscript editor Barbara Rappaport, all of which have contributed to a better book. Special thanks go to Colleen Fournier, the author's supremely capable secretary and assistant, for conscientious preparation of drafts and manuscripts and cheerful performance of many other tasks in generating this volume. Without the encouragement, support, and forbearance of the author's wife, Deborah Murray, and his family, this book could never have been written.

Basic Trial Advocacy

1 The Training of Trial Lawyers

A. How Trial Lawyers Were Trained in the Old Days

Traditionally, which means until about twenty years ago, trial lawyers received virtually no formal training, either in law school or afterward, in how to try a case in court. The typical law school curriculum offered at most a laid-back once-a-week seminar-type experience in which a local practitioner would discuss assorted topics of trial tactics or strategy from a largely anecdotal standpoint. These courses were of minimal value in imparting to law students either the theory or the skills of preparing and presenting cases at trial.

In those bygone days lawyers were expected to develop the necessary skills and knowledge through the time-honored sink-or-swim method following actual entry into law practice.

"So you want to be a trial lawyer. Here's your start." The senior partner would hand the tyro a stack of grubby files, the "dogs" of the office. These assorted small cases were considered grist for the mill of training the young trial advocate. The notion was that the new lawyer would take on the fender-benders, the drunk driving cases, the evictions, and similar relatively minor litigation matters. He (there were few female trial lawyers in those days) would work on them for countless hours in order to gain experience and "get into court." Typically, little or no supervision was provided. The young lawyer was supposed to learn by doing. If he got into a jam, presumably he could ask advice from a senior partner or more experienced lawyer.

Timorous and terrified, the lawyer in training would take his cases to court. The court might be the police court, the district court, or even the state court in which jury trials were held. Watching older lawyers, listening to courthouse rumor, gossip and lore, and trial and error made up the learning process. The skills of the trial advocate were picked up largely by osmosis. Habits and techniques were assimilated without the lawyer knowing why they were effective or in what kind of situations they should be applied.

Slowly, ever so slowly, the survivors of this baptism of fire would get the hang of it. Slowly, painfully, self-confidence would be developed. Over a considerable period of time and after a large number of outings, with failures as well as successes, this kind of purely experiential training process would produce a trial lawyer. And so it went for countless past generations of practitioners.

There were many casualties. Sometimes the buffettings to self-confidence would be so severe that the young lawyer would sink rather than swim. After a few disastrous experiences, some would-be trial advocates found that other areas of the law were more to their liking and apparent aptitude.

Traditional sink-or-swim training gave most trial lawyers very little understanding of the "whys" of their craft. The ability to try cases was often attributed to inherent talent rather than a process of learning. The techniques of trial lawyering were usually described by time-worn (and sometimes shop-worn) adages and proverbs passed on from generation to generation of seasoned practitioners. Writings on trial advocacy tended to be anecdotal, focusing on the exploits of great practitioners rather than providing an actual analysis of why their techniques worked.

Prior generations of trial lawyers trained by the sink-or-swim method swear by its efficacy in much the same way as medical doctors proclaim the virtue of seventy-two-hour stints "on the floor" during their internships. Regardless of the value of this kind of purgatorial training in medicine, it is a poor way to train trial lawyers. Uninformed and unguided experience is a very slow and inefficient way to gain an understanding of any aspect of a lawyer's work. We do not train engineers to build highway bridges by sending them out to build footbridges on their own. In-court experience remains a vital component in the seasoning and development of trial lawyers. But it is no longer the exclusive method by which they learn the basic skills and theoretical underpinnings of their profession.

B.   How We Train Trial Lawyers Now

The sink-or-swim method is no longer the way trial lawyers learn their craft. Present-day law practice no longer provides many "dog" cases where the client's legal interests can be safely entrusted to the fumbling of a neophyte. The number of available trial exposures per lawyer has dramatically decreased with the mushrooming of the size of the bar. Inexperienced young lawyers are paid far too much to permit them to fritter away their billable and nonbillable time in trying to figure out the basics of trial practice by experimenting on small cases. Most important, other more efficient and effective methods for training trial lawyers have become available.

Systematic simulated trial advocacy training began in earnest with the work of the National Institute of Trial Advocacy (NITA). Beginning in the early 1970s, NITA developed and conducted intensive one- to three-weeks-long "institutes" during which young lawyers performed simulated witness examinations, openings, and closings subject to on-the-spot and video critiquing by experienced practitioners and judges. The intense observation and feedback alone produced dramatically improved results. It suddenly became evident that trial advocacy could be taught as well as learned. The NITA phenomenon swept the country. Soon intensive NITA-type training programs became established in many law schools, in bar association CLE programs, in large law offices, in government agencies, and in an ongoing series of national and regional institutes conducted by NITA itself.

Further developments have occurred. Gradually, trial practice teachers are advancing from simple prescription of recognized trial advocacy techniques to more systematic analysis of the trial process itself and the underlying reasons why particular techniques are effective or ineffective. The state of the art in simulated trial advocacy training now combines both practical and theoretical or systematic elements.

The practical approach usually consists of simulated trial exercises performed by the students and critiqued by instructors. Often the instructors are successful trial lawyers who have been trained to provide meaningful and helpful on-the-spot critique. This practical training is informed by an explanation of the reasons and systematic functions for the techniques which are being taught.

On the one hand, there is no substitute for actually "doing" trial advocacy, especially when the performances are thoughtfully and systematically critiqued. On the other hand, an understanding of the why's of advocacy enables the student to generalize the training received to apply to a variety of situations. The slope of the learning curve is increased.

At one time it was asserted by a leading authority that a trial lawyer could not learn how to perform effective cross-examination without personally conducting at least twenty-five jury trials. "How am I ever going to get twenty-five jury trials in this day and age?" became the plaintive cry of the trial-lawyer trainee. Now it is clear that effective trial advocacy training can bring proficiency with a lower number of actual hands-on experiences. Experience is more useful to the lawyer in training if it is informed by some understanding of what is really going on, what should work, and why.

Trial advocacy texts have followed the development of trial advocacy teaching. Early classics such as Francis Wellman's, *The Art of Cross Examination*[1] were rich in anecdotes about trial successes of the authors and other famous lawyers of the day. However, they provided little real understanding of why the techniques recommended by the masters are or are not effective.

In more recent years this approach has been supplemented by efforts to articulate general rules, such as "Never ask a question on cross-examination if you don't know the answer." Often these prescriptions have been supported by largely anecdotal examples demonstrating the applicability of the rule in a colorful situation. Another approach has been to organize and present copious examples of transcripts of different kinds of examinations, sometimes accompanied by commentary on their overall effectiveness.

As we learn more about what we are teaching, more systematization is possible. Going beyond anecdotes and prescriptions, it is possible to describe the function of different techniques as elements of the trial process itself. Rather than simply saying that one should not ask a cross-examination question without knowing the answer, we can now explain the importance of control devices in witness presentation, what kind of devices are available, and how they can be used to control a less than cooperative witness.

[1] Macmillan (1903).

Similarly, in constructing and organizing curricula for trial advocacy training, it is now possible to develop the curriculum around a pedagogical theory or theme. We can elaborate a model of a trial as a competitive presentation of images of events, conditions, or circumstances from real life.

At the present state of the art, the best recipe for a successful trial advocacy training course combines simulated experiential training with systematic understanding of trial techniques and their function in the trial process.

C.   Where This Book Comes In

This text provides descriptions and explanations of the principal techniques by which trial lawyers make their presentations. It is the author's hope that using this book in connection with a program of simulated trial practice exercises will enable trial advocacy students better to generalize their experience and to understand the function of the techniques they are learning in the context of a systematic whole. The text identifies and recommends specific techniques and approaches, but its primary thrust is not intended to be prescriptive. The idea is to understand the function of the techniques and to attempt to assign a reason for what is done.

Of course, the state of knowledge in trial advocacy is imperfect at best. Trying a case is one of the most complex of intellectual functions. It involves psychology, communication, language, drama, artistry, and several kinds of legal and fact analysis. The hope, however, is that inquiry into the central elements of the trial process will provide greater understanding of how and why it works. Such understanding will help us to teach trial lawyering to future generations of practitioners and to reform the trial process to meet the needs of our evolving society.

Chapter 2 The Task of the
Trial Lawyer

What does a trial lawyer really do? What makes the trial lawyer's work different from that of lawyers who negotiate contracts, draft deeds, or advise clients on the law? Why is it something special to be called "a real trial lawyer"?

Most people's image of the trial lawyer is derived from television, detective fiction, and similar sources in the popular culture. Often the trial lawyer is cast in a heroic role as the defender of someone mistakenly, or even unjustly, accused of a crime. Courtroom scenes are usually moments of high drama. In the character of the trial lawyer there are elements of a detective, an actor, a strategist, and a gladiator. What a difficult and exciting line of work!

The popular image, of course, is a much exaggerated and romanticized version of the real thing. Neither literature nor drama gives much attention to the thousands of routine criminal and civil trials that take place every day in courtrooms across the country. Rarely does one find a TV show about a run-of-the-mill prosecution for breaking and entering or drunk driving. Popular literature does not focus on commercial trials or patent cases. Yet it is these more mundane cases that form the bulk of the work of the trial lawyer.

Now and then every trial lawyer gets a moment to shine. The ferreting out of deception by shrewd cross-examination is likely to be a dramatic moment in any trial. Most trial lawyers can cherish the memory of at least one case in which their efforts saved a client from injustice, if not worse. Adrenalin, the drug of habit of trial lawyers, can give its heady rush in many a contested situation.

While it may be exciting to think of the trial lawyer as detective, actor, strategist, and gladiator perhaps, for the purpose of learning the craft, less dramatic images will do. How about storyteller and teacher, planner and organizer, analyst of fact and law, and vigorous representative of the client's rights and interests? The complex science of trial advocacy involves some of all of these demanding functions, sometimes all at once.

A.   Legal Analysis and Fact Analysis

When one thinks of the analytical function of a lawyer, one usually starts with legal analysis, the practice of finding and applying an appropriate legal rule to fit a given fact situation. Counselling a client often requires the lawyer to determine what legal rule will be applied to a particular scenario so the client can be warned to prepare for the consequences of what she has done or is considering doing. Similarly, appellate advocacy involves the process of analyzing and applying legal rules to the facts determined in the court below. The appellate lawyer argues that, for reasons of policy, logic, consistency, and precedent, her proposed legal rule should be applied in the given fact situation in preference to the rule proposed by her opponent.

Much of pretrial motion practice is similarly involved with questions of law. The moving party places before the court, by affidavit or otherwise, a largely undisputed fact scenario. The issue then is to determine what rule of law should be applied. Considerations of consistency, logic, precedent, and policy are invoked in favor of the competing legal rules.

In every law school curriculum the students are taught the tools and techniques of legal analysis. The case method of instruction focuses on the study of appellate decisions and the analysis employed by appellate courts to choose rules of law to fit the fact pictures of the decisions under review. This process is typically carried forward in moot court exercises in which the law students themselves argue real or simulated appellate cases applying competing legal principles to a given body of facts. The process of legal analysis emphasizes logical, analytical thinking, often in the abstract, designed to appeal to our sense of order and predictability.

The function of the trial lawyer is quite different. Her task is to develop from the available unstructured information surrounding some event or condition that took place in real life the fact picture to which the legal rules will be applied. The trial lawyer then

recreates an image of that event or condition in the consciousnesses of the factfinders in the courtroom. That image becomes the
"what happened?" of the case.

B.   The Trial Lawyer as Storyteller

The trial lawyer's task can be analogized to the role of raconteur at
a social party or similar informal gathering. The storyteller enter-
tains his audience by recreating in the consciousnesses of the listeners an image of an event or episode from another time and place.
The image must be sufficiently clear, concise, and credible so the
audience gets the point without being bored in the process.

A successful storyteller conjures up a visual image by the use of
words and other media so essential features spring spontaneously
to life in the minds of the listeners. Success is a laugh or a murmur
of appreciation; failure is an awkward silence, incomprehension,
or the listeners' drifting away before the point is reached.

The tools of the raconteur are words, the voice used to communicate them, gestures, any available props, eye contact, and the force
of personality. The raconteur uses these tools to create the desired
image as colorfully and efficiently as possible.

The assignment of the trial lawyer is very similar: she strives to
create in the consciousness of the factfinder (whether judge or jury)
a clear and authoritative image of an event, episode, condition, or
situation that occurred at some other time and place. The scenario
must be communicated accurately enough so that the factfinder
will be able to understand and recognize all of the essential features of the fact picture. Where the factfinder is a member of a jury,
the image must be clear enough so that all of the jury members will
be able to agree on the important elements.

The portrayal must be performed efficiently so that it can be done
within the available time. Even the simplest and shortest of events
contains a myriad of potential details. Sometimes the interval available for in-court presentation is smaller than the time period over
which the events occurred in real life. The trial lawyer must rigorously select those details that are essential to the image to be presented and must find efficient ways by which to convey them.

The presentation must be authoritative so that the factfinder
will be able to rely on the scenario presented as the basis for an

important decision. This means that the material must come from sources that the factfinders will find reliable and that the picture presented must accord with the factfinders' own experience with the real world.

In comparison with the role of the storyteller, the task of the trial lawyer is considerably more demanding. The distinctive features of a particular scenario at trial may be much more subtle than the point of an entertaining story. Apparently small differences in fact image can require the application of vastly different rules of law.

For instance, the image of a person carefully driving an automobile down the street and accidentally hitting a pedestrian emerging from between two parked cars can be associated with a legal rule of nonliability for accidental harm. However, if the image is very slightly altered to depict the driver glancing away from the roadway to look at a dog on the sidewalk or some other distraction, the applicable legal rule may be wholly different; it may instead be a rule that negligently caused harm results in financial liability. The gross outlines of the two images might be the same, but a flickering of the driver's eyeball could be the difference in fact image over which the case would be fought.

A storyteller is seldom burdened by procedural rules other than human consideration and good taste in the handling of the media and the communication of the tale. The trial lawyer, however, has to create the desired fact image while contending with a complicated series of evidentiary and procedural rules designed to ensure fairness and reliability in the proceedings.

The raconteur typically controls the media directly. He picks the words, makes the gestures, and uses his own voice to add color and authority. The trial lawyer, on the other hand, must work by remote control. Most of the components of the trial lawyer's fact picture must be derived from and communicated by witnesses who are under examination. These witnesses have varying storytelling abilities and personalities, and each witness may be able to supply only a piece of the overall picture. The lawyer must organize, guide, and prompt the witnesses to develop the overall fact image in the form preselected by the lawyer to fit the desired legal rule.

It is rare that a storyteller has a spoiler who seeks to shout down, criticize, or compete with the presentation. The trial lawyer by definition is faced with an opponent, whose task is to impede the lawyer's presentation, to denigrate what the lawyer has done, and to promote a competing image differing in some legally crucial respect. For these reasons being an effective storyteller does not guarantee success as a trial lawyer . . . but it helps.

The focus of the trial lawyer's presentation is not on attacking her opponent. Trial advocacy is competitive presentation, not hand-to-hand combat. The persona of the trial lawyer is that of the impresario, oriented to the audience and intent on creating an impression on it.

C. The Trial Lawyer as Teacher

In a real and fundamental sense, a trial lawyer is a teacher: she is bringing information about the outside world into the consciousness of the factfinders, just as a teacher brings information into the consciousnesses of his students. The trial lawyer's job is to teach the facts.

Success comes to the trial lawyer when the factfinders understand the lesson being taught. Regardless of what a teacher does, or how he does it, in the final analysis it is the students' understanding that matters. Like the teacher, the lawyer must focus not on her own presentation, but on the image that is created in the understanding of the factfinders.

D. The Trial Lawyer as Persuader

Another image that is often associated with a trial lawyer at work is that of a salesperson. The lawyer must not only describe the facts and teach the fact picture but also persuade the jury that the picture she is presenting is the right and authentic one. The lawyer has a stake in the factfinders' acceptance of her pitch similar to that of a salesman trying to make a sale to a skeptical customer.

One cannot forget that a trial is a competitive presentation. The spoils go to the lawyer who is able to persuade the factfinders that the fact picture portrayed by her and her witnesses is the best reflection of reality, so far as the issues in the case are concerned.

It is said that a salesperson cannot sell his products unless he believes in them. The same is true of the trial lawyer. It is very hard for a lawyer to persuade a jury that her version of the facts is the accurate one unless she believes that that is the case.

E.   Preparation for Fact Presentation

As the first stage of the fact investigation, the lawyer analyzes the available raw information to see whether there is a potential fact picture that will fit a legal rule with consequences favorable to the client. The lawyer attempts to get as much information as possible about the events or issues of concern to see what actually happened. Taking into account the opponent's anticipated presentation, the lawyer chooses from among the potential scenarios the version that (1) fits a rule favoring the interests of the client and (2) would likely be accepted by the finders of fact. The analysis and selection is based on the information available.

The investigation and the sifting of information concerning an event to determine potential fact scenarios is an important part of the work of a trial lawyer. Because the focus of this book is on in-court presentation, however, detailed discussion of the investigative function is omitted.

The process of developing an image from the available information to be presented to the factfinders is often referred to as developing the "factual theory" of the case. The assignment for the trial lawyer is to then recreate this fact image in the minds of the jury at the trial.

Real life furnishes no event, condition, or circumstance that can be recreated in each and every detail within the kind of time available for presentation in court. Even the site of a simple automobile collision contains so many potential environmental details that re-creation of the scene with complete fidelity could take a great deal of time. These details range from the prominent to the subtle, from those of great significance to those which matter scarcely at all. Any moment of reality, any locus in the real environment, has almost infinite complexity. Attempting to recapture the full detail and to replay it in court is logistically impossible.

This is true particularly when the re-creation relies on such inefficient methods of communication as oral description. Oral communication is, of course, one word at a time, spoken and heard. It must rely on often ambiguous language references and allows reliable re-creation of relatively few details. For these reasons the trial lawyer must be selective in determining which facts will be utilized efficiently to create an authoritative, accurate, and compelling picture.

For instance, in the case of a pedestrian accident, such elements as the color of the automobile, its make, the material of the pavement, the architecture of nearby buildings, and the activities of uninvolved passersby would all be elements of a faithful re-creation of the accident scene. But these details might be entirely immaterial to the essence of a picture of a negligent motorist hitting a pedestrian. On the other hand, such details as the driver's state of mind, the location of parked cars, the movements of the pedestrian, the existence of distractions might be important in shaping a picture with legal consequences. The trial lawyer has to figure out what facts matter in creating the desired fact image. The lawyer must focus the limited resources of time, available media, and factfinder attention on those facts that will establish a necessarily oversimplified picture selected for its favorable legal consequences.

Any effective fact presentation in court incorporates this kind of analysis and selection. However, most of this part of the process should occur long before the trial. It is before the trial begins that the lawyer must decide on the precise fact image to be created and the evidence that will be used as the building blocks to form that image.

The process of turning the facts over in the mind and trying to consider them from different perspectives continues throughout the trial preparation process. Sometimes the lawyer does not really assimilate all the facts until they are unfolding at trial. By then it is too late, unfortunately, to make provision for unfavorable slants or untoward inferences.

F.   Control of the Fact Presentation Process

At the trial itself, the key word is "control." The lawyer does not communicate the facts directly except in her opening and closing statement. Instead, she must rely on witnesses and exhibits in

evidence. [1] That does not mean, however, that she is not orches-
trating and controlling the entire presentation. That control is the
art of trial advocacy, the exercise of various techniques to guide
the presentation of the factual material to recreate the desired
image, to teach the facts.

The trial lawyer's presentation and control function and the
various techniques employed will be discussed at length in later
chapters. The principal means by which a controlled presentation
is made are 1) by selection and pretrial preparation of the witnesses, the communications media, and the order of proof; 2) by
the form and language of oral questions on direct and cross-
examination; 3) by objections to opposing evidence; and 4) by
body language and force of personality. By using sources of information and various control and presentation techniques with the
available media, the trial lawyer can create the desired image in the
consciousness of the factfinders that they can accept as authoritative and agree on in all material respects.

G. Oral and Visual Media

Trial advocacy and fact presentation also differs from appellate
advocacy and legal analysis in the choice of media. With appellate advocacy and legal analysis, the medium of choice is words,
liberally employed both in written briefs and in oral argument. In
fact, the law is largely concerned with words, and often the issue
in a case is about the meaning of these words as they can be
applied to specific fact situations.

But that does not mean that words are necessarily the medium
of choice for fact presentation at a trial. Most people think about
episodes or events as visual images. When one considers something
that has occurred in another place or at another time, it is usually a
picture of the event that is formed in the mind. Most people do not
think of events as strings of text. But sometimes the only route by
which the image can be conveyed from reality to the courtroom is

---

[1] The classic phrase "in evidence" is preferred to the currently more common but less
grammatical "*into* evidence." Evidence is not a place into which something goes or is
placed. It is a status or state of being. A thing is either "in evidence" or "not in evidence"; it
is not "into evidence" or "out of evidence."

by verbal description. Thus the trial advocate must be completely conversant with the use of words to create visual images as well as to convey abstractions.

Words, however, are subject to certain limitations as conduits in the courtroom. First of all, verbal communication is slow. The listener must associate each word or a group of words with some kind of image from his own experiential glossary. An unfamiliar word can cause a temporary blockage, distraction, or short circuit, and the capacity of the memory to absorb purely verbal communication is limited.

There is a considerable risk that the individual factfinders may each have a different or imprecise association with the words chosen. For instance, the word "crawfish" would summon up an image of a small delicious crustacean to a juror in Louisiana. But the same word might leave a juror in Maine unable to associate anything with the word. For these reasons, modern trial advocacy is laying ever greater emphasis on the use of visual and nonverbal media.

Even during the golden age of oral advocacy of Webster, Clarence Darrow, and the other great orators of bygone days, the records of trials reveal the use of demonstrations, maps, and such other visual media as the then-existing technology would permit. Since that time, technological advances have provided the trial lawyer with a wealth of powerful visual media with which to make accurate and authoritative fact presentations. A trial lawyer in the past was limited to drawings or paintings or slate boards for recreations of elements of a fact picture. Today, photographs, paper and computer graphics, and video are only a few of the available methods by which a trial lawyer can communicate the fact picture to the factfinder.

There can be no doubt about the power of visual image. It can take hours to try to describe in words what can be instantaneously depicted with almost 100 percent accuracy by a photograph, a drawing, or even a simple demonstration in court.

Suppose that a witness says, "Yesterday I caught a fish twenty-seven inches long." The listeners will each have his or her own estimate of how long twenty-seven inches is. Each listener will go through some mental comparisons to translate the twenty-seven-inch fish into a visual image. "Is that the length of my leg — or my arm? It is very likely that of a dozen jurors, each one will have a different impression. There also will be at least some confusion and a lack of certainty in the minds of some of the factfinders. The image of the fish will be imperfectly recreated. But if the witness merely says, "Yesterday I caught a fish this long" (indicating with his hands), immediately each and every one of the factfinders will receive the same mental image of the size of the fish. The image will be one in which the factfinders can have a good deal of confidence (at least as much confidence as one would ever have in a fish story).

Modern trial advocacy recognizes and embraces the power of the visual media. An increasingly important part of successful trial advocacy today is the creative and professional use of visual media as a crucial part of the trial presentation.

In planning any presentation, the trial lawyer must select among the available media those that are best calculated to communicate different aspects of the fact picture. Some choices are obvious. For instance, information about space relationships, appearances, directions, sizes, and shapes can best be communicated with visual media. The lawyer should utilize visual media as the primary means of communication in situations where these elements are important. On the other hand, verbal communication may be required where a person's state of mind or a progression of events over time must be described.

But abstract factual material, such as trends and relationships, can be illustrated by graphs, charts, and the like. The success of graphics in advertising makes clear the applicability of these visual media in trial advocacy.

The communications media used in court are subject to evidentiary rules to ensure fairness and reliability. Sometimes lawyers are dissuaded from using visual and other nonverbal media because of concern about the application of these rules. However, the power of these media is such that they cannot be safely ignored. Once the lawyer is comfortable with the use of visual media to convey elements of the fact picture, an important tool has been brought to hand.

H.   Bench Trials and Jury Trials

To most trial lawyers "trial advocacy" is the process of teaching, persuading, or creating an image of the facts for a jury in a civil or criminal trial. This book and most other texts on trial advocacy and its techniques focus largely on the function of the trial lawyer in the context of a jury trial. "Factfinders" can usually be read as "jury." In popular as well as classical literature it is the jury trial, with its fascinating combination of law and human values, that has captured the imagination as to what goes on in court.

Jury trials are but a small portion of all formal court hearings. They represent an even smaller portion of all the court and administrative hearings in which lawyers portray competing fact pictures before a factfinder. The great bulk of lawyering goes on before judges and administrative hearings officers, not juries.

It is not the purpose of this book to discuss the differences in approach or technique between jury and nonjury trial lawyering. The trial lawyer's assignment is the same in both forums. The task of the trial lawyer is to recreate an authoritative fact image in the consciousness of the factfinder, whether it is an administrative hearings officer, a judge, or a jury.

It is true that the requirements for presentation to a jury are likely to be more rigorous than those for a judge or other fact-finder. Certainly the rules of evidence are applied more stringently if the factfinders are a group of lay people than if a trained jurist is hearing the case. Procedural rules that are designed to protect the jury from making improper inferences based on inadmissible evidence do not apply to trials before a judge or to administrative hearings. Most trial lawyers would agree that presenting a case to a judge is likely to be technically easier than presenting the same case to a jury. It has been said that "If you can try a case to a jury, you can try it to a judge."

On the other hand, judge trials have certain hazards all their own, the primary one being that the trial lawyer is presenting her picture to a single individual, with that individual's unique background, psychological makeup, prejudices, and interests. If a judge takes a bad slant on a case, there are no other factfinders to straighten the judge out during deliberations. With a jury, one can hope for a spectrum of pre-existing views that will provide a composite background for the lawyer's picture. With a judge one must take her chances.

Judges also have the right to see the evidence they are ruling on. The factfinder is forced to see that which he may rule to be legally inadmissible. Although judges assert that their decisions are based only on the admissible evidence, some pictures, once formed, are very hard to forget, no matter how legally inadmissible the source.

Within the courtroom, the energy flows according to whether the trial is to a jury or to the bench. The lawyer has to adjust her stance and orientation, as well as those of the witness, in order to direct the image to the judge. The presentation may be more informal in some senses but more formal in others. After all, the lawyer is not speaking to fellow citizens from the community but to a jurist who will decide the law as well as the facts of the case.

These, and many other differences between jury and bench trials, should not obscure the essential sameness of the trial lawyer's function, whether in a jury trial, a bench trial, or an administrative hearing. In all three contexts the trial lawyer is doing the same thing: teaching someone about something that happened somewhere else at another time, with enough authority, clarity, and precision so the other person will be able to make an important decision based on the image created. In the first and last analysis, that is what trying cases is about.

Chapter 3 Trial Lawyers' Ethics

Trial lawyers are confronted with difficult issues of ethics on a daily basis. Many of these are the same ethical problems that are encountered by all lawyers. Others are unique to the trial process and the role of the trial lawyer in it.

The trial lawyer's special function, representing a client in a formal proceeding to determine the objective truth, often creates ethical dilemmas. On the one hand, the lawyer must be a faithful and effective exponent for the client. Our complex legal system requires that parties involved with the law have trained and dedicated representatives to protect their interests and preserve their autonomy. On the other hand, the purpose of the system is to find the truth. The role of the lawyer is an integral part of that system. Most people have a positive regard for truthfulness and an abhorrence of deliberate falsehood. These values are important in our culture.

Many ethical issues are either created or exacerbated by the potential for conflict between the roles of the lawyer as client representative on the one hand and as an independent human being and officer of the court on the other.

A. Ethical Issues at Trial

A thorough discussion of the many ethical issues regularly confronted by trial lawyers would fill a book far larger than this volume. Moreover, the often conflicting ethical obligations of trial lawyers are already the subject matter of a considerable body of scholarly and practical literature. On the other hand, without some attention at the outset to the difficult ethical issues raised by trial lawyering and the ethical rules by which trial lawyers live and

19

work, it is possible for the student of trial advocacy to get the impression that presenting fact cases in court is very like a game and that presenting a winning image is the only thing that counts.

Is the image the trial lawyer seeks to recreate only an illusion? Does the trial lawyer have any obligation to pursue objective "truth" in that which she presents to the factfinders? Is the standard of accountability limited to what the lawyer can "get away with" without offending either judge or factfinder?

Our adversary trial system, which gives the lawyers almost the entire responsibility for presenting the fact image in court, also puts them under great pressure to win for their clients. Trial lawyers also want to win for themselves. Sometimes the lawyers, as they seek to represent their clients effectively, seem more like sporting contestants, or even combatants, than serious seekers after truth.

The trial context raises its own unique variety of ethical issues because of the nature of the trial itself. The trial is fundamentally an exercise in which the lawyers for each of the opposing sides attempt to present fact images about an event, circumstance, or condition that occurred outside the courtroom. The fidelity and accuracy of the in-court fact presentations are vital to the integrity of the process.

Despite the value of cross-examination as a tool to uncover falsehood, there is often no way of objectively validating a particular assertion or image. It is possible to present an image that is false, fundamentally or in some detail, and not get caught. Does the trial lawyer's duty to the client mean that the lawyer may or should present such an image when it is possible and expedient to do so?

The tension between effective presentation of facts from the standpoint of a client's interest and the presentation of the facts in an objectively accurate fashion is ever present. Each case is likely to involve two versions of what really happened. It is rare that both versions are objectively true. And the presentation process itself can involve deception and tactics that may seem unfair. There are few issues in the presentation of a case on trial that do not involve serious questions of whether what the lawyer is doing or might do is ethical.

Another difficulty with trial lawyer ethics is that there is some variation and disagreement among the trial lawyers themselves as to what is and what is not ethically permissible. Of course, there are black letter rules that apply to everyone, but in the large area of practice that does not fall squarely within the requirements of a black letter rule, there is room for wide disagreement. This lack of unanimity among sincere and conscientious scholars and practitioners on what is ethically required means that some trial lawyers ultimately fashion their own ethical codes within the overall bounds of the formal rules.

It should be also kept in mind that trial lawyers are confronted with difficult ethical issues not in the comfort of their offices and libraries but in the heat of battle, the give and take of the courtroom. Under these conditions of fierce competition, if not combat, deliberate and detached consideration of reason and policy is sometimes difficult, and it can be easy to do something impulsive that is later regretted. An understanding of the ethical quandaries faced by participants in the trial process and how those quandaries are resolved — whether by formal rule, by unwritten custom, or by the lawyer's own sense of honor and integrity, is an indispensable prerequisite to basic trial advocacy.

B. The Formal Ethical Rules

Formal rules governing the activities of trial lawyers can be considered in two groups. The first group consists of the many rules of ethics that explicitly regulate specific functions of the lawyer in the trial process. These rules, with their various articulated rationales, are applications to the trial specialty of the rules of ethics that govern lawyers generally.

The second group of rules are more general in form. They address issues such as candor, truthfulness, and honesty in dealings with court, client, and opposing parties. Some of these apply primarily, if not exclusively, to the activities of trial lawyers presenting their cases in court. They implement policies in favor of accuracy and integrity of court proceedings. Often they are difficult to apply in borderline situations.

Every state and federal jurisdiction has adopted ethical rules and regulations that are binding on law practitioners in that jurisdiction. Many of these codes are versions of either the Model Code of Professional Responsibility (ABA Code) or the Model Rules of

Professional Conduct (ABA Rules), both originally sponsored by the American Bar Association. These rules have the force of law, and violations are subject to official sanction. All lawyers, including trial lawyers, must abide scrupulously with both the specific and the general rules as interpreted and applied in their governing jurisdictions.

1. Specific Rules That Apply to Trial Lawyering

Almost all of the many specific ethical rules contained in the governing codes have some application to the trial setting. For example, rules requiring confidentiality between client and lawyer apply to all lawyers. [1] In the context of the work of the trial lawyer, these rules often have poignant application. Well known are the cases in which lawyers learn from their clients information about other unsolved crimes, but the lawyers are barred from disclosing their knowledge to baffled law enforcement officials or even next of kin of deceased victims.

Ethical rules regulating conflicts of interest apply to representation in litigation and at trial as well as in other contexts. [2] Litigation tends to sharpen conflicts and to sensitize parties about the implications of actions taken on their behalf or on behalf of others. Rare is the case where a trial lawyer can ethically represent more than a single, clearly defined interest in a litigation situation. Often the situation is presented where the trial lawyer may be subject to claims of potentially conflicting interests of clients, witnesses, and others.

There are also specific rules that apply primarily to the trial context. For instance, the rule that prohibits a trial lawyer from expressing a personal belief on the merits or on the credibility of a witness at trial [3] is generally considered a rule of ethics and is codified along with ethical rules governing lawyers. Similar rules regulate trial publicity (and even literary rights), communications by the lawyer with the judge, other trial participants, witnesses, and jurors, and the special responsibilities of the prosecutor.

[1] See ABA Code DR 4-101; ABA Rule 1.6.
[2] See ABA Code DR 5-101–5-107; ABA Rules 1.7–1.11.
[3] See ABA Code DR 7-106(C)(4); ABA Rule 3.4(c).

These specific rules must be and are generally complied with. When they are not, there is usually not much question about the appropriateness of sanctions. Trial lawyers should know all of these rules well and take care to avoid infractions. The application of some of these rules to common trial situations is discussed below.

2.   General Rules of Candor and Truthfulness

The other, and much more troublesome, group of ethical rules with which a trial lawyer must be concerned are the overall prohibitions against fraud and the presentation of false evidence. [4] These rules appear in somewhat more general terms in the official codifications. They represent attempts to require by rule a minimum level of candor, fairness, and objective factual integrity in trial presentations. By their terms, they directly address the trial lawyer and what she is doing when she organizes, orchestrates, and directs the presentation of a fact image in behalf of her client.

For instance, Disciplinary Rule 7-102 states that a lawyer shall not "conceal or fail to disclose that which he is required by law to reveal" or "counsel or assist his client in conduct that the lawyer knows to be illegal or fraudulent." Model Rule 3.3 prescribes that a lawyer shall not knowingly "fail to disclose a material fact to a tribunal when disclosure is necessary to avoid assisting a criminal or fraudulent act by the client" or "offer evidence that the lawyer knows to be false." Compliance with these rules may often be perceived to conflict with effective representation of client interests and the lawyer's own desire to win. These rules have proven extremely difficult to apply in some situations presented by trial practice.

In fact, there is debate among scholars and practitioners about what these rules really mean. What does it mean when the ABA Code of Professional Responsibility says that a lawyer shall not "Participate in the creation or preservation of evidence when he knows or it is obvious that the evidence is false"? [5] Does this mean that a lawyer has an obligation to make an independent determination of the objective truth of that which she is presenting and only present what she is convinced is objectively true? Does this rule

---

[4] See ABA Code DR 7-101–7-102, 7-106; ABA Rules 3.1–3.5.
[5] ABA Code DR 7-107(A)(6).

forbid a lawyer from advising her client as to the legal consequences of potential versions of the facts? When does a lawyer
"know" that evidence is false? How does this rule apply to attacking evidence proffered by the other side?

On the other hand, what do the rules mean when they say that a
lawyer *may* "refuse to aid or participate in conduct that she believes is unlawful, even though there is some support for an argument that the conduct is lawful"?[6] Can a lawyer refuse to argue an
inference that she does not believe in? Can a lawyer pull punches in
cross-examining a witness who is telling the truth? How should a
lawyer balance the interests of her client against her own commitment to the truth?

These and other provisions of the rules that relate to the candor
and integrity of the lawyer's presentation have been interpreted
and reinterpreted by lawyers, judges, and scholars over and over
again. No final answer has been found.

The more recently drafted Model Rules of Professional Conduct
have attempted to address trial candor and integrity more specifically and less ambiguously than did the Model Code. But even the
Model Rules are not wholly successful at establishing clear guides
to the trial lawyer in planning a presentation in court. According
to the Model Rules, a lawyer shall not "in trial allude to any
matter that the lawyer does not reasonably believe is relevant or
that will not be supported by admissible evidence. . . ."[7] What
kind of standard of objective truth is "reasonable belief"? Although one of the prime purposes of the Model Rules was to
remove ambiguities found in the Model Code and to make applicable standards more explicit, experience with the Rules has shown
there is still room for difference and doubt as to the meaning of
some of the key formulations.

It is not the purpose of this chapter to attempt to construe or
parse, or to find ambiguities in either the Model Code or the
Model Rules. These rules provide the profession's most authoritative articulation of the trial lawyer's obligation of candor in the
representation of clients in court. Understanding the requirements
of these rules and obeying them scrupulously is a basic necessity to
effective trial advocacy.

[6] Id., DR 7-106(B)(2).
[7] Model Rule 3.4(e).

C. The Obligation to Present the Truth

As discussed above, a trial is a process of recreating an image of an event or circumstance from real life in order to apply to that fact picture certain rules of law. In order for the trial process to apply the law reliably to real life happenings, it must produce a fact picture that faithfully reflects the reality that is the subject matter of the presentation. It is claimed that the adversary system, by which contending and cross-examining adversaries submit competing versions of the truth to a more or less passive factfinder, produces a composite image of high accuracy.

The question is whether the participants in that process, particularly the lawyers, have any obligation to present only information that they know, or at least believe, is accurate. On the one hand, it seems basically wrong for a person to be knowingly presenting false information to a tribunal that is supposed to be finding out the truth. On the other hand, lawyers function in court not as judges but as partisan representatives who are loyal to the interests of their clients. It is asking a great deal of lawyers to sit in judgment of their clients' cases even before putting them on. The basic tenet of the adversary system requires that the lawyer present the version of the truth to which the client subscribes and that the court determine the "real" truth from the clash of the competing partisan presentations.

Both the Model Code and the Disciplinary Rules attempt to mediate between the duty to the client and the need to maintain some standard of candor in court presentations. Without parsing the words of the Code or Model Rules and, at the risk of gross oversimplification, the trial lawyer is required by both formulations to observe a certain level of objective candor on certain key matters including questions of law and the fact evidence and testimony that are actually presented by the lawyer in court. The lawyer is thus ethically responsible for the law given to the court and for the facts that she has a hand in presenting.

1. Questions of Law

On questions of law, the trial lawyer is required to maintain a high standard of objective candor, even to the extent of disclosing to the court legal authority known to the lawyer to be contrary to the position the lawyer is advancing in behalf of her client. [8] This obligation is well understood by most lawyers from the time of their first moot court argument in law school. Rarely is a lawyer called to task for knowing failure to disclose unfavorable legal authority.

2. False Testimony and Evidence

According to both the Code and the Model Rules, the lawyer's duty of candor also applies to any evidence or testimony the lawyer presents in court. [9] It is safe to say that both formulations forbid a lawyer from attempting to create a false factual picture with evidence or testimony that the lawyer knows is false. Both the language and the apparent policy of these provisions would appear to be fairly clear, but not all lawyers agree on how they should be applied.

In a civil case, virtually all would agree that a lawyer cannot ethically present testimony that the lawyer knows is false, and almost all would agree that a lawyer is barred from adducing false testimony from a nonclient witness in a criminal case as well. However, there is a significant difference of opinion when it comes to presentation of evidence through the testimony of the criminal defendant himself. The predominant view is that knowing presentation of perjured testimony of a criminal defendant in violation of both the Code and the Rules is clearly unethical and improper. On the other hand, there are respected scholars and practitioners who argue that the defendant's right to effective assistance of counsel requires that a criminal defense lawyer be permitted to offer the defendant's own testimony, regardless of whether it is known to be true or false. [10]

Even lawyers who state that they would never call a perjurious witness to testify acknowledge that they may go to some pains to avoid knowing whether a criminal defendant's proposed testimony is true or false. Ignorance is never a good preparation for the rigors

[8] ABA Code DR 7-106(B)(1); Model Rule 3.3(a)(3).
[9] ABA Code DR 7-102; Model Rule 3.3.
[10] See M. Freedman, Understanding Lawyers' Ethics 109-141 (1990).

of a trial. Sometimes the need to know enough to present a defense without knowing too much leads to strange interview techniques:

> Q. Now, Mr. Client, don't tell me what happened, just tell me what you think the State is going to say happened.

or

> Q. Maybe you could tell me what your worst enemy would say that you did. . . .

Other lawyers ask their clients for the facts straight out, but not until they have warned the client of the consequences of being candid with his lawyer:

> Counsel. Now before we get into your version of what happened, you should know that as a lawyer I am under an ethical obligation not to present testimony that I know to be false. So if you tell me something now, I will not be able to let you get on the witness stand and tell the jury something else. You should tell me the truth, of course, but you should also know that whatever you tell me is what we have to go with if you testify at your trial.

Such "Miranda warnings" can be confusing to the client at best and, at worst, may invite the client to make up the "official" story before telling anything to the lawyer.

To some lawyers, the constitutional right to effective assistance of counsel entitles a party to a lawyer's advice before the party is asked, "what happened?"

> Counsel. Now before we get into your story, you should know the legal consequences of various versions of what might have happened. If you saw the victim before you hit him, even if you saw him just a moment before, you would probably be guilty of murder. Of course, if you didn't see him, you could not have formed the necessary intent to kill him, and it would be an accident. In that case the worst you could be guilty of would be negligent homicide.

This kind of counseling has an obvious potential for assisting the client in the formulation of a perjurious story that would best serve the client's interests. The line between appropriately providing a client with legal advice and facilitating the creation of perjury, which is expressly forbidden by Code and Rules [11] is not always a distinct one.

The United States Supreme Court has ruled that the constitutional right to counsel does not require appointed defense counsel to permit a criminal defendant to testify falsely at his own trial. [12] Whether this right would protect from discipline a lawyer who knowingly permits her client to testify falsely in his own defense is still an open question. [13]

The prohibition of presentation of false testimony is limited in both Code and Rules to "knowing" presentation of false testimony. If the lawyer in good faith does not know that the testimony is false, it is not unethical to put it on. It is all right to accept the statement of a client or witness relatively uncritically. It is all right to present the testimony even if the lawyer has her suspicions as to its truthfulness or is somewhat skeptical.

If the witness believes his own testimony to be true but the lawyer knows that the witness is mistaken, is it ethical to present the testimony? If the defendant confessed to his lawyer that he was the person who mugged Linda Loomis on the night of May 14, may his lawyer present alibi testimony given in good faith, but erroneously, by the defendant's employer? Although the question is not free from doubt, most lawyers read the word "false" in the Code and Rules to cover only evidence and testimony known by both lawyer and witness to be false. If the witness in good faith believes the evidence to be true, most lawyers would say that the lawyer can put it on, even if the lawyer "knows" that it is wrong.

In the final analysis, if a lawyer's duty of candor in trial presentation is to have any meaning, the Rules and Code prohibitions should be read to forbid any presentation by the lawyer of evidence or testimony that she knows is false, regardless of the source

---

[11] ABA Code DR 7-102(6), 7-102(7); Model Rule 3.4(b).

[12] Nix v. Whiteside, 475 U.S. 157 (1986).

[13] But see Board of Bar Overseers v. Dineen, 481 A.2d 499 (Me. 1984) (constitutional rights of accused did not excuse deliberate use of the accused's perjured testimony by his counsel).

of the testimony or the belief of the witness. Nor should a lawyer who intends to comply with the minimum rules of candor feel obligated to warn her client at the outset. The requirement that a lawyer cannot present false testimony is inherent in the system under which the representation is being provided to the client. There is no reason why a lawyer should feel compelled to assist the client in evading that requirement. Finally, a lawyer's duty to advise a client on the legal consequences of conduct that has already occurred does not require that the lawyer brief the client before the client relates the facts to the lawyer.

Although the foregoing propositions do not command universal agreement, they do follow the black letter rules and they do establish a meaningful minimum level of lawyer integrity in the fact presentation process. Any lower standard that would permit either knowing use of false evidence or conscious efforts not to know is likely to lead to a slippery slope on which any responsibility for the presentation of objective truth is quickly lost.

3. False Inferences and Arguments

While the Code and Rules rather clearly prohibit a lawyer from creating a false fact image by presenting false testimony and evidence, there is considerably more latitude permitted in creating and arguing questionable or even false inferences from testimony not known to be untrue. The prohibitory language of both Code and Rules refers only to "testimony" and "evidence" "known" to be "false" or "fraudulent." By negative inference as well as by long-established professional consensus, generating and arguing false inferences or conclusions from true proven facts is not unethical.

For example, if the criminal defense lawyer knew that her client had seen the decedent lying on the sidewalk before running over him with his car, that lawyer would be barred from calling the defendant as a witness and permitting him to testify that he had not seen anything. However, the lawyer would not be barred from bringing up other evidence that would support the inference that the defendant did not see anything. Nor would the lawyer be precluded from arguing in summation that it was too dark for the defendant to have seen the decedent and that, because other witnesses had been unable to see the decedent, it was unlikely that the defendant could have done so.

The rules requiring candor do not restrict a lawyer from trying to cast doubt on witness testimony that the lawyer knows to be true, both by cross-examination and by argument. Even if the defendant has told his lawyer that he was the assailant who mugged the elderly victim in the hall outside her apartment, the lawyer may cross-examine the victim in an effort to undermine her identification of his client:

> Q.   You customarily wear glasses, don't you, Ms. Loomis?
>
> A.   Yes, I do.
>
> Q.   You didn't have your glasses on on the evening of May 14, did you?
>
> A.   That's right, I had left them in the apartment.
>
> Q.   The only light in your hallway is a small bulb at the end of the corridor, isn't it?
>
> A.   If you say so.
>
> Q.   And you saw this person who grabbed your purse for only a second, right?
>
> A.   Yeah, I guess so.

All of this examination is calculated to support the inference that the victim might have misidentified the perpetrator, an inference that the lawyer knows is false.

This latitude extends even to calling witnesses to give truthful testimony that leads to a false conclusion. For instance, in the example above, defense counsel would be ethically permitted to call a character witness to attest to the defendant's reputation for honesty and nonviolence. These traits are ones chosen by the lawyer as inconsistent with the conclusion that the defendant committed the crime.

> Q.   And now, Reverend Grimes, what is Mr. Thomas's reputation in your congregation for honesty and nonviolence?

> *A.* His reputation for honesty and nonviolence is good. He
> is an honest and gentle young man.

As long as the witness is telling what he thinks is the truth, the
lawyer may ethically present his testimony even in aid of a false
argument or conclusion.

By the same token, the lawyer is also permitted to argue from
facts known to be true for a conclusion known to be false. In
summation:

> *Defendant's Counsel.*   Members of the jury, how could Ms.
> Loomis have seen the man who grabbed her purse well
> enough to be able to identify Jeff Thomas as that man? It
> was dark in that hall. She didn't have her glasses on, and
> the whole business lasted for just a split second.
>
> You heard Mr. Boilard. He's Jeff Thomas's boss at the
> Rosebud saloon. Jeff wasn't at 24 Washington Avenue at
> 10 P.M. on the night of May 14. He was at the Rosebud
> washing dishes.
>
> And we all remember Reverend Grimes, the minister of the
> church where Jeff and his mother are members of the congre-
> gation. He told us that Jeff is simply not the kind of person
> who would do anything like take anybody's pocketbook.

In criminal cases, the moral authority for this latitude with the
known truth is the right of the criminal defendant to "put the government to its proof." It is the government's obligation to prove guilt
beyond a reasonable doubt. Hence the defendant's lawyer may generate false inferences and arguments in a criminal case.

This rationale, of course, does not apply to civil cases or to the
conduct of the prosecutor in a criminal case. It is clear that a
prosecutor who knowingly maintains a false prosecution by use
of false inferences from true facts is in violation of at least the
more stringent standards of prosecutorial conduct. Whether a
lawyer can argue false inferences in a civil case is much less clear.
Some lawyers read the prohibitions against false and fraudulent
fact presentations narrowly as limited to the actual facts but ex-
cluding inferences. Others would refuse in any case, criminal or

civil, to employ any argument or inference known to be false, regardless of the truth of the underlying facts."

D. Observing a Higher Level of Candor Than the Rules Require

The blurring of the official rules standard and the absence of agreement among scholars, judges, and practitioners give rise to the risk that the externally imposed standards of candor for in-court presentation will be set at the lowest common denominator. It is not surprising that some experienced trial lawyers counsel law students to do "what you can get away with" in the courtroom and tell them that it is okay to play fast and loose with the truth so long as one is not obviously putting on blatant perjury.

Trial lawyering is a competitive exercise. Competition drives activity to the edge of its efficiency. The assumption is that obligations of candor are ethical burdens on the ingenuity and virtuosity of counsel in developing a trial presentation to suit the interests of the client. Based on these premises, some argue that a client should be entitled to a lawyer who will observe the lowest acceptable standards of in-court truth and integrity to obtain a favorable outcome for the client.

Some trial lawyers have reacted to the less than definitive state of the official rules on in-court candor by formulating and following their own personal codes of ethics. These personal codes are not written down. Usually they are more a mind-set or perspective. The lawyer simply determines to adhere to a level of candor and integrity in court that will provide ethical satisfaction to the trial lawyer in practice.

One example of such a personal code of ethics can be expressed in the following terms:

- I will not represent any fact that I do not believe to be true.

- I will not seek to generate an inference that I do not believe in.

- I will not seek to convince other than by logic, reason, and public policy.

- I will not use trickery to confuse or distort what I know to be fact.

- I will not seek to circumvent the requirements of procedural or evidentiary rules.

A code of personal candor as stringent as the foregoing is in no way required by the explicit rules or by any consensus among trial lawyers as to what is or even should be required of all lawyers. Some lawyers and law teachers question whether such individual lawyer codes are fair to clients. Should a client's interests be subjected to moral or ethical scruples of an individual lawyer that are not required of all lawyers?

The point is that some lawyers may conclude that their own sense of self and their personal integrity will be compromised by operating at the minimum permitted by rule and custom. Some lawyers may feel uncomfortable in seeking to suggest by inference, if not explicit fact, what they know is not true. Such lawyers need not swallow their scruples and go as far as the written rules allow to obscure and warp what they know is objective truth.

In the last analysis, lawyers are people who have to live with themselves and sleep at night. Telling the truth has always been a very important value in our society. There is nothing about being a lawyer that should prevent a person from prizing, and telling, the truth.

Although there is little in the ABA Code that addresses the lawyer's right to live by a code any more demanding than the required minimum, the Model Rules are somewhat more explicit. Rule 3.3(c) specifically authorizes a lawyer to "refuse to offer evidence that the lawyer reasonably believes is false." Rule 1.16(b) further authorizes a lawyer to withdraw from representation if the client "persists in a course of action involving the lawyer's services that the lawyer reasonably believes is criminal or fraudulent" or even "insists upon pursuing an objective that the lawyer considers repugnant or imprudent."

This does not mean that the ethical trial lawyer will never use a ploy or deception in the representation of her client. As will be discussed below, tricks and trial stratagems can be used to reveal the truth as well as to obscure it. There are some contexts when an apparent deception will result in uncovering the true facts. In these circumstances, a degree of apparent duplicity may be consistent with the highest personal standards of candor.

E.   The Lawyer's Ethics and the Client's Interests

There is no question that in certain situations the regulations requiring candor of lawyers in presenting evidence in court may operate to the disadvantage of the interests of the lawyer's client. If indeed the client has an interest in maintaining an image that is in fact false and wants the lawyer to help in the undertaking, the client's short-run interests will be adversely affected by the lawyer's ethical requirements. If the client's false testimony is what is needed to convince the jury not to convict, the lawyer's ethical scruples can be seen as a real burden on the client.

Those ethical obligations set forth in, or reasonably inferred from, the written rules are inherent in the justice system under which the client's guilt or innocence is being determined. There is no need or reason for the lawyer to be apologetic about them or to warn the client before the client is committed to a story. These obligations are givens.

On the other hand, a lawyer who adopts a personal ethical code that is more demanding than the minimum required of the profession as a whole should make it clear to her client at an early stage of the litigation that she is adhering to standards of candor and integrity more stringent than are demanded by the official rules. She should advise the client of the effect of her ethical standards on the conduct and prospects of the case. If the client does not wish to bear the burden of his lawyer's more rigorous scruples, he can seek assistance from a lawyer who works closer to the official line.

It is sometimes difficult for a lawyer to advise the client, whose fortunes are at stake in the litigation, of potential or actual restrictions on the lawyer's permissible activities arising from official or personal ethical requirements. If the requirement comes from the official rules, the lawyer can say "I *can't* ...". However, if the ethical scruple is personal to the lawyer, the lawyer is saying, in effect, "I *won't* ...". Many a lawyer's scruples are put to the test when advising the client of things the lawyer just won't do, even if permitted by the official rules.

On the other hand, lawyers who assume that their clients will automatically demand the lowest level of permissible conduct sometimes do not expect enough of their clients. The school of experience teaches that most clients are understanding and supportive of both official and unofficial ethical requirements of candor and honesty. Some clients expect their lawyers to serve as their consciences. Many are willing to accept the fact that legal employment does not include participating in a fraud or even creating a misleading impression.

Frequently a trial lawyer may feel reluctant to base a decision affecting the client's fortunes on the lawyer's personal ethical responsibilities. Often a lawyer is shy about imposing her ethical standards on activities that so directly affect the interests of the client. Too often the lawyer feels obliged to justify a decision required by ethics in terms of ethically neutral strategic or tactical considerations. Such lawyers believe that the client will better accept a course of action or restraint if it is based at least ostensibly on the client's interests rather than on the lawyer's ethical requirements.

Strategic or tactical advice that masks an ethical concern of the lawyer is bad advice. The lawyer is operating from a conflict of interest. The real considerations are not on the table. The lawyer is essentially manipulating the client. If a client later finds out the advice was not what it seemed to be at the time, the client will have just cause for complaint. It is always far better for the lawyer frankly to disclose to the client the lawyer's scruples about any aspect of the case. They can be discussed and evaluated for what they are, not in the guise of strategic or tactical advice.

F. The Unwritten Rules of Legal Ethics

Traditionally, the written rules and precepts regulating lawyer conduct have been supplemented by unwritten rules of custom and local practice that often have ethical implications. These sometimes seem more like courtesies than ethical rules and are likely to be most significant among relatively small groups of practitioners who all know each other and encounter each other repeatedly in daily practice. In environments containing large numbers of diverse lawyers, unwritten rules are less common and less effective.

Due process is seldom involved in the enforcement of unwritten rules and customs among lawyers. If a lawyer offends a local standard of conduct that is not the subject of a written rule, the best that can be expected is a word of advice from a more seasoned practitioner:

> *Seasoned Practitioner.* Perhaps you did not know that it is customary in this county to call your opposing attorney before seeking sanctions for failure to comply with discovery requests. Maybe you want to withdraw that Rule 37 motion and call Ms. Jones before filing another one. . . .

Violations of unwritten rules are usually noted in the "black books" kept by other practitioners in the locality. The repeat offender finds it difficult to obtain the usual courtesies and cooperations necessary to the everyday practice of law. Ultimate alienation and ostracism can be the final result of inability or unwillingness to abide by the unwritten local codes of lawyer conduct.

Overall, it is probably safe to say that such unwritten customs of civility are of far less significance today than they were in the law practice of past generations. Nostalgia at their passing should not obscure the fact that these codes were often used as means to perpetuate traditional power structures and values and to stifle nonconformity and dissent. Sometimes the loss in traditional good manners is outbalanced by a gain in diversity of lawyer style and viewpoint and wider participation in the legal process.

Recent efforts of lawyers and judges to reverse a perceived decline in lawyer civility have resulted in the promulgation by bar associations and even courts of written formal and informal codes of lawyer practice. These codes often address conduct that was previously governed by unwritten custom or common understanding when trial bars were smaller, more homogeneous, and more cohesive. At this point it is hard to say whether these written codes will succeed in regenerating real consideration and courtesy among trial lawyers or whether they will simply add to the intricacy of the degenerating struggle. They underscore the fact that sometimes the borderline between formal ethical obligations and human consideration and sensitivity is a narrow one.

G. How Ethical Issues Arise

Issues of candor and fairness in trial representation arise in a variety of contexts, large and small. Many of the most stringent ethical quandaries arise in the course of witness preparation. This is when the lawyer begins to feel uncomfortable if she suspects that her client is fabricating a story that the lawyer will be expected to present as the truth, and when she may be tempted to give the client the legal advice necessary to craft a false exonerating scenario. This is also when the lawyer has the opportunity to consider the ethical consequences of her fact presentation outside of the hurly-burly of the trial itself and to make the tough decisions and to structure her presentation along ethical lines.

During the actual trial, the lawyer will also encounter many situations in which her loyalty to honesty and candor will be tested. The trial process is replete with opportunities to take advantage of circumstances and to unfairly create a false impression. Many lapses of candor and integrity never become the subject of any kind of disciplinary proceeding. They often go undetected and unpunished and are matters solely between the lawyer and her conscience.

To a large extent, trial lawyers must police themselves. Techniques of communication and presentation are imprecise. It is easy to "unintentionally" misquote testimony. It is sometimes hard to resist the temptation to waft an unwarranted innuendo in the direction of the factfinders. A hardball move from the other side often evokes a response of the same tenor.

Some violations are serious enough to attract the attention of opposing counsel but are too minor to justify intervention by the court or by a disciplinary body. These cheap shots may cause the other lawyer to make a note in his mental "black book" list of lawyers to watch in the future. In a small bar, where the lawyers are likely to be meeting each other again and again, this kind of informal discipline can be very effective in maintaining high standards of conduct. Other seemingly trifling compromises may bring down the wrath of the court, depending on the circumstances and on who the judge is.

When all is said and done, the only way one can be sure is to follow the spirit as well as the letter of the rules scrupulously. There are never circumstances that justify departing from truth, candor, integrity, and honesty in dealings in court.

H.   Ethical Lapses in Court

The following are illustrative of the many common situations in which trial lawyers sometimes depart from high standards of truthfulness and fair dealing in their courtroom activities. The history of trial advocacy has documented the infinite variety of ingenious fact presentations of which the human mind is capable. It has also recorded a tremendous variety of lapses in the level of candor and consideration that are necessary to the effective functioning of the trial process.

1.   Improving the Testimony

Sometimes the lawyer may be tempted to resort to a number of ploys to try to "improve" the testimony as it is being given in court. On both direct and cross-examination, the lawyer has opportunity to improve the testimony given. For example, on direct examination:

Q.   What happened next?

A.   The car hit us.

Q.   How did you feel when the car smashed into you?

The witness's word 'hit' has been transformed into the direct examiner's "smashed into" via her next question. And on cross-examination:

Q.   You hit the Clark car in the middle of the intersection, didn't you?

A.   Yes.

Q.   After you smashed into the Clark car, your car ended up on Mrs. Godard's lawn, didn't it?

The cross-examiner has improved the answer in the body of his followup question.

Sometimes this kind of misquotation is the result of innocent mistake; sometimes it is an effort of the lawyer to get away with whatever she can. Whether innocent or intentional, misquotation of prior testimony in later questions is objectionable as a matter of trial management. Counsel's license to incorporate prior testimony into later questions is limited to an exact repetition of the incorporated evidence. It cannot be improved.

> *Opposing Counsel.*   Objection! Cousel is misquoting the prior testimony of the witness.
>
> *The Court.*   Sustained. Counsel, please make sure that you quote the witness's exact words in your follow-up questions.

When done on purpose, misquotation in a later question of the previous testimony is likely to be a violation of the Code and Rules prohibitions on allusions to matters not in evidence. [14] Such conduct is indefensible as a matter of trial ethics.

A variation on this practice is the "When did you stop beating your wife?" question used on cross-examination. Such a question buries the examiner's assertion with which the witness does not necessarily agree in the predicate of the question, where it is not readily accessible to be denied.

Sometimes the buried assertion is subtle:

> Q.   Mr. Maxfield, after you ran over and killed Mr. Savage there on the sidewalk, you drove back out onto Jackson Street, didn't you?
>
> A.   Well, I . . .
>
> *Opposing Counsel.*   Objection! That is an unfair question, Your Honor. The implication is that Mr. Maxfield consciously ran over and killed the decedent, whereas his testimony is exactly to the contrary.
>
> *The Court.*   Sustained. Please rephrase your question, Counsel.

The court's ruling here is a close call. The defendant did indeed run over and kill the decedent, but he claims that he did not see the decedent beforehand and did not even know that he had hit

---

[14] See ABA Code DR 7-106, EC 7-25; Model Rule 3.4.

anybody until sometime afterward. The questioner, however, combines in the same breath the defendant's running over and killing the decedent and his later driving back into the street. The later action was concededly conscious and intentional. This juxtaposition raises the implication that both actions were conscious and intentional.

On the one hand, it can be argued that this is just good trial advocacy and helps the factfinder to assess the credibility of the driver's claim of innocence. On the other hand, is the question fair to the witness? Does he have a fair opportunity to address the damaging implication in his answer to the question asked? In ruling on a borderline question such as this, the trial judge may well be influenced by her overall appraisal of the quality of the lawyer's tactics throughout the trial.

2. Leading and Prompting Witnesses on Direct Examination

On direct examination counsel are not supposed to ask leading questions containing the information that the witness is supposed to supply. The rule against leading questions reflects a policy in favor of getting the information directly from the witness and in the witness's terminology so long as the lawyer can remain in control of the proceedings. A lawyer should be able to control a friendly or neutral witness sufficiently by the use of open questions that focus on the kind of information requested without providing the actual facts. Leading questions are usually permitted to refresh the witness's recollection when it has been exhausted.

The leading question on direct examination is one of the most common breaches of the rules of evidence and trial procedure. Objections to leading questions are frequently made and frequently sustained or overruled. Usually the objection is cured by rephrasing the question in proper form.

The use of leading questions can be abused. Some lawyers will ask a leading question in words carefully chosen to cue the witness with the exact words to be used in the answer. Even if the objection to the question is sustained, the witness has gotten the message. Appropriately primed, the witness answers the follow-up open question in the words selected by the lawyer.

Q. When the doctor told you about the possibility of a future operation, did you feel concerned and upset about that?

Opposing Counsel. Objection! Leading.

The Court. Sustained.

Q. How did you feel when the doctor told you about the possibility of a future operation?

A. I felt concerned and upset.

This kind of cuing of the witness will occur to some extent with all leading questions. It becomes a vice if the lawyer asks the objectionable question purposely to alert the witness. Although some trial lawyers actually will counsel this ploy "if you can get away with it," alerting the witness is in fact unethical. Deliberately violating the evidence and procedural rules governing leading questions in order to coach a witness is a violation of Model Rule 3.4(c), which prohibits a lawyer from knowingly disobeying rules of court, and of Model Code DR 7-106(A), of similar import.

Such tactics also should be avoided for another reason. Judges and factfinders notice if this kind of pattern occurs more than a very few times. The credibility of both lawyer and witness will suffer.

3. *Good Faith Questions on Cross-Examination*

On cross-examination, typically all of the information is contained in the questions. The answers are usually merely affirmations or denials of the assertions contained in the cross-examiner's questions. This circumstance makes it possible for the trial lawyer to create factual misimpressions from questions alone, regardless of the witness's answers. If a lawyer cross-examining a witness asserts facts in a question that reflect adversely on the witness, the factfinders may credit the assertion and discredit the witness's denial. This is especially true if the assertion is detailed and positively stated.

Q. You and your buddies were drinking that afternoon at the Blue Goose, weren't you?

    A. Eating and drinking.

    Q. In fact, you each had three beers, didn't you?

    A. No, we didn't. It was one or, at the most, two.

    Q. And you smoked marijuana earlier that afternoon, didn't you?

    A. No, we didn't.

Even though the witness has denied the number of beers and the marijuana, the factfinders may be left with the impression that maybe the college-age youths did drink several beers and smoke pot on the afternoon of the accident.

Because of the potential of cross-examination questions themselves to waft innuendo to the factfinders, a cross-examiner may ask a leading question only if he has a good-faith basis for believing it is true.

A good-faith basis for a cross-examination question is just that. The lawyer must have some reason for believing in good faith that the fact asserted in the question is true. It need not be a certainty, but it must be more than a guess or suspicion.

A good-faith basis is not the equivalent of a control device. It is possible to have a good-faith basis for believing that facts are true without having any usable device for requiring the witness to admit them. On the other hand, if the cross-examiner possesses the ability to "prove up" any relevant assertion made in cross-examination, he has complete protection against any charge of lack of good-faith basis for the question.

Asking questions on cross-examination without a good-faith basis violates the rules that regulate trial procedure and is a breach of trial lawyer ethics. Disciplinary Rule 7-106(C)(4) states that a lawyer may not

> (1) State or allude to any matter that he has no reasonable basis to believe is relevant to the case or that will not be supported by relevant evidence.

or

(2) Ask any question that he has no reasonable basis to believe is relevant to the case and that is intended to degrade a witness or other person.

Model Rule 3.4(e) contains a similar prohibition.

Cross-examination questions posed without a good-faith factual basis are likely to encounter vigorous objection and to be dealt with firmly by the court.

> *Opposing Counsel.*   Objection! Lack of good-faith basis for the question. May we be heard at sidebar?
>
> *The Court.*   Come to sidebar.
>
> *Opposing Counsel* (at sidebar).   Your Honor, there is no good-faith basis for that question. There is not a shred of evidence of any suspicion of drugs in this case. The unfair prejudice is clear. We request a curative instruction.
>
> *Cross-Examiner.*   Your Honor, who knows. These are young college kids. Maybe they did have some pot.
>
> *The Court.*   Objection sustained.
>
> (to the cross-examiner).   Watch it, Counsel.
>
> (to the jury).   Ladies and gentlemen, you are to disregard that last question entirely and are to draw no inference from it whatsoever.

This also is the kind of violation that is sometimes not caught and punished. That does not make it any less unethical.

A variant on the "no good-faith basis" question has the lawyer holding some kind of paper as he puts the damning question to the witness. For instance, assume in the foregoing line of questioning the lawyer was holding and looking at something that looked like some kind of official report form.

> *Q.*   Well, didn't you tell the police that you had been drinking and smoking marijuana earlier that afternoon?
>
> *A.*   No, we didn't.

Despite the denial, the factfinders are left with the misimpression that some official police report has recorded admissions by the witnesses that he and his associates were drinking and using drugs. Yet the paper in the hands of the lawyer could be a mock-up. Or it could be the real police report but without any mention of the drinking or drugs.

This kind of escalation of a misimpression without a good-faith basis is a serious ethical breach. It is hard to excuse as unintentional. If detected, it can subject the lawyer to discipline.

Use of a fake prop to create a false impression without any good-faith basis can be contrasted to the use of a prop as a control device for facts known or believed by the lawyer to be true. Sometimes a lawyer will ask questions that the lawyer believes are true and should be admitted by the witness while holding a paper that resembles the witness's deposition or statement. Even if the paper does not support all of the assertions the lawyer believes to be true, the witness may be afraid to fabricate if he believes that the lawyer has in hand the "goods" to impeach or discredit him. In that context, some deception of the witness in the aid of the disclosure of the truth may be permissible.

4. Tricks in Court

Lawyer stories and trial anecdotes occasionally record instances in which a lawyer used an in-court trick or deception to win a case or even uncover the truth. A famous example involved a defense counsel's substitution of a handwriting exemplar before cross-examination of the prosecution's handwriting expert. The unknowing expert continued to insist on cross-examination that the bogus exemplar matched the handwriting of the perpetrator of the crime. Disclosure of the stratagem resulted in the acquittal of the defendant. It also resulted in the suspension of the successful lawyer. [15]

Another trick sometimes employed to confuse an identification witness is to substitute another person, similarly dressed, for the defendant or other person to be identified in court. It can be argued that such a stratagem merely tests the accuracy of the identifi-

[15] See In re Metzger, 31 Hawaii 929 (1931).

cation, but such a ploy can also be seen as a shoddy misuse of the lawyer's role in court.

The line between deception to force the truth and deception to create a misimpression is a very narrow one. Tricks can backfire. In case of doubt, the better path is right down the middle.

5. Ethical Problems with Objections

Counsel's right to state an objection in the middle of her opponent's presentation can be misused. The proper purpose of an objection is to seek a ruling from the court on an issue of evidence or trial procedure. The objection process, however, allows counsel to interrupt the opponent's presentation and to comment on the quality of the evidence. If counsel uses this license for an improper purpose, a breach of ethics may be involved.

Sometimes an examination or cross-examination can acquire a sort of momentum that seems to contribute to the effectiveness of the presentation. An objection, even if not well-founded, can break this momentum and throw the other lawyer or the witness off-stride. The value of an interruption in the opponent's presentation might properly motivate a lawyer to lodge a well-founded objection, but a legally baseless objection cannot be justified by the desire to break up the other side's presentation.

Some lawyers use objections to cue the witness. If the witness seems to be straying into a dangerous area on cross-examination, an objection is sometimes used — improperly — to warn the witness of an impending peril.

> Q. Mr. Borak, Exhibit 6 is a picture of the corner of Wood and Vale, is it not?
>
> A. Yes, it is.
>
> Q. (showing picture to witness). And looking from the stop sign down Wood Street, you had a perfectly clear view on the day of the crash?
>
> Opposing Counsel.   Objection! That picture wasn't taken on the day of the accident. The foliage is different; there are no parked cars. You can't tell anything from that picture.

The Court.   Overruled. You may answer.

A.   Well, it wasn't really quite like that on the day it happened.

"Speaking objections" are sometimes used as mini-arguments addressed to the credibility of the evidence as well as its admissibility. Counsel should, and often can, argue objections to evidence "out in the pit," in front of the judge and within the hearing of the jury. However, in making such arguments, the lawyer must be sure to use words of art that do not involve comments on or a summary of the evidence. It is one thing to say, "Objection! Irrelevant." It is quite another to argue,

> *Opposing Counsel.*   Objection! What Ms. Mercer was able to see just before the accident has no bearing on what Mr. Maxfield could see. Ms. Mercer was at a different location and had been focusing on the place where the decedent lay in the darkness. It is, however, Mr. Maxfield's behavior that is at issue here. Mr. Maxfield had been driving down the street in a Ford Mustang, swerved to the right, and bumped up on the curb. There is no showing whatsoever that Mr. Maxfield ever was in a position to see what Ms. Mercer saw. Without such a showing this testimony is irrelevant, incompetent, and immaterial.

If the purpose of making such a detailed argument on the objection is to blunt the effect on the jury of the anticipated evidence, the objection and argument are unethical. If it is important to discuss the facts in order to effectively make the objection, the only appropriate choice is to approach the bench and request a sidebar conference to make the objection out of the hearing of the jury. If the other lawyer seems to be making a speaking objection, it is permissible and sometimes necessary to interrupt and request that the objection be heard at sidebar.

> *Counsel.*   Objection! What Ms. Mercer was able to see just before the accident has no bearing on what Mr. Maxfield could see. Ms. Mercer was at a different location . . .

Opposing Counsel. Your Honor, may this objection be heard at sidebar?

The Court. Counsel will approach the bench.

If it is possible to anticipate an objection, either party may try to avoid interruption in the presentation by seeking an advance ruling *in limine* before the trial starts or during a recess.

6. Misuse of Voir Dire

"Voir dire," meaning, literally, "to see to say" or "to see what he will say," is a term that is used in two senses in trial advocacy. Jury voir dire is a preliminary examination of the jurors or potential jurors during the course of jury selection at the beginning of the trial. In many jurisdictions the judge conducts the voir dire of prospective jurors. The questioning is usually limited to the prospective jurors' qualifications to sit impartially on the case. In some jurisdictions jury voir dire is conducted by counsel. In these jurisdictions voir dire often is the important first lawyer-juror interaction and is used by effective trial lawyers to commence the process of teaching and image building that is the trial.

Despite its importance in those jurisdictions in which it is still in widespread use, jury voir dire is not discussed in this book. Trial lawyers practicing in jurisdictions where lawyer voir dire of the jury panel is permitted should consult some of the growing body of literature on that subject.

The term "voir dire" as used in this book refers to the opportunity given to the opposing counsel to interrupt an ongoing witness examination to ask questions on a limited preliminary issue usually involving admissibility of evidence. Voir dire is not a matter of right. It may be permitted in the discretion of the court. A lawyer who plans to object to a question or to the admissibility of evidence may request the opportunity to voir dire when the objectionable question is asked or the proposed exhibit is offered.

Q. Doctor, what is your opinion as to the percentage of permanent impairment suffered by Mr. Cluney as a result of the car crash?

>   *Other Lawyer.*   Objection! May we have a brief voir dire,
>   Your Honor?
>
>   *The Court.*   Yes, you may.

The purpose of the voir dire is to elicit facts that have not yet
come out in the witness's testimony and that are helpful to the
pending objection. The pending examination is interrupted to permit these facts to be brought out at the time of the objection. The
request to voir dire contains an implicit representation that the
lawyer has a good-faith basis for believing that the witness may
have knowledge of facts that, if established, may support sustaining the objection.

Sometimes there is a temptation to request voir dire when there
is no real hope of getting the objection sustained. Counsel may be
aware, however, of something that might diminish the impact of
the anticipated testimony or exhibit. Waiting for the direct to be
completed and for cross-examination will give the testimony a
long time to sink in before it can be assailed. If the opposing lawyer
uses voir dire to make the compromising point on the spot, the
effect on the presentation will be more immediate. And if the
presentation seems to have some momentum, an interruption is
always welcome to the opponent.

Misuse of voir dire as an early mini-cross-examination or as an
interruption of the opponent's presentation is a violation of the
ethical prohibitions against intentional violation of procedural
rules. It is also the kind of cheap shot that is noticed by the judge
and by opposing counsel. Misuse of voir dire on one occasion may
make it difficult for the lawyer to obtain permission for voir dire in
the future.

7.   *Lawyer Commentary and Expressions of Personal Belief*

The lawyer's conviction of the rightness of her cause is an essential
component of an effective presentation. How can someone expect
factfinders to credit an image being created for them unless the
creator makes it very clear that she herself believes in the image as
well? A sense of the personal conviction of the presenter is essential
to the success of any presentation.

At the same time, explicit statements of a lawyer's personal opinion of the rightness of a position, the guilt or innocence of a defendant, or the credibility of a witness are improper and unethical.

> *Counsel* (in summation).   Men and women of the jury, when
> all is said and done, I know that you will believe, as I do,
> that the defendant could not have committed this crime.
> He is simply not the kind of person who would ever take
> the life of another human being.

> *Opposing Counsel.*   *Objection!* Your Honor, Counsel is ex-
> pressing a personal belief in the outcome of this case.

> *The Court.*   The objection is sustained. Members of the jury,
> please disregard any statement by counsel of his personal
> belief in the guilt or innocence of the defendant. You may
> proceed, Counsel.

The ABA Code and Rules both condemn such statements. According to DR 7-106(C)(1) and 7-106(C)(4), a lawyer may not assert
personal knowledge of facts in issue or a personal opinion of just-
ness of a cause, the credibility of a witness, or the guilt or innocence of a defendant. Model Rule 3.4(e) forbids the same conduct.

In the heat of trial it is easy for a lawyer unintentionally to
violate this rule. It is easy for the lawyer's implicit confidence to
become explicit without the lawyer even being aware of it. Improper expressions of personal opinion are particularly likely to
slip into the final windup of a closing:

> *Counsel.*   Mr. Maxfield told it like it is. He didn't try to hide
> anything. His testimony had the ring of truth. When all is
> said and done, I think we have to believe Mr. Maxfield's
> testimony.

or

> *Counsel.*   I don't think you have any choice, Ladies and Gen-
> tlemen. I can't believe that the evidence that you have heard
> can convince you beyond a reasonable doubt that Bob
> Maxfield had any intention of hurting or killing anyone.

A lawyer can generally avoid unintentionally expressing a personal opinion during trial by avoiding use of the first person singular in trial discourse. The "I" is what injects the lawyer expressly into the proceedings. Very rarely does the first person singular enhance a trial presentation, and frequently it can detract. The persona of the lawyer is best felt as the self-effacing presenter of the image. It is that which is being presented, not the presenter that matters. If a lawyer adopts a habit of never using "I" during a trial, the risk of an improper personal opinion will be reduced to nothing.

> *Counsel.* Mr. Maxfield told it like it is. He didn't try to hide anything. His testimony had the ring of truth. When all is said and done, we have to believe Mr. Maxfield's testimony. Do you have any choice, Ladies and Gentlemen? The evidence that you have heard cannot convince you beyond a reasonable doubt that Bob Maxfield had any intention of hurting or killing anyone.

A particularly sensitive area for lawyer comment is the truthfulness of parties and witnesses. The rules specifically forbid explicit expression of a lawyer's opinion of the credibility of a witness. At the same time, it is permissible and often important to argue and even attack the credibility of a witness on summation. Sometimes the line between permissible argument and impermissible injection of the lawyer's own opinion is a hazy one. For instance, in some courts an argument such as

> *Counsel.* Alex Hood was lying. He lied when he told us that he was not at the Suisse Chalet. He lied again when he said that he didn't even know why he was in Portland. His past record of convictions shows that he is a liar.

would be improper prosecution summation. Courts condemning such argument usually refer to the rules prohibiting lawyer opinions on witness credibility. It may seem illogical to apply this rule to arguments that do not expressly state the lawyer's opinion or belief. On the other hand, an express accusation of lying is seldom made unless the accuser really believes it. Such an accusation may by its very nature invoke the personal credibility of the accuser and make it an issue. While the sensitivity of courts on this issue varies, it is safe to say that trial lawyers should be cautious about direct accusations of untruthfulness in their questioning and argument.

This brief chapter cannot catalog all or any large portion of the temptations faced by lawyers presenting fact cases at trial. When does an aggressive presentation become misrepresentation? When does an argument go too far? These questions trouble lawyers with every trial.

Trial lawyering is not a game. Winning is important, but it is not the only thing. No degree of dedication to a client's short-term interests can justify conduct that corrodes and undermines the legitimacy of the very process itself.

Although the official rules do not provide all the answers, a trial lawyer must abide scrupulously by their letter and their spirit. Sometimes in the heat of battle it is hard to remember chapter and verse. But if the trial lawyer presents as fact only that which she believes is true, if she uses the licenses granted her scrupulously for the purposes for which they were intended, if she creates no trick or deception in the process, she will not go far wrong.

4 Developing a Fact Theory of the Case

A. Developing a Theory of the Case

The process by which the trial lawyer develops the fact "theory of the case" could be the subject of an entire book. It is at the core of effective trial advocacy.

Before the trial lawyer can even begin to determine whether her case is worth trying, she must analyze the available factual material found in the frequently ambiguous, fragmented impressions derived from the unstructured facts and uncertain inferences. She must then attempt to discern the outline of the potential fact pictures or scenarios that fit within the legal rules.

The theory of a case, then, is the fact picture to be presented and the references to logic, consistency, and, above all, human experience, that support acceptance of that fact picture by the fact-finders. "What happened, and why do we believe it?" is the fact theory of the case. In order to make an effective trial presentation, the lawyer must carefully think out and analyze the potential alternative theories that can be developed from the available information. Usually the next step is to choose the theory that 1) fits the available facts and 2) is associated with a legal rule favorable to the side that the lawyer is representing.

For instance, assume that the prosecutor learns from the investigation of a potential murder case that the defendant and the decedent had a quarrel on the defendant's front porch on a residential street at about 9 o'clock on the evening of the incident. The defendant goes into the house, and the decedent leaves. The decedent, drunk, staggers down the street and falls on the sidewalk under a tree. A few moments later the defendant drives rapidly down the street, up onto the sidewalk, over the prone body of the decedent, and then back onto the street.

From these facts the prosecutor develops her theory of the case: The defendant saw the decedent and ran over him intending to kill him. This theory of the case seems to fit the fact material available to the prosecutor. Some of this theory is supported directly by witness observation or physical evidence. The fight on the porch and even the car driving up on the sidewalk and over the recumbent body of the decedent can be portrayed directly by witnesses. But some of the crucial elements of the theory must be supplied by inference. The prosecutor has no direct proof that the defendant intended to run over the decedent or that he even saw him as he was lying on the sidewalk. The blanks in the picture not provided by direct evidence must be filled in by inference. Human experience suggests that people do not drive up on the sidewalk unless they have a good reason for doing so. Human experience also teaches that a person who has been humiliated in a confrontation on his porch could very well wish to do his assailant serious harm, and would have a good reason to pursue him and drive over his body on the sidewalk.

A fact theory is considered viable if the available facts and likely inferences will build a picture that the lawyer can present to the factfinders with the confidence that they will accept it. A viable fact theory is worth presenting if the picture generated is associated with a legal rule favorable to the lawyer's client. In this case, the picture of the angry? disgruntled? humiliated? defendant deliberately driving over the recumbent body of his recent assailant is not only factually viable but can be associated with the legal rule defining the crime of murder — "intentionally causing the death of another."

The process of developing the fact theory begins early in preparation of the case and continues until the end of the trial. As the case is prepared, and sometimes even as it is being presented, careful investigation and study of the facts is necessary to refine the theory. For instance, in the example above, the prosecutor might find that the most likely fact image would be of the defendant leaving his home determined to seek, catch, and kill the decedent. The "theory" would be that the defendant decided to kill the decedent while the defendant was in the home and left with that intention. As the prosecutor learns more facts and thinks about them more, the initial fact theory may appear flawed. A more plausible picture might be that of the defendant leaving his home seeking merely to locate the departing antagonist but then suddenly forming the murderous intent when he sees the decedent lying helpless on the ground. This theory would be that the defendant formed the intent to kill just before hitting the body.

In the same example, if the police investigation disclosed that the defendant had called the police at the time he went into his house, the prosecutor might conclude that it would be difficult or impossible to recreate a convincing picture of the defendant forming the intent to murder the decedent or do him harm at the same time as he was calling the police. Who would call the police to come and witness the caller in the process of killing someone? Most people do not go out and kill someone right after they have asked the police to come and deal with the matter. The information that the police had been called might make more plausible a fact theory that the defendant did not form the intent to kill until he was driving down the street and saw the decedent on the sidewalk.

On the other hand, the image of the defendant's car accelerating continuously in the direction of the decedent as soon as it left the defendant's driveway would suggest that perhaps the murderous intent had been formed at an earlier time.

The prosecutor will have to make a choice. Which of these two alternative theories will be adopted will depend on the prosecutor's assessment of the available facts that can be presented and her ability to recreate a picture that has the maximum chance for acceptance by the factfinders.

Successful theories are usually relatively simple, sufficient to explain all of the known facts, and in accord with human experience. Fact pictures that are complicated, that do not understandably incorporate all of the known facts, or that are not in accord with human experience are hard to sell.

As it is being developed, tested, and refined by the lawyer, the fact theory becomes the outline of the overall picture and its most important elements. It is then for the trial lawyer to organize the presentation of this picture in such a manner that the fact theory is taught to the factfinders with the greatest impact, accuracy, and credibility as the resources allow.

B. Supporting Themes

Once the trial lawyer has decided on the theory of the case, it is time to identify supportive fact patterns or themes that will be used in the presentation to make the theory more plausible. Unlike a theory, a theme is not an outline of the story itself but is a fact element or pattern in the story that may make the overall picture more credible or acceptable to the factfinder. Most cases have more than one theme. Some themes appeal to the conscious and reasoning mind; others are designed to reach the subconscious thought processes. Some themes are even calculated to play on potential prejudices or emotional reactions of the factfinders. Although opinion is not unanimous on the issue, the use of themes to exploit factfinder prejudices and to appeal to their emotions is subject to serious ethical question.

In a prosecution for murder, where the defendant ran over the decedent as he lay passed out on the sidewalk after an unpleasant confrontation, the prosecutor might structure her presentation to emphasize the theme of the defendant taking the law into his own hands. The defendant might be likened to a vigilante who short-cuts the processes of justice in favor of revenge. The defense might play on a theme of a homeowner who had been assaulted in his own home and was acting to protect his family.

These themes are not themselves relevant facts but are ways of understanding the facts and the paths to the desired inferences. For instance, the vigilante theme may tend to explain and make understandable the defendant's attack on the decedent, even after the police had been summoned.

Themes often play on common psychological traits. In order to make the defendant's otherwise uncharacteristic rage more understandable, the prosecutor might point out the challenge to the defendant's masculinity represented by the front-porch confrontation between the two drunks.

Sometimes a theme may play on emotion and prejudice. In a blue-collar town, the prosecutor might subtly emphasize the upper-middle-class status of the defendant, as opposed to the working-class origins of the decedent. Although it is never actually articulated, the theme of oppression of blue-collar people by white-collar supervisors might influence the factfinders' understanding of the prosecution's fact picture of how the alleged murder took place.

Themes can be expressed in symbols or by analogy. In a civil suit for accountant malpractice, for example, the defendant accounting firm auditing the records of a failed corporation was analogized to the captain of the Titanic, ignoring warning signals and steaming into the iceberg. In another case, personnel of a hospital were portrayed as the crew of a "ship of birth," who failed to act to save the innocent mother and child from harm at the hands of a demented doctor captain.

Sometimes the theme can be as simple as a visual pattern or symbol. In an insanity defense to bank robbery, the defendant's prior head injury commenced a spiral of mental dysfunction, causing anxiety, causing greater dysfunction, engendering increased anxiety, heightening the dysfunction, and so on and so on until the defendant snapped and committed the crime. During opening statement, witness testimony, and closing, a spiral was repeatedly used in the visual aids and by hand gestures to illustrate the progress of the defendant's mental state. The theme of the spiral served to unify and make understandable the expert witnesses' various technical explanations and to relate them to the defendant's fact theory of a progression of mental deterioration and lack of criminal responsibility.

Picking the fact theories and the available themes of the case is a vital part of the lawyer's task of fact analysis. The lawyer must study all of the available facts in order to find the most understandable and persuasive image that can be recreated in court. Fact analysis is not confined to review of files in the law office or discussions with other lawyers or witnesses. Driving a car, taking a shower, dozing off to sleep at night, a lawyer who is developing and refining a theory for trial thinks about the facts all the time. The facts and inferences and how they can be articulated and proved are never out of the lawyer's mind. Frequent mulling of the facts, testing alternative theories and hypotheses, fitting pieces together and relating them to experience are usually necessary in order to develop a truly authoritative fact theory that can be presented at trial and can withstand the challenge of the opponent. That image is likely to be the truth.

C.   Theories, Themes, and Available Resources

Developing and refining a case requires consideration of not only what the facts are but how they can be effectively presented. Even though a particular theory might seem logically persuasive to the lawyer, unless it can be effectively portrayed with the existing resources it will not win in the face of opposition. The task is to choose a theory that can be well portrayed. Thus, as the lawyer develops a theory, she is also thinking of how it lends itself to a presentation using the available witnesses, information, and media.

Sometimes the resources necessary to present the fact picture are obvious and are readily at hand. Friendly witnesses who can relate an observed event, physical evidence that can be associated with a given happening or state of affairs, established events that are consistent in human experience with the picture sought are all obvious resources to present a fact theory. However, such resources are not always available. Sometimes a party or his counsel may have a good-faith belief of how things happened but be without resources to show it in court. This may mean that the fact theory is simply not viable. But sometimes by digging a little deeper, the lawyer can discover less obvious resources that will make it possible to present the fact theory after all.

In an intersection collision case, assume that the plaintiff's theory is that the defendant failed to look down the street before starting into the intersection. If no witnesses come forward to say they saw the defendant entering the intersection without looking and the defendant asserts that he did look, the plaintiff may be hard-pressed to establish this theory, regardless of the strength of his conviction in the truth of that picture. The lawyer thinks, "Hmmm; why did I come to the conclusion that the defendant probably did not look?"

The lawyer realizes that when he examined the scene, he noticed that the street with the right-of-way was long and straight. The corner with the stop sign was by a vacant lot. A person sitting at the stop sign would have had a good view down the street from where the plaintiff's car was coming. The answer becomes obvious: if the defendant had looked, he would have had to see the oncoming car. The collision itself is the proof that he did not look.

The resources for the development of this theory are not the testimony of the witnesses but the physical layout of the streets and the relationships between time, speed, and distance travelled. Photographs and diagrams thus become the primary vehicles to build the plaintiff's case. Mathematical computations and appeals to human experience in driving technique may take the place of witness testimony in establishing a fact picture associated with the desired legal rule.

D.   The Process of Developing the Fact Theory

One can look at fact theory development as a two-step process. The first step is taken at the time the case is first organized and undertaken. From the available sources of information, usually the lawyer's own client and sources within the client's control, the lawyer has to figure out whether there are the potential elements of a viable fact picture, usually without much thought as to how that picture can or will be presented. In the often unorganized and miscellaneous facts that attend any event or transaction, the lawyer tries to visualize a pattern or outline that (1) has favorable legal consequences and (2) is likely to be acceptable to factfinders.

Once it has been determined that the circumstances of the case contain a potential fact picture that is worth presenting, the lawyer will investigate the facts and undertake discovery. This is the second step in the development process. The purpose of discovery is to see if there are other facts that will add to or detract from the picture that the lawyer has fastened on as the tentative theory of the case and to identify and locate potential resources that can be used to present the fact theory in court.

Sometimes the results of the investigations and discovery will lead the lawyer to modify or give up on a prior theory and develop a new theory. The lawyer may find that the picture initially chosen just "doesn't hold water," and that may be the end of the case. Many a lawyer has had to abandon or settle a case or cop a plea when her initial theory of the case "didn't pan out."

In the murder prosecution in our earlier example, the prosecution's initial theory was that the defendant got mad at the two assailants and decided to kill them while they were all still on the porch. Then the prosecutor learns that the defendant was with his girlfriend moments later when she called the police. The initial prosecution theory seems a little less probable. Is it really likely that the defendant would intentionally go out and try to kill the men knowing that the police were on their way?

Initially the decedent's companion tells the police that the defendant struck the decedent with his car while the decedent was running along the sidewalk. Later, however, an account by an eyewitness and an analysis of the condition of the car make it much more likely that the decedent was lying on the ground at the time he was struck.

Out of the wreckage of the prosecutor's original theory a new theory is born. The prosecutor can accept the defendant's explanation that he got into his car to follow the men so that the police could arrest them, and that it was not his intention at the outset to kill them. As the defendant drove down the street, the decedent, lying in the shadow of a big tree, was invisible. But then, suddenly in the glare of the headlights, the former adversary appeared, lying on the sidewalk, at the defendant's mercy. In a split second the necessary intent was formed, the wheel was turned, and the murder was committed.

As the lawyer moves forward, testing theories against the available facts and resources, she must remain flexible to possible changes in the picture to be portrayed. Dogged insistence on an obsolete theory can be the ruin of a good case. Right up to the time of trial the theory should always be provisional and subject to refinement and change based on the facts and resources at hand.

E. Determining How the Fact Theory Will Be Presented

As the trial lawyer is developing her fact theory, testing it, and changing it based on her growing knowledge of the available facts, she is simultaneously figuring out how best to present the fact picture. This is a process of analysis and resource selection.

As suggested before, accurate portrayal of all aspects of any event would require that a vast number of impressions be communicated and recreated in the consciousness of the factfinders. Using conventional presentation techniques, faithful re-creation of all details of even simple events would be long and boring procedures. Trials, however, should never be boring. They should always be no longer than necessary to convince the factfinder. It is therefore up to the trial lawyer to

1)   select those details of the image that are important to the theory or its acceptance by the factfinders for portrayal, and

2)   choose media that will convey important information as rapidly, accurately, and authoritatively as possible.

Details that matter are those that directly contribute to the fact image to be recreated or that make the image portrayed more understandable and credible. These details should be conveyed using media that will transmit them to the consciousness of the factfinders as clearly and efficiently as possible. The choice of details to include in the presentation and what kind of media to use to present them is an important part of the work of the trial lawyer. How can this fact theory be best taught from the available resources? Here there is room not only for careful fact analysis but for real creativity in planning and designing the overall presentation as well as its component details.

F.   Choosing the Important Facts and Details

In selecting details from the actual incident or circumstance to be recreated in court, it is easy to eliminate those that obviously do not matter. In presenting an automobile accident case, for example, many of the details of the scene of the accident and of what happened before and after might pass the test of relevance as a matter of the law of evidence. Many of these details, however, should be screened out.

The color and make of the eyewitness's car are details from the actual scene of the accident, but it is unlikely that the lawyer for either the plaintiff or the defendant would bother to take the time to include them as part of the case of either party. A large number of extraneous details such as these must be screened out as a matter of efficiency and impact in case presentation.

There are also a large number of details that do not figure directly in the events in question and therefore are not directly elements of the picture to be portrayed. They can affect how the picture is received, however. Thus, for instance, the make of the eyewitness's car may be a detail worth using if there is a potential issue of the perspective of the witness. Giving the factfinders an image of the place from which the eyewitness saw the accident may make the witness's testimony more "real."

Trial lawyers often include key details that do not seem to have direct legal significance but give their presentations more reality and make them more acceptable to factfinders. One class of information that is sometimes scanted in trial presentations is the details about the parties and witnesses as people, their backgrounds, occupations, relationships, and lives. Humanization of the parties and witnesses is a part of every examination. Too often, however, the lawyer asks the humanizing questions in a routine and uninterested manner, usually as a preliminary to the important facts about the case itself. But human facts about the parties and witnesses are some of the most important aspects of the case. What kind of a person is this? Most people find this question a very important one in assaying any information given by or about another person. In real life we all make important decisions based on our assessment of another person as a person.

A lawyer should not forget this when going to court. Giving the factfinders a picture of the party or witness as a human being helps them to decide whether to accept what the witness is saying and whether the party is someone whom they like and want to help.

Preparation for the trial should include selection of information about the parties and witnesses that will promote the factfinders' acceptance of their testimony and a desire to help. It is easier for the factfinders to assess and accept testimony from someone who seems to be like them than from someone who seems to be different or whose life is a cipher. Details that fill in the persona of the party or witness can be the most mundane ones; residence, marriage, military service, occupation, children, and the like. If those personal details are familiar to or shared by the factfinders, there is a feeling of kinship and trust that is helpful to the factfinders' appraisal of the party or witness. People want to believe and help other people like themselves.

Regarding the accident itself, details that make the event understandable in light of the common experience of the factfinders are the most helpful to achieving acceptance of the picture. In a trial for a murder committed by driving a car over the victim while he lies on the sidewalk, the prosecution might well show in detail a confrontation between the defendant and the deceased a few minutes before the incident. The fact that the defendant stood quietly by while the decedent insulted the defendant's girlfriend could be an important one. It might assist the factfinders to believe in a portrayal of the defendant as humiliated and enraged enough to take such drastic and deadly action.

In an automobile accident case, the fact that the defendant was on his way home in the early evening after spending the afternoon collecting from his customers over a familiar route might be proffered to assist the jury in understanding an image of him crossing a through street without stopping completely at the stop sign. On the other hand, the defense might want the factfinders to know that the defendant's route was familiar to him in hopes that they would accept an image of the defendant stopping at the stop sign in the same almost reflexive manner he had for decades before.

Although they may be necessary to a 100 percent accurate recreation of an episode at issue, many facts are not needed to recreate those aspects of the scene that are important to one legal theory or the other. For example, many details of the knife, such as its color, age, the manner in which blades other than the primary blade are opened, probably have no consequence to the legal theory involving the use of the knife as a weapon. There is no need to elicit those facts as a part of the presentation at trial. On the other hand, some features of the knife, such as its size, weight, blade length, and manner of opening the principal blade, relate directly to the central issue.

Fact images can be transmitted individually or in bundles. For instance, the word "desk" conveys a more or less defined bundle of facts that define a certain kind of furniture. Because the term is a general one, the image that will arise in the factfinders' minds will differ based on their own experiences. But there is a sufficient common experience so that "desk" does convey to most individuals an overall image that includes many individual facts.

In selecting the facts to be portrayed, the lawyer will look to the theory of the case and those facts that will make the theory more plausible. While the theory itself may be a stark outline, enough facts have to be included to give the events a sense of reality. The lawyer should include enough background and accrediting facts about the incident on trial so that the factfinders are satisfied that they have an understanding of an event and its circumstances.

G. Choosing the Media

Once the image has been chosen and the salient facts to convey and accredit that image have been selected, the trial lawyer must decide what media and resources to use to recreate the image in court. This choice involves considerations of power, accuracy, efficiency, availability, and cost.

The kind of information to be conveyed requires the most suitable medium for its presentation. For instance, information about a scene is almost always best conveyed by visual media. If the appearance of a particular scene is important to a case, for maximum effect there is no substitute for a blown up photograph. Whenever the geographic layout of a scene is involved, an appropriate diagram or plan of the area, with the significant details included or added at trial, will best enhance the factfinders' understanding. If the diagram is neat and is drawn to scale, its authenticity will be enhanced. If it is obviously crude or not to scale, its value as a direct source of information will be limited.

Almost all cases involve something that needs to be visualized. For such evidence, visual media are clearly the best way to convey information; oral testimony comes in a distant second. But, if the subject matter of the case is a progression of events, or if a state of mind is involved, there will likely be much greater reliance on oral testimony, with charts, diagrams, or other illustrative aids to augment it.

The power of the visual media is so great that the resourceful lawyer will strive hard to incorporate visuals in the key parts of her presentation. Thus, in a damages claim presentation, financial data illustrated graphically will likely have a much greater impact than the same information presented only through oral witness testimony.

The universal acceptance of television and video in American life means that information presented in court via these media is likely to receive a positive reception by factfinders. Thus a witness who may be unimpressive in person is likely to look better on video. Expert testimony offered by video deposition was once considered a poor substitute for having the expert appear in person. However, many trial lawyers now believe that a witness properly presented on TV carries greater weight and authority than when that witness testifies in person.

Those parts of the presentation that rely on oral testimony should be analyzed for potential ambiguity. Words and expressions should be chosen for their associations and for their lively images. Amorphous and colorless wording should be avoided. Words that evoke sharp and unambiguous images are ordinarily more effective. Thus the plaintiff's lawyer might use the word "crash" to describe the same event that the defense lawyer calls a "collision." The prosecutor refers to the defendant "killing" the victim with his car; the defense prefers to suggest that the decedent died as the result of an "accident."

Words that can be used thematically are particularly helpful. If the same key words used by the lawyer in the opening are used again by an important witness when testifying and once again by the lawyer in closing, those words and the images associated with them are likely to be graven into the consciousnesses of the fact-finders. For example, in an opening statement:

> *Counsel.*   And when he was thrown backward and forward in that crash, the L-2 vertebra in Mr. Cluney's back was crushed and shattered into several pieces.

During the direct examination of the plaintiff's expert:

> *Q.*   Doctor, what do you mean when you say that Mr. Cluney had a "comminuted compression fracture of the L-2 vertebra"?
>
> *A.*   Mr. Cluney's L-2 vertebra was crushed and shattered by the impact.

During cross-examination of the defendant's medical expert witness:

> *Q.*   And that means, Doctor, that Mr. Cluney's L-2 vertebra was crushed and shattered, doesn't it?
>
> *A.*   Yes, broken in several pieces.

During closing argument:

Counsel.   And what is fair to compensate Mr. Cluney for the
crushed and shattered L-2 vertebra in his back?

Repetition of colorful key words will make the image conveyed
indelible in the consciousnesses of the factfinders.

Although courtroom presentations are traditionally thought of
as exercises in oral communication, in reality they are multimedia
events. Even a purely oral witness account of an incident can be
enhanced by gestures, demonstrations, the use of visual aids, and
the reference to exhibits. The trial lawyer's responsibility to plan
and control the presentation extends to everything that will happen
in the courtroom. There is no detail that is not worthy of consideration in the interest of the most effective overall presentation.

Chapter 5 Courtroom Conduct and Manners

Trial advocacy is competitive fact presentation and teaching, controlled and conducted by the lawyers. This presentation and teaching takes place in the special, artificial environment of the courtroom under the direct control of the judge. The lawyers' conduct during their courtroom presentations is governed by a host of written and unwritten rules designed to make the process as fair and accurate as circumstances permit. The written rules are those of evidence and procedure, with which every trial lawyer must be intimately familiar. These rules merge imperceptibly into a body of trial law and courtroom custom, etiquette, and tradition, which are almost as important. Knowledge and understanding of these rules and customs enable the trial lawyer confidently to exercise considerable freedom to spread the fact picture before the factfinders as effectively as possible.

Since many of the rules of courtroom courtesy and manners are unwritten and customary, they vary from jurisdiction to jurisdiction, from county to county, and from judge to judge. The teachings of any book such as this must be taken with a grain of the local salt. The important lesson from all of these practices is that trial lawyers are expected to perform their work with a high degree of professionalism and to accord respect and courtesy to all participants in the trial process.

A. The Courtroom as a Stage

Effective trial presentations make full use of the space of the courtroom to aid in the process. In a sense, the courtroom is a stage on which the lawyer makes a presentation. The courtroom is an all-encompassing space in which all the participants have places and roles that must be accommodated and respected.

The authority of the presentation is usually aided by the lawyer's apparent command of the courtroom and the flow of energy within that space. Just as a teacher asserts command over the classroom and makes that space serve the purposes of the class presentation, so must the trial lawyer control the courtroom space and dynamics during her presentation.

This does not mean that the lawyer has an unfettered right to restructure the courtroom space to suit the presentation. She does not have absolute freedom to move about or cause witnesses or other participants in the process to move about during the trial. Customs and practices affecting utilization of courtroom space vary from jurisdiction to jurisdiction and, indeed, from judge to judge. In every context there is a point at which the trial lawyer's command of the courtroom spaces is subject to the overall control and supervision of the judge. Within the scope allotted the lawyer by rules and customs, written and unwritten, she must take control of the space and make it serve her presentation.

1. Acknowledging the Judge

The degree to which a trial lawyer is expected to express deference to the trial judge varies, both among jurisdictions and among judges. In many jurisdictions it is customary for the lawyer to acknowledge the judge by saying, "May it please the Court" before beginning a presentation to the jury. In many jurisdictions the trial lawyer is expected to ask the permission of the court before having the witness leave the witness stand to use a visual aid or demonstrate in front of the jury.

> Q. Your Honor, may the witness approach the blackboard?

or

> Q. With the permission of the Court, Ms. Mercer, would you go to the blackboard and draw for us a sketch of the area of Jackson Street where you live?

Some judges expect the lawyer to ask permission before leaving the podium or other place of examination to approach the witness:

Q. Your Honor, may I approach the witness?

When the purpose of the lawyer's approaching the witness is obvious, the judge may consider a request for permission superfluous.

Q. Your Honor, may this be marked as Exhibit 1 for identification?

The Court. Yes, Exhibit 1 for identification.

Q. Your Honor, may I approach the witness?

The Court. In this courtroom, Counsel, it is not necessary to ask the Court's permission to approach the witness to show her a proposed exhibit.

And if a lawyer's movements in the courtroom are unduly intimidating or show a lack of consideration of the court, jury, or opponent, the opponent can appeal to the court for remedial action.

Opposing Counsel. Your Honor, we object to counsel hanging over the witness that way.

Or, more irritatingly,

Opposing Counsel. Your Honor, Counsel is blocking my view of the witness!

Q. Your Honor, it is all right with us if Plaintiff's counsel moves to another place in the courtroom from where she can have an unobstructed view of the witness.

Although local rules or custom may require acknowledgments of the suzerainty of the judge as a part of the presentation, the trial lawyer should be anything but tentative in her command of the courtroom space. The "requests" to the court for leave to approach the witness or to have the witness leave the stand, for example, are usually made in a tone that is more declarative than interrogative.

> Q. Your Honor, may the witness leave the stand to show the jury the part of his back that was injured in the crash?

usually ends in the downbeat inflection of a statement rather than the upbeat of a genuine question. The idea is simply to acknowledge the overriding authority of the court while maintaining firm control of the space.

2. Focusing on the Factfinders

Even while the lawyer acknowledges the overall authority of the judge, the main focus of the presentation should always be on the factfinders. It should be clear from the first sentence out of the lawyer's mouth that the jury is the chief object of her interest, and all the elements of the visual and oral presentation should be aimed primarily at the jury as factfinders. While the lawyer defers to the judge as a matter of courtesy, the members of the jury are the ones who will have to get the picture being taught by the lawyer. The lawyer should make sure that the jury has the best view of visual presentations and can easily hear what is said by the witnesses. She should telegraph by word and action how important the factfinders are to her and her client and how much she wants them to see and hear every element of her presentation.

B. Effective Positioning for Presentation

Once the lawyer has taken control of the courtroom space, it is up to her to use it to the best advantage. Throughout the presentation, the lawyer will position herself at various spots so as to enhance the particular parts of the presentation. Sometimes local rules require lawyers to remain seated at counsel table during examination or to use a podium when examining witnesses or addressing the factfinders. Subject to these considerations, the trial lawyer should position herself, the witnesses, and any visual media she uses in such a way as to have maximum impact on the factfinders. Where will witnesses and aids be positioned to make sure the factfinders can see them? How can the lawyer maintain effective eye contact with the witnesses and the factfinders? How should the projection screen be positioned to make sure that the jury and perhaps the judge as well can see it, yet so that it will not obstruct other activities in the courtroom? Is there enough light so that people can read things placed before them? These questions and many more must be addressed by the trial lawyer planning her use of space in the courtroom.

1.   Energy in the Courtroom

Teachers, storytellers, and entertainers emit a kind of energy that is beamed at their audiences. Transmitted by body language, tone of voice, and eye contact, this energy is an unconscious but important part of any presentation. Storytellers and entertainers orchestrate their performances to make use of this energy for maximum effect; a trial lawyer must do the same. The lawyer must also make sure to arrange the presentation so that the positive energy of lawyer and witnesses will be directed at and effectively reach the factfinders.

The lawyer helps the witnesses beam their energy toward the factfinders by the form and tone of the questions and by the lawyer's position and body language. A question asked in an encouraging and interested tone is more likely to encourage the witness to give an animated, energized response than one that is asked in an indifferent or aloof manner. If a lawyer and her witness are engaged in an intense give and take, say, up in front of a blackboard, the back and forth flow of the exchange may include the participants but conspicuously exclude the factfinders. The factfinders become onlookers rather than participants in the give and take of persuasive energy. A factfinder who is only looking on is more likely to lose interest and be distracted than one who is in the path of the flow of energy emanating from the lawyer and her witness.

A teacher's skills are enhanced by the energy that his students absorb as a part of his presentation. The same is true of presenting a case at trial. Like the teacher, the lawyer must make sure that the participants in the presentation are in the best positions to maximize energy flow in the right direction — toward the factfinders.

2. During Opening and Closing Statements

a. Where to Stand

During the opening statement, when the trial lawyer is first exposed to the factfinders and is first describing the image that will be recreated, she usually stands directly in front of the factfinders. She delivers her opening directly to them, and pays very little attention to the judge and none to the opposing lawyer. She stands close enough to the factfinders to maintain good eye contact and to be easily heard but back far enough so that she is not invading their space. [When visual aids are used she positions herself near these aids so that she can effectively use them to teach the factfinders.]

Closing arguments involve considerations similar to those of opening statements. The lawyer wants to communicate with the factfinders as directly and effectively as she can, so her positioning is similar to that for the opening—usually right in front of the factfinders.

Movement by the lawyer during her opening statement and closing argument, as in any other part of the trial, should be purposeful. How she moves around within the courtroom space can have a strong impact in terms of emphasis and drama. Repetitive and nervous motion and pacing can easily distract the factfinders and divert attention from the focus of the presentation.

b. Using a Microphone

Many courtrooms have poor acoustics. Sometimes microphones are provided at counsel table, at a podium, and at the witness stand. The additional volume from the microphones may diminish the intimacy of the address and cause a loss of flexibility in movement and positioning. These competing considerations have to be weighed by the lawyer in planning the presentation.

c. Using a Podium

Opinion is split on the use of a podium during opening or summation. Some see the podium as a helpful, stabilizing factor, a place to perch notes and to anchor oneself. Others regard the podium as a extraneous element. It restricts the lawyer's ability to move around and to use her whole body effectively, and it tends to make the opening or closing more of a speech and less of a conversation. Is the lawyer hiding or hanging on? While the podium can provide security, it can also inhibit one's ability to enhance the presentation with physical gestures and demonstrations.

Experience in the teaching of trial advocacy suggests that the claimed virtues of a podium are the result of habit. Lawyers who have been trained to use a podium in court often feel naked and nervous without it, but lawyers who work without a podium are able to be more animated and natural and can throw their whole bodies into the presentation process.

3. During Direct Examination

During direct examination, the lawyer will usually wish to position herself so as to help project the witness's presentation and energy to the factfinders. In many conventionally designed courtrooms, a good position for counsel is beyond the end of the jury box, farthest away from the witness. The lawyer-witness dialogue thus forces the witness to look and speak toward the jury. The likelihood that the witness will establish and maintain positive eye contact with some of the factfinders is increased, and the witness's positive energy is directed toward the factfinders.

If the lawyer stands and examines from the far end of the jury box, the witness is also automatically encouraged to speak loudly enough so the lawyer can hear from the other side of the jury. This usually means that all of the factfinders will hear as well.

Most important, as the lawyer conducts the examination from behind the jury box, she is experiencing the witness's presentation from the perspective of the factfinders. The lawyer can appreciate the witness's effect on them and can modify her cues and instructions to maximize that impact. From her position she can instantly tell whether the factfinders can see or hear what the witness is doing or saying. She can tell the witness to

Q. Please speak up so that all of the members of the jury can hear you.

or she can cue the witness to show the jury an exhibit or visual aid:

> Q. Officer Anderson, can you please make the "P" beside
> where you drew the box to represent the Clark car a little
> bigger and a little darker so we can all see it clearly?

A position near the jury box makes it easy for the lawyer to include herself in with the factfinders in the form of her questions.

> Q. Ms. Mercer, please show us where you live.

The "us" refers to the examining lawyer and the factfinders. The other lawyer and his client, sitting at the counsel table across the room, are, by unconscious implication, excluded.

Sometimes courtroom design or local rules or customs require the lawyer to conduct direct examination from a podium or other fixed location that does not naturally tend to make the witness project to the jury as he responds to the questions. The lawyer must then take extra pains, both by speech and by body language, to cue the witness to speak and project to the jury.

> Q. Ms. Mercer, would you please tell the members of the
> jury [lawyer looks in the direction of the jury] what you
> saw when you looked out of your window?

or, even more explicitly,

> Q. Ms. Mercer, would you please speak directly to the mem-
> bers of the jury and tell them what you saw when you
> looked out of the window?

4. *During Cross-Examination*

While conducting a cross-examination or voir dire of an opposing witness, the examining lawyer makes herself the center of attention. Most of the time during cross-examination, all of the information being elicited is in the questions put by the lawyer, and most, if not all, of the energy is coming from the lawyer. It is the lawyer to whom the factfinders are to pay attention, not the other side's witness. The role of the witness is reduced merely to confirmation of the lawyer's questions. There is a saying among trial lawyers that "Cross-examination is an aria, sung by the lawyer, to which the witness merely mutters affirmances."

The cross-examining lawyer usually stands where she will be fully visible to and will project to the factfinders as she poses her questions. Although the cross-examination questions are nominally posed to the witness, the information in these questions is really for the factfinders, so the lawyer must place herself where the energy and impact of her questions will reach the jury most effectively. This is usually right out in front of the factfinders, where they can all see and hear the lawyer. From this position she can best observe the factfinders and get feedback by eye contact with them.

The lawyer must also be in a position to exercise effective eye contact and voice control over the witness, however. As discussed in greater detail in Chapter 8, lawyers exercise control on cross-examination by position, eye contact, and body language as well as by leading questions.

At the same time, the cross-examining lawyer wants the persuasive energy of the witness to be muted and directed away from the jury. The lawyer should be standing where the witness cannot establish eye contact with the factfinders as he attempts to parry her questions. The witness should be forced by the lawyer's position to look away from the factfinders as he answers.

Occasionally, a lawyer cross-examining someone may approach a step or two closer to the witness to give added emphasis to a particular question or to put more pressure on the witness to give an affirmative answer. This technique can be overused: the intimidation conveyed by the lawyer's hostile movement toward the witness may spill over to the factfinders and make them side with the witness. In rare instances a lawyer might wish to hint at her lack of respect for a witness's integrity by the tone or manner of her cross-examination.

Under appropriate circumstances, however, the lawyer may seek to dramatize her cross-examination by moving around the courtroom as she asks the questions. Sometimes the lawyer may demonstrate with body language as she puts the question:

Q. And, Mrs. Godard, the next thing you did was to bend down and pick up your paper [lawyer bends down and picks up an imaginary paper from the courtroom floor], didn't you?

Sometimes such demonstrations require the examining lawyer to turn away from the witness temporarily. In almost every case, however, after completing the movement, the lawyer will pause to fix the witness in her gaze before ending the question and calling for the affirmation. The practice of dramatically turning away from a witness while posing a cross-examination question can be over-used. Turning one's back on someone is a sign of disrespect. Any perceived condescension or lack of respect by the lawyer toward any witness will generate a reaction by the factfinders adverse not to the witness but to the lawyer.

Sometimes the lawyer's movements and antics can become seriously distracting both to the factfinders and to the lawyer herself. Many a young trial lawyer has dramatically turned her back on the witness to pose her cross-examination questions to the far corner of the courtroom and thereby has lost one of her primary tools of control over the witness. Although the lawyer may be asking a leading question her failure to look at the witness as the question is being asked may relieve the witness of the implicit obligation to give a fair answer. The price for such a lapse in control is usually paid on the spot in the form of an undesired and damaging response from the witness.

5. Using Exhibits and Illustrative Aids

When the lawyer is using exhibits or illustrative aids during the presentation, whether it be direct examination, cross-examination, opening or closing, the paramount consideration is the ability of the factfinders to see the visual media easily and to observe what the witness or counsel is doing with it. The witness using the exhibits and visual aids should be positioned to use them effectively and to direct her energy to the factfinders at the same time. This may require the lawyer to bring the witness down from the stand and direct her to stand in a particular position with respect to the illustrative aid.

    Q. Mrs. Mercer, with the Court's permission, would you
       please come down from the stand and over to the dia-
       gram there on the easel in the middle of the courtroom?
       [Witness comes down and goes over to the diagram on
       the easel.]

    Q. Now, Mrs. Mercer, would you please show us with the
       aid of the diagram where your house is on Jackson
       Street?

The lawyer should not hesitate to reposition the witness or give
the witness directions in order to make sure that the factfinders can
easily see what is going on.

    Q. Excuse me, Ms. Mercer, would you please move a little
       bit to the side so that all the jurors can see where you are
       pointing?

During cross-examination it is the lawyer who becomes the
teacher using the visual aid. The lawyer projects her energy and the
information regarding the aid toward the factfinders while the witness remains confined to the witness chair. It is just as important
that the factfinders can see well during the cross-examination and
that the cross-examining lawyer not block their view.

Sometimes it is difficult to position exhibits, visual aids, projection screens, and the like so that judge, factfinders, and opposing
counsel can all see well. In such cases the factfinders clearly must
come first, with the judge's ability to see a distant second. Most
judges are understanding on this issue and will be content with a
poor or partial view. However, the lawyer should not obviously
ignore the judge and should not assume that the judge is willing to
be left out of the visual presentation. Sometimes a simple acknowledgment or inquiry is in order:

    Q. Your Honor, would the Court be inconvenienced if we
       moved the screen a little closer so that the jurors could
       all read the figures being projected?

    The Court. That's all right, Counsel; I can move down to this
       end of the bench to see the slides when you project them.

A trial lawyer should not feel that she must compromise the impact of an exhibit or illustrative aid so that opposing counsel can see it from counsel table. If, in order to give the factfinders a good view, it is necessary to position the illustrative aid or exhibit where opposing counsel cannot see it well, common courtesy would be to invite opposing counsel to move to a position from where they can get a better view.

> Q. Your Honor, if Opposing Counsel wishes to move over to our table so that they can see the visual aid, that is fine with us.

Sometimes a polite suggestion to this effect will forestall an objection and potential disruption of the presentation.

C. Body Language

Lawyers must also be conscious of how their posture and activities within the courtroom space reflect on their presentations. How trial lawyers conduct themselves in the courtroom frequently sends messages to the factfinders. If the lawyer's posture and movements are perceived as sloppy and lackadaisical, it is likely that some of that impression will rub off on the lawyer's case. The lawyer's conduct, of course, contributes to the image being presented. That image should at all times express forthright confidence and belief in the strength of the case.

1. Posture

Standing solidly upright on both feet, with hands used purposefully or positioned out of the way, projects an image of confident professionalism, which enhances a presentation. Slouching or leaning on the podium or jury rail may telegraph to the factfinders a feeling of physical weakness or instability. This association may carry over to the factfinders' perceptions of the lawyer's case.

By the same token, when the lawyer is seated, she should sit upright at counsel table, with her feet on the floor and with her legs under her so that she can rise on a moment's notice to make an objection or address the court. If a lawyer is leaning back in her chair or sitting with crossed legs, it may look as though she is not attentive or does not care what is going on. It should also be noted that it is very hard to spring to one's feet from these positions in the event of a need to object.

2. Hands

One of the questions most frequently asked by trial advocacy students and inexperienced lawyers is, "What do I do with my hands?"

Many people feel some awkwardness about their hands when they are addressing groups of people such as a jury. There is the feeling that the hands are just there, that they get in the way, that something has to be done with them. Ultimately, each lawyer has to use her hands in a way that is comfortable and effective for that lawyer and that does not appear awkward or distracting to the factfinders.

Some common hand positions, though, are believed to convey certain messages. A lawyer standing in the courtroom with her hands crossed in front of her chest may be conveying aloofness or forbidding stubbornness, an image that is unlikely to be appealing to the factfinders. On the other hand, the picture of the lawyer standing with hands clasped or in a praying position may be associated with tentativeness and insecurity.

Hands in pockets may suggest nonchalance and will inhibit gestures and demonstrations using the hands. Hands in pockets may also unconsciously jingle keys or coins. It is even more distracting, however, for the lawyer to attempt to keep her hands occupied by toying with a pen, a pad, or a pair of glasses. A lawyer can unknowingly provide a sideshow that can so distract the factfinders that they fail to hear a word being said.

Some lawyers find relief from "the hand thing" by firmly grasping the sides of a podium during their entire courtroom presentations. This approach makes it impossible to use one's hands for gestures or demonstrations. By coming to depend on the podium as a crutch, the lawyer might risk extreme discomfort if required to function in a space without a podium.

No particular hand position can be prescribed as best for all

people in all situations. However, a novice trial lawyer would do
well to become accustomed to speaking and asking questions with
her hands held quietly at her sides and raised only for some ascer-
tainable purpose.

3.   Space Management

a.   The Courtroom Environment

Like in the classroom, the management of the space in the courtroom maximizes the impact of what is being presented and minimizes the distractions. There are many elements that are potential
distractions, including mannerisms of a lawyer or witness, repetitive movements or gestures, the use of notes and handling of pens,
glasses, or other intentional or unintentional props. Other distractions can come from extraneous elements such as a buzzing fly,
noisy air conditioners, coughs from the audience, or noises from
the street. These can divert precious attention from what the lawyer is trying to teach the factfinders. The lawyer must see to it that
they are minimized during the important parts of her presentation.

Courtrooms vary widely in design, layout, and the facilities
available to assist the trial lawyer in her presentation. Frequently,
courtrooms are plagued with poor acoustics, noisy or inadequate
ventilation systems, dim lighting, and intrusive sounds from traffic
or other activities happening outside. Yet the space of the courtroom is the environment in which the lawyer must recreate her
picture to win the case. This means that the trial lawyer must tailor
her presentation to take into account the imperfect conditions
under which it will be made. Poor acoustics may mean that she will
have to rely more on microphones, which may affect where she
and her witnesses can stand. Presentation of visual evidence must
be planned in the context of the lighting conditions. Sometimes it is
difficult to darken the courtroom to permit effective presentation
of projected slides or film, which might mean that the lawyer will
have to rely more on pre-prepared boards or photographic blow-
ups to convey visual information. The idea is to plan the presentation in light of the conditions under which it will be made.

The last stages of trial planning usually involve a visit to the courtroom in which the trial will be conducted. This enables the lawyer to visualize how the elements of the presentation will be handled in the actual courtroom environment. Plans can be made for the positioning of witnesses and visual aids. Possible problems due to courtroom layout or facilities can be anticipated and provided for. Acoustics and sight lines can be tested.

b.   Counsel Table Placement

An issue that sometimes arises in planning for trial is the allocation of counsel tables to the respective parties. Often one of the counsel tables is closer than the other to the bench or the factfinders. Sometimes the tables are placed side by side, with one nearer to the jury than the other. In other courtrooms, the counsel tables are positioned one behind the other, so that the lawyers for one side are located in front of their opponents and between them and the bench. Depending on the planned presentation, the position of the counsel table from which the lawyer will be working can be either a significant perceived advantage or a drawback.

The allocation of counsel tables among the parties is usually covered by local rule or custom. The most frequent rule is that the party with the ultimate burden of proof on the case in chief is entitled to sit closer to the judge or the jury, meaning that in a courtroom with side-by-side counsel tables ordinarily the prosecution or the plaintiff will be entitled to the table that is nearer to the jury box. In a courtroom with the tables positioned one behind the other, the prosecution or plaintiff would usually get the front table, with the defense sitting behind. This rule of counsel table allocation is not followed in all courts. In some courts, the tables are up for grabs. The party who arrives first and claims a particular table is entitled to use it during the trial.

In some courts, the use of electronic recording devices determine where counsel sits. Each device has a separate track, and the individual trial participant must use the table that is wired with a designated track.

It is up to counsel to find out in advance the ground rules for the use of counsel tables. If there is some opportunity to claim a table that is well placed for counsel's anticipated needs during the trial, counsel should take advantage of the opportunity to secure the table by arriving well in advance and getting set up. Otherwise, she should find out which table is allocated to her under the local rules and plan her presentation with her counsel table location in mind.

If the arrangement of the counsel tables is such that counsel will be seriously impeded in her presentation by the usual arrangement of the tables, it is not unheard of for counsel to request in advance that the tables be rearranged for the trial.

Q. (in chambers before the start of trial).   Your Honor, we note that counsel tables in the main courtroom are usually arranged forward and back, with the plaintiff in front and the defendant in back. In this case we plan to use a number of overhead transparencies that will need to be projected so that the jury, the court, and Opposing Counsel can see them clearly. Would it be okay if we move the counsel tables so that they are side by side and so we can position our screen here [showing simple diagram]? That would enable us to project the slides so that everyone can see with the least fuss and feathers.

The Court.   Is there any objection to this proposal?

Opposing Counsel.   Well, Your Honor, ordinarily we would be nearer to the Court . . .

The Court.   Yes, but in this case it makes sense that everyone should be able to see these slides. You may go ahead and rearrange the counsel tables as requested.

Effective use of the courtroom space is an important part of making a winning presentation. The lawyer should be knowledgeable about the courtroom layout and integrate the presentation with the available space and facilities and make use of them to enhance the presentation as much as possible.

D.   Lawyers' Language

The lawyer's courtroom language should be familiar and readily understandable to the factfinders. A common error of inexperienced lawyers is the importation of "lawyerese" into courtroom presentations.

> *Q.* Tell us — when, Sir, did the Defendant exit the vehicle?

or

> *Q.* Where was Ms. Farris positioned during this altercation?

There are at least two drawbacks to the use of such language. First, it distances the lawyer from the factfinders. Factfinders are rarely impressed by the use of "highfalutin" language by the lawyers who are appearing before them. If the language used by the lawyer is unfamiliar to the factfinders, they will perceive that the lawyer is different from them. People tend to distrust other people who seem to be different.

Second, if the vocabulary the lawyer uses is not readily understood, the message is not getting through unimpeded. While the witness is answering or the lawyer is continuing with the next question, some of the factfinders may still be thinking, "What did he mean by a 'vehicle'? Is a vehicle a truck?" or "Hmm. . . . What is an altercation, or was it an alteration?"

While the factfinders are trying to puzzle out strange and complicated lawyer language, they are probably not paying attention to the next pieces of the presentation.

> *Q.* Tell us, Sir, when did Mr. Borak get out of the car?

or

> *Q.* Where was Ms. Farris during the argument?

would be better choices of words at trial.

It is said that the very best trial lawyers are consummately articulate with words with no more than five letters and two syllables.

At the same time, it is very important for the lawyer not to "talk down" to witnesses or factfinders at trial. Trial discourse is at all times among equals and is marked by respect and consideration. The least whiff of perceived condescension in a lawyer's manner or speech is likely to be severely damaging to her relationship with the persons whom she must convince with her presentation.

E. Lawyer Palaver and Commentary

Usually there is no occasion for the lawyer to make lengthy statements to the witness or factfinders during witness presentation. Simple "headnotes" to accomplish focusing or transition are sometimes appropriate, but lengthy introductions of witnesses or subject matter during an examination rarely contribute positively to the presentation and are often improper. Witness examination is the lawyer's opportunity to present a picture through testimony, not to argue inferences or to comment on the presentation.

1. "Preambles" to Witness Examination

Some lawyers might start a cross-examination with something like the following.

> Q. Good morning, Ms. Mercer. I have only a few questions
> to clarify what you said on your direct examination.
> Please listen to my questions and then answer them
> "yes" or "no."

This apparently harmless lead-in to the questioning is undesirable in several respects. First, although a simple greeting is usually harmless, it is also redundant and distracts from the focus of the examination. The appropriate time for such greetings has usually passed by the time the witness takes the stand. The factfinders know what the purpose of the questioning is, and any effort to remind them of why the lawyer is asking the questions is likely to be a waste of energy and precious attention span.

Second, most nonlawyers consider "a few" to be two or three. When a lawyer says she has only "a few" questions, the factfinders mentally adjust their attention span to two or three inquiries. When the questioning continues for longer than the number of questions promised, the factfinders' human reaction is to resent the unexpected imposition and possibly pay less attention.

Third, it is unlikely that the real purpose of the cross-examination is "to clarify" the witness's direct testimony. It is more likely that the purpose of the questions on cross-examinations is to blur and discredit the direct examination rather than clarify it. The insincerity of such a statement soon becomes apparent. And it is possible that after the eighteenth question one might hear from the judge,

> *The Court.*   Counsel, I thought you said that you had *a few* questions on cross-examination.

It is usually better for the lawyer not to promise anything or attempt to characterize what she is about to do when she starts her examination.

Finally, lecturing the witness on how to answer the questions ("yes" or "no") is not likely to be effective, at least not at the outset of the examination. On cross-examination it is the obligation of the lawyer to pose questions that can fairly be answered "yes" or "no." If the lawyer does not do so, no amount of preliminary instructions can control the witness's responses. There is even the possibility that such an instruction by the lawyer might draw an adverse comment from the judge,

> *The Court.*   The witness may answer the questions in any way she needs to do so.

2.   *Commentary During Examination*

Lawyer commentary during examination can range from unconscious repetition of a witness's answer to actual comments by the lawyer on the accuracy or credibility of the testimony.

> *Q.*   So what were the two men doing?
>
> *A.*   They were standing there talking. One seemed to have his hands up in the air.
>
> *Q.*   — hands in the air. What was he doing with his hands in the air?

> A. He seemed to be waving them at the house.
>
> Q. Okay, he was waving them at Ms. Farris's house. How long did he do this?
>
> A. For a minute or two, I think.
>
> Q. Right, and what did he do then?

This kind of commentary is a kind of heavy-handed control of and encouragement to the witness. Although usually well-meant or entirely unconscious, this kind of commentary sooner or later becomes noticeable to the listeners. The lawyer is perceived as intruding on the exposure of the witness, and doubt is seeded in the factfinders' minds as to the spontaneity of the witness's responses. Sometimes the lawyer will enhance or change the answer in the repetition. If this is intentional, it is an ethical breach. If it is unintentional, or unconscious, it is poor form and distracting.

Lawyer commentary and feedback during examination are objectionable as improper argument. Inserting running commentary during witness examination can become a habit that is very hard to break. The lawyer should reserve comments until final argument and should confine the examination to clean questions and answers.

> Q. So what were the two men doing?
>
> A. They were standing there talking. One seemed to have his hands up in the air.
>
> Q. What was he doing with his hands up in the air?
>
> A. He seemed to be waving them at the house.
>
> Q. Which house did he seem to be waving them at?
>
> A. Ms. Farris's house.
>
> Q. How long did he seem to be waving them at Ms. Farris' house?
>
> A. For a minute or two, I think.
>
> Q. What did he do then?

On cross, it is sometimes hard to resist the temptation to express skepticism or some other reaction to the witness's responses.

Q.   The two men were drunk, weren't they?

A.   They looked that way.

Q.   You bet they did. And you know a drunk when you see one, don't you?

Opposing Counsel.   Objection. Move to strike Counsel's comment.

The Court.   Sustained. Counsel's comment will be disregarded.

Comments are but one way in which a lawyer may attempt to inject her reaction to a witness's testimony. As discussed in Chapter 7, on direct examination the examining lawyer should support and encourage her own witness by the tone of her questions and by her body language as she poses the questions and listens to the responses. However, such support must be expressed subtly and in such a manner so as not to distract the factfinders. Nods of approval, murmurs of "right" or "okay," excessive repetition of a part of the last answer (". . . hands in the air") can be distracting habits on direct and can add to the impression that the witness presentation is coached. When carried to extremes, such mannerisms can lead to censure by the judge.

The Court.   Counsel will refrain from nodding her head in response to the witness's answers!

Conversely, on cross-examination mugging, eye-rolling, scowling, and headshaking in disbelief are usually ineffective and are always improper. These lawyer's antics seldom accomplish their purpose and are often resented by both the factfinders and the judge.

Opposing Counsel.   Your Honor, we object to Counsel's rolling her eyes in disbelief whenever the witness attempts to answer her question.

> *The Court.* Objection sustained. Counsel, you should know
> better than that.

Sometimes a lawyer may be tempted to express a verbal or
nonverbal reaction to a question or answer during the opponent's
examination or cross-examination.

> *Q.* As you approached the stop sign, Mr. Borak, what did
> you do?
>
> *A.* Came to a complete stop, looked to the right, and looked
> to the left.
>
> *Opposing Counsel* (seated at counsel table, *sotto voce*).   Like
> fun!
>
> *Q.* What did you see when you looked to the right and to
> the left?
>
> (Opposing Counsel rolls eyes in disbelief.)
>
> *A.* Nothing.
>
> *Opposing Counsel.*   Likely!
>
> *Q.* Your Honor, may we approach the bench?
>
> *The Court.* Yes.
>
> *Q.* Your Honor, would the Court admonish Opposing Coun-
> sel for commenting by words and facial expressions dur-
> ing my examination?
>
> *The Court.* Yes, I've noticed that. Counsel, I don't want to
> see or hear anything from you while Ms. Hartwell is con-
> ducting her examination.

It should be obvious that any such commentary during an opponent's examination or argument is highly unprofessional. When a
lawyer is given the stage to make her presentation, she should not
be subject to cheap sniping from her opponent. The truly professional lawyer sits impassively at counsel table during her opponent's presentation and does not betray any reaction, either verbal
or by facial expression, to the testimony of the opponent's wit-

nesses or the statements of counsel, other than to make an objection if properly called for. The manner of making objections is dealt with below.

F.   Using Notes in the Courtroom

One of the issues in trial advocacy about which there is no unanimity of opinion among lawyers and teachers is the proper use of written notes during courtroom presentation. Some lawyers scorn the use of notes at any time during the trial; others find notes indispensable to a methodical and detailed presentation and to a feeling of security. Both positions have merit. A trial lawyer should be sensitive to the potential for distraction posed by notes and prompting devices. At the same time, notes can often assist in organizing the presentation and ensuring that the lawyer will not omit some important element or suddenly draw a blank.

1.   Pluses and Minuses of Notes in General

Because fact presentations are complex and require a high degree of accuracy, all trial lawyers rely to some extent on written notes of various kinds in making their presentations. The discipline of recording the subject matter of examination or argument on paper and even writing out the questions can force the lawyer to concentrate on articulating the ideas to be covered. Proper notes can be helpful to keep track of the subject matter to be covered, to prompt specific areas of examination or discussion, and to recapture exact words, numbers, or phraseology. Notes are useful as insurance to guard against unexpected "blanking" of memory.

But the use of notes can have several drawbacks. Excessive use, particularly questions or argument read from notes, can destroy any spontaneity in the presentation and can compromise the lawyer's eye contact with witnesses and factfinders. The lawyer's handling of a note pad, cards, or the like can also be a cause of distraction to the factfinders. Excessive reliance on notes might also contribute to rigidity in presentation in the face of changes in focus or themes. Notes may also tend to keep the lawyer thinking in terms of words

and abstractions rather than working directly from the visual image
in her own mind to present to the factfinders.

2. During Openings and Closings

On balance, increased factfinder impact and freedom from distractions tend to favor delivering the opening statement and the closing argument without obviously or frequently resorting to notes.
The opening and closing are when eye contact with the factfinders
is most important. Because the lawyer is the center of attention,
these times hold the greatest potential for distraction by the lawyer's mannerisms and handling of notes. These are also the times
when the lawyer's own personal confidence in the image being
projected should be conveyed most strongly. For these reasons,
during openings and closings the trial lawyer should make a special effort to maintain continuous, undistracted, and direct communication with the factfinders.

This does not mean that the lawyer should try to make up and
retain the details of the opening or closing entirely in her head. As
suggested before, it is usually desirable to write out key elements
just to make sure that she can properly convert images effectively
into words. The use of notes may assist in structuring the presentation and marshaling the important ideas, but once the opening and
argument are prepared, the trial lawyer is usually better off wean-
ing herself from the notes and speaking to the factfinders from the
image in her consciousness rather than from the words on a page
in front of her.

3. During Witness Examination

Frequently the lawyer might need prompts on subject matter for
questioning and for precise phraseology during the course of direct
or cross-examination. During these phases of the trial the lawyer is
not relating as directly with the jury as during opening statement
and closing argument. The challenge of eliciting details in the testimony of either a friendly or hostile witness can be lessened by the
use of cribbed notes.

At no time is it effective to read questions from a script, however. This seriously compromises the lawyer's spontaneity and the infusion of the lawyer's own personality into the presentation. If the lawyer refers to notes for the subject or the phrasing of a question, she should always look up and at the witness before beginning the question in order to establish eye contact and ensure the witness's attentiveness as the question is being posed.

4. Where to Put the Notes

During opening and closing, when counsel is attempting to relate directly to the factfinders without notes, simple outline notes can be kept on counsel table, a nearby podium, or some other convenient place. From such a position, the notes are available to remind the lawyer of a subject matter that should be covered, or to rescue the lawyer if things suddenly go blank. The important thing is for the notes to be in a position where they are reasonably accessible but not immediately in front of the lawyer or in a position where they will distract the lawyer in her presentation to the factfinders or the factfinders in their attention to the lawyer.

It is not necessary for the lawyer to be able to refer to the notes on a continuous basis during delivery. If she needs to refer to the notes, it is all right for her to, in effect, excuse herself in order to do so. The notes should be just a few steps away, such as on a podium to the side of the lawyer or on the lawyer's counsel table, and should be positioned so that they can be easily referred to if necessary. If the lawyer suddenly forgets the subject matter or the next segment of the presentation, the notes are available for a quick prompt.

> Counsel (during opening statement).   May I have a moment, Your Honor?
>
> (Counsel pauses, goes over to counsel table, and looks for a moment at outline notes there.)
>
> Counsel.   Then we will also hear from Dr. Mortimor Haven. Dr. Haven will tell us . . .

During witness examination the direct relationship with the fact-finders is less important. If the subject matter of the examination is complex or if the ideas are tricky to articulate, the lawyer might want to have the notes nearer at hand for more frequent reference. In any event, the notes should not be permitted either to convert the examination into a reading exercise or to interfere with the lawyer's ability to relate directly with witness or factfinders. If the examination is being carried out from a podium, the notes can be left on the podium and referred to as necessary to get the right ideas or even the right words. Otherwise, the notes can be placed on counsel table, or even the other counsel's table if necessary, so they are in a position to be used as needed.

Q. Your Honor, would it be all right if I use the corner of opposing counsel's table for my notes during my direct examination?

Opposing Counsel. We have no objection to that, Your Honor.

G.   Courtesy

Courtesy to the court and to opposing counsel is the hallmark of the professional trial lawyer. The trial is a competitive but not combative process. The point is to make a better presentation than the opponent, not to hurt the opponent. Trial presentation may include comments about the accuracy or credibility of the presentation made by the opposition, but such criticism should never be shrill, overstated, or personal.

1.   Courtesy to Opposing Counsel

Although trying cases is a keenly competitive activity in which the stakes can be very high, it is necessary for a trial lawyer at all times to display complete courtesy to opposing counsel as well as to all other participants in the trial. In the eyes of the factfinders, courtesy to the opponent is a sign of strength, not weakness and must be real, not exaggerated or tinged with sarcasm.

The courteous and professional trial lawyer always seeks to address the other side's presentation, not the other side's persona. Factfinders and judges are just as likely to side with the person attacked as with the attacker. On the other hand, critical comments directed at the other side's image, contention, argument, or brief can be very strong without giving offense.

> *Counsel.*   Your Honor, that argument is absurd. There is no basis for the application of punitive damages in this case.

This is likely to generate more light with less heat than

> *Counsel.*   Your Honor, the other lawyer doesn't know what he is talking about. He has not given you any reason to apply punitive damages in this case.

In almost all courts, the lawyers are required to address all statements and remarks to the judge or (during opening or closing) to the factfinders. Direct colloquy between counsel during the trial is forbidden.

> *Counsel.*   We offer Exhibit 5 for Identification.
>
> *Opposing Counsel.*   Objection. Your photograph was taken with a flash. You know that doesn't fairly and accurately reflect the lighting on the night of the accident. You are trying to . . .
>
> *The Court.*   Counsel! Please address your remarks to the Court.
>
> *Opposing Counsel* (embarrassed).   We beg your pardon, Your Honor. Your Honor, we object to Exhibit 5. As the Court can clearly see, that photograph was taken with a flash. It doesn't fairly and accurately reflect the lighting and visibility on the night of the accident. The danger of unfair prejudice substantially outweighs the probative value.

When challenging the opponent's presentation, the professional trial lawyer addresses the argument to the court and attacks the presentation, not the presenter. One of the purposes of this rule is to put all communication between the competitors under the direct control of the court, thus defusing unnecessary conflict and avoiding sharp exchanges between the competitors.

Courtesy to opposing counsel does not mean affecting a sloppy camaraderie around the courthouse during trial. When a lawyer kids and jokes with the lawyer on the other side, say, as they leave the courthouse after the trial, clients and factfinders who see them may begin to wonder if they really meant what they said during the trial. The image of contending advocates putting down their briefcases and walking out of the courthouse arm in arm, in sight of the jurors and other trial participants, is an unsettling one to those whose fortunes are at risk in the trial and to those who must decide the issues.

A degree of courteous and professional distance should characterize a lawyer's behavior toward the adversary in the courthouse. Jokes, hugs, and beers should be reserved for the bar association picnic.

2. Courtesy to the Court

Trial lawyers should show appropriate respect for the judge. Even if put upon unfairly by the judge, it never pays to show discourtesy or rudeness to Her Honor. Factfinders almost always respect and often come to like "their" judge. A perceived lack of respect or courtesy on the part of one of the lawyers may bring down on that lawyer not only the displeasure of the judge but the dislike of the factfinders as well.

In many courts it is customary to address the judge as "the Court" or as "Your Honor."

> Q. If the Court please, may the witness approach the blackboard?

or

> Q. Your Honor, may the witness approach the illustrative aid?

"Judge" is usually considered a more informal form of address, which might not be acceptable in all courts.

> Q. Judge, may we approach the bench?

"You" is almost never used when addressing the judge.

Appropriate respect for the judge does not mean obsequiousness. Excessive deference and apparent efforts to curry favor by fawning over the judge usually backfire. Nor is it effective to attempt to create the impression of special friendliness and rapport with the judge. Either the judge or the factfinders or both (and certainly the opposing lawyer) will be turned off by such displays.

One common manifestation of excessive obsequiousness to the judge is the practice of thanking the judge after a ruling during the trial. Some lawyers may do so out of an extreme of politesse. Others sometimes thank the judge in an effort to increase the impact of a favorable ruling. Some even thank the judge for unfavorable rulings in hopes that the factfinders will misapprehend the defeat for a victory.

> Q. What did the children say, Mr. Maxfield?
>
> *Opposing Counsel.* Objection, hearsay.
>
> Q. That is not for the truth, Your Honor. It's for the defendant's state of mind.
>
> *The Court.* Objection overruled. The witness may answer.
>
> *Opposing Counsel.* Thank you, Your Honor.

This practice, whether innocently motivated or not, is improper.

> *The Court.* It is the Court's duty to rule on objections. It is not appropriate to thank the Court for a ruling, Counsel, especially when the Court has ruled against you.

Nor should the trial lawyer feel unduly intimidated by the power and role of the judge. Sometimes the judge will miss the point of an argument or will rule before the lawyer has a chance to make her point. Sometimes judges are simply impatient, rude, or inconsiderate.

The lawyer has a responsibility not to let the vagaries of the judge interfere with a full and fair presentation of the case. It is the lawyer, after all, who must put on the case. This may mean that the lawyer must insist on objections or points despite the judge's adverse attitude. Sometimes the lawyer's only protection is the stenographic or electronic record of the proceedings.

Counsel.   We offer Exhibit 5 in evidence.

Opposing Counsel.   Objection!

The Court.   Overruled.

Opposing Counsel.   May we be heard, Your Honor?

The Court.   Yes, briefly.

Opposing Counsel.   Your Honor, we object based on Rule 403. May we be heard at the bench?

The Court.   All right, but let's not take all the time in the world.

Opposing Counsel (at sidebar).   Your Honor, the photograph marked as Exhibit 5 was taken with a flash. It distorts the light. The amount of light and visibility is a crucial issue in the case. May we have a brief voir dire?

The Court.   Denied. I've had enough of this.

Opposing Counsel.   Your Honor, if permitted, voir dire would have shown that the picture was taken with a flash and that it shows the scene as considerably brighter than it was in reality on the night in question.

Polite but firm persistence will more likely win the respect of the judge and the factfinders than will craven crumbling in the face of judicial impatience or arbitrariness.

6 Opening Statements

The first event in the process of fact presentation in court is usually the opening statement, given by the lawyer to the fact-finders. In the opening statement the lawyer sets forth the case, which will be proved by the exhibits and witnesses she presents during the trial. She portrays herself as a sincere and reliable source of the information.

A. The Importance of the Opening

The importance of the opening statement cannot be overstated. Some consider it the most important part of the lawyer's trial presentation. The opening is usually the lawyer's first real opportunity to 1) lay out before the factfinder the fact image to be recreated and 2) accredit herself and her witnesses as a source of information that can be accepted and believed by the factfinders. Studies in psychology and effective communications have demonstrated that our first impressions are stronger and more durable than generally assumed. Thus it is very important to make a good first impression. If jury voir dire is permitted, the same policy holds true. Many lawyers make effective use of the voir dire process to precondition the jurors interviewed with a favorable image of their particular case.

The notion that factfinders sit throughout an evidentiary presentation and suspend their own judgments and impressions until they have heard all of the evidence and received the charge of the court is a fiction. Current thinking on how juries function is the exact opposite. Many factfinders make up their minds about the whole case largely based on the narratives presented to them in the opening.

The opening is the first opportunity for the lawyer to function as a teacher, spreading out the material before the factfinders so that they can understand the facts and recreate an accurate image in their own consciousnesses. During the trial the lawyer must paint the picture by remote control, through witnesses and exhibits. In the opening, however, the lawyer can function as a raconteur, working directly with the media to create the best possible first impression, which will be reinforced by the witness testimony and closing argument.

For these reasons, it is rarely appropriate to waive the opening statement. For the party with the burden of proof, the opportunity to start carrying that burden with a good strong beginning cannot be dispensed with. It is safe to assume that no single witness will have the comprehensive information, the perspective, and the ability to tell the whole story as effectively as can the lawyer. The opening is the lawyer's opportunity to get the story out in front of the factfinders, to be accredited, supported, and proved by the testimony and evidence to come.

In criminal cases tactical considerations of the defense may sometimes weigh in favor of waiving the opening, or at least deferring it until after the prosecution has rested its case. However, even if the defense counsel does not plan to offer much evidence, the opening is a good time to start to establish a relationship of trust and confidence with the jury. Such a relationship can make a difference in how the jury receives their impressions at trial from any source.

Nor should the opening be confined to the time-honored "road map" presentation. Traditionally, counsel would preface opening statements with introductions such as

> *Counsel.*   This opening statement is not evidence. You should consider this opening statement as a road map that will enable you to understand the evidence as you hear it from the witnesses.

This approach needlessly de-emphasizes a very important part of the trial presentation. Probably the judge will have given the factfinders a brief introduction to the trial process in which he has told them that the openings are not evidence. And the analogy to the road map does not really hold up. The opening should be the actual image that will be presented, not some kind of set of directions on how to get there.

The trial lawyer takes advantage of the opportunity of the opening to set forth the relevant fact picture completely and in some detail. Using colorful but accurate narrative, enhanced if possible by visual aids, the lawyer strives to generate a powerful picture of the case. By the end of the opening the pertinent features of the picture should have been well described. The presentation of witnesses and exhibits following the opening will then fortify and support this initial image.

Because of the importance of the opening statement, it is usually wise to take the time to do it well. Sometimes this means that the lawyer will have to resist efforts of the judge to "move things along" by allowing too little time for a complete or effective opening statement. The lawyer's response to such efforts is that the purpose of the opening is to assist the jury,

> *The Court.* Counsel, we have to move this trial along. You may each have ten minutes for your opening.
>
> *Q.* Your Honor, with all due respect, a more complete opening statement will be of great assistance to the jury in understanding the evidence in this complex case.
>
> *The Court.* How much time do you need then, Counsel?
>
> *Q.* Well, Your Honor, it will take a good twenty minutes to give the jurors the kind of picture they should have to understand the evidence in this case.
>
> *The Court.* Very well, Counsel; please try to keep it to twenty minutes.

B. Accrediting the Lawyer

A primary purpose of the opening is the accreditation of the lawyer. It is an opportunity for her to communicate to the factfinders her sincerity, her knowledge of the facts, and her commitment to helping the factfinders understand the case as well as possible.

There are many techniques available to the trial lawyer to develop rapport and a feeling of community with the factfinder. One technique traditionally recommended by trial lawyers and trial practice teachers is the "courtroom introduction." Here the lawyer uses part of the opening statement to introduce the jurors to some or all of the personalities and procedures of the trial. This puts the lawyer in the position of assisting the factfinders to understand everyone's role and what will be happening during the trial. This role may carry over to enhance the lawyer's credibility on the merits of the case.

Traditional trial advocacy texts often recommend stories, such as those that Abraham Lincoln would tell in court, to bond with the jury and to gain their interest and confidence. A good story that illustrates a trait of human character has value in generating a feeling of commonality with any group of people. This is apart from the value that an anecdotal approach may have in generating understanding of the controverted aspects of the case on trial.

At the same time, it is easy to use up the crucial first few minutes of the factfinder's undivided attention with introductions, anecdotes, and similar palaver. If the lawyer seems to be slow to come to the point, the factfinders may get the notion that she may not be that confident of the merits of her case. For these reasons, courtroom introduction and anecdotal openings are now perceived to be less effective than in the past.

If the main purpose of the opening is to develop an authoritative image of what is going to be shown at trial, the best accreditation for the lawyer comes from a well organized, clear, and colorful narrative describing relevant facts and testimony right from the start. This will create a plausible and interesting picture that the factfinders can easily understand and accept.

Factfinders are quick to detect a lawyer's conscious effort to ingratiate herself with extraneous conversation and interpret such efforts as being "talked down to." This is always dangerous — to the lawyer. When in doubt, she is better off relying on her command of her case and her ability to describe it than on stories or gimmicks to try to gain the factfinders' interest and trust.

C.   Describing the Fact Picture

The bulk of the opening should be devoted to a description of the fact picture that the lawyer intends to develop a trial. The purpose is to generate the desired image with as much authority as possible.

It is true that the opening is not evidence itself; it is, however, a prediction of what that evidence will be. The opening is sometimes referred to by trial lawyers as "a promise" of what the picture will be. If a strong and reliable image is to be developed in the consciousnesses of the factfinders, this first impression must be clear and positive, and the evidence to follow should consistently track the predictions made in the opening.

The opening should be delivered in a tone that is firm and definite, not tentative or even expectant. It should convey a definite image presented with complete confidence.

> *Counsel.* On October 10, 1992, Robert Maxfield killed Roscoe Savage by running over him with his 1987 Ford Mustang. The evidence the State of Ames will present will show beyond any reasonable doubt that Mr. Maxfield killed Mr. Savage intentionally or knowingly. Here is how it happened. . . .

rather than

> *Counsel.* I think the evidence will show . . .

or

> *Counsel.* We are hoping to hear . . .

The opening should be organized so as to make the picture easy to understand. Depending on the subject matter, the opening can be organized chronologically, on a witness-by-witness basis, or in some other manner. The point is to create the clearest image in the most understandable way and to predict the confirmation of that picture by the evidence admitted at the trial.

In cases involving events, the chronological organization is usually most effective. Even though the testimony may be given out of chronological order, most people think of events as running in a sequence. Telling the story as it happened enables the lawyer to take the various disjointed perspectives of the witnesses and weave them into an overall picture, complete with a case theory and perhaps some significant themes. Chronological sequence is a well understood and accepted manner by which people keep track of events and remember them.

Sometimes the sequence of events is simple or the issue has little to do with the sequence of the action. If the identity and credibility of the witnesses is more significant to the factfinders' acceptance of the lawyer's fact pattern, a witness-by-witness opening might provide a more effective first impression. But if there are several witnesses to an ongoing event, describing their individual testimonies one by one might suggest potential discrepancies. Furthermore, a witness-by-witness presentation does not take advantage of the opportunity to create an overall consistent picture into which the individual witnesses' contributions will be fit.

One way of organizing the opening suggested by some authorities in the past is the "cast of characters" approach: the lawyer introduces each of the witnesses without describing any of the anticipated testimony. The lawyer then proceeds with a chronological description of the events in which the witnesses played their various roles. The problem with this format is that during the vital first few minutes, the factfinders learn the names of several witnesses without knowing how they figured in the action. Without presenting an image at the time of their introduction, the witnesses are about as relevant to the action as are the printed names in a playbill. It is usually just as easy to introduce the witnesses as the action is being described.

Often the best form of opening is a simple narrative:

> *Counsel.*   On November 30, 1986, Robert Ramirez spent the evening with some of his friends. Mr. Ramirez drove home from work at about 5:00 P.M . Shortly afterward he met his friend Louis Cantelmo at Mr. Cantelmo's house. The two men had something to drink, a couple of beers, and went over to join their friends. . . .

In legal terms, of course, the opening statement of counsel is not "evidence"; it is only a prediction of the picture that will be established in the consciousnesses of the factfinders from the evidence they will see and hear during the trial. Traditionally it has been thought necessary to couch the opening in terms of "what the evidence will show" rather than to state something as an established fact. Under this view, an occasional "the evidence will show . . ." or "we will hear . . ." or words to like effect will remind the court and opposing counsel that the narrative is indeed only a prediction of future testimony rather than established fact. The more recent view is that, if counsel focuses her opening statement on a factual recital of the picture to be established, there seems to be little reason to use this artificial terminology.

D.   Use of Illustrative Aids and Exhibits

Like any fact presentation, the opening should be enlivened wherever possible by the use of visual aids. Simple gestures can accomplish much. A lawyer who "talks with her hands" has the ability to supplement verbal communication with useful visual prompts.

In addition to hand gestures, when the trial lawyer prepares an opening statement, she should consider using the illustrative aids and exhibits that will be offered during the trial to enhance the narrative.

The clarity and completeness in the image imparted by the opening statement is vital to the smooth development of the proof at trial. If the image conveyed by the opening statement is fuzzy or incomplete, the factfinder must constantly revise it as the proof comes in, absorbing some of the factfinder's attention and energy and causing the feeling of the image's overall reliability to be undermined. If, on the other hand, the opening statement clearly lays out the entire picture, the proof will corroborate and reinforce the initial image without creating doubt or distraction.

Thus, if the trial involves something visual, it is helpful to get as exact an image as possible of what is in controversy before the factfinders. Inferences made from a verbal description will always need revision during the trial when the factfinders see a photograph or diagram, but if they are given the opportunity to see a diagram or photograph during the opening they will be able to form the intended impressions right from the start.

The lawyer describing the fact picture in an opening statement is functioning as a teacher, an authoritative image in most people's experience. The analogy is greatly enhanced during opening statement when the lawyer approaches a blackboard or similar aid and "teaches" the factfinders what the case is going to be about. Illustrative aids such as diagrams, charts, graphs, and blackboards are usually not offered or admitted into evidence, but they may be used in opening statements as long as they do not unfairly distort what they purport to depict.

Any object that will be offered as an exhibit may also be used in opening statements as long as the proponent of the exhibit is confident that it will be admitted in evidence. If there is a potential issue of admissibility, either party would do well to resolve the issue before the opening begins to avoid a possible interruption by an objection to the later presentation.

The use of exhibits and illustrative aids is addressed in greater detail in Chapters 10 and 11.

E.   Avoiding Argument

The purpose of the lawyer's opening statement is to describe what the fact pictures will be, not to suggest why the factfinders should accept one fact picture in preference to another. Discussions of why a particular image should be derived from the proof at trial is a form of argument. As a matter of trial procedure, argument is not permitted in opening statements. If a lawyer tries to use an opening statement to argue her case, the opponent may object.

> *Counsel* (during Plaintiff's opening statement).   And how do we know that Mr. Ramirez was lying on the ground when Officer Levy fired the shot? Because the angle of the bullet came down from above, not at right angles to his back.
>
> *Opposing Counsel.* Objection! That's argument, Your Honor.
>
> *The Court.* Sustained. Stick with the facts, Counsel.

Although excessive argumentation is a common flaw in opening statements, the line between appropriate description and forbidden argument is not necessarily a difficult one. For instance, the statement

> *Counsel.* Mr. Maxfield went into the house and heard his girlfriend calling the police on the telephone. He then went out of the back of the house and got into his car.

would be proper opening. The lawyer is describing in narrative form what the evidence will show happened. This can be contrasted with

> *Counsel.*   This is the best evidence that Mr. Maxfield never intended to kill the decedent. If Mr. Maxfield had decided to kill someone, he certainly wouldn't have done so when the police had been called and were on the way.

This kind of commentary is generally considered to be improper in an opening statement. An argumentative statement is one that attempts to suggest a particular inference based on the fact picture or to argue why one particular fact picture should be accepted rather than another.

A rhetorical question in opening is likely to be argumentative:

> *Counsel.*   Would Mr. Maxfield actually have decided to kill someone when he knew the police were on their way?
>
> *Other Lawyer.*   Objection, Your Honor; that's argument.
>
> *The Court.*   Objection sustained. The jury is instructed to disregard Counsel's rhetorical question.

The rule against express argument does not mean that the opening should not be as convincing as possible. The facts should suggest the appropriate inferences without the need for arguing them.

> *Counsel.*   Mr. Maxfield heard his girlfriend calling the police when he went into his house. He knew she was calling the police when he went out to get into his car.

Of course the factfinders hearing these facts will start to ask themselves, "Well, if he knew the police were coming, why would he go out and try to kill the victim himself?" It is the fact picture the lawyer describes that permits the conclusion, not the lawyer's argument. The picture portrayed by the opening statement should sell itself rather than require conscious argument.

Chapter 7 Direct Examination

In most cases the bulk of a party's affirmative presentation is made by testimony and other evidence provided by that party and by friendly or nonadverse witnesses. Although an adverse party or a hostile witness can be called and questioned on direct examination, such an examination usually involves issues of control and presentation more akin to those of cross-examination than conventional direct. The discussion in this chapter will be limited to the examination of the lawyer's own client and friendly or nonadverse witnesses.

A. Purpose and Importance of Direct Examination

The purpose of direct examination is to present the witness's contribution to the overall image to be conveyed under the control and guidance of the lawyer. The importance of direct examination cannot be underestimated. Although cross-examination may be more dramatic, the bulk of a party's own fact picture must usually be presented by the party's own testimony or the testimony of friendly or other non-adverse resources. This is particularly true for the party that bears the burden of ultimate persuasion on the fact case. Rarely can one rely on the testimony of the opposite side to build one's own case.

There is a saying among trial lawyers that "Cases are won on direct examination," meaning that direct examination provides the basic impressions out of which the winning picture is created. The basic outlines and elements of the picture must be supplied by a party's own and allied resources. It is usually impossible to get a factfinder to accept a party's version of what happened in real life unless the party is able to present a clear and persuasive picture of that version in court. Cross-examination, while important, usually goes little further than to discredit part or all of the opponent's picture or to provide relatively small supporting elements of the examiner's own scenario.

B.   The Role of the Lawyer

The role of the lawyer conducting a direct examination is not that of an interrogator seeking information from the witness. Direct examination is not meant to be discovery. The lawyer is not asking questions to which she does not already know the answers. Instead, the lawyer's role is that of a facilitator or a guide to assist the witness in making his presentation to the factfinders. In direct examination the lawyer's task is to have planned her presentation ahead of time and then to cue the witness so that he can give the testimony most effective to the overall case.

Effective direct examination gives maximum exposure to the witness. Information about an event is most persuasive if it comes from sources close to the event without intermediation or translation by third parties. The effects of bias, language, and honest mistakes in transmittal are familiar to all factfinders and are taken into account in the assessment of all presentations. A participant's or witness's own narrative carries more authority than that of a person who is passing on what he has been told.

The lawyer's own party and witnesses are presumably ready, willing, and more or less able to make their contributions to the picture so long as the lawyer can help them do so in the most effective manner. However, most witnesses are not professionally trained or oriented to provide even a part of an overall picture under courtroom conditions. On direct examination the lawyer seeks to present the witness's information as directly as possible while at the same time maintaining control so that the presentation develops as planned.

While the lawyer must have a sufficient presence to maintain control of the examination, her role vis à vis the witness should be supportive and somewhat self-effacing. It is the witness's credibility that is to be projected. Although the lawyer is not allowed to explicitly assert her belief in the credibility of her witness, her conduct and tone of questioning will demonstrate her belief implicitly.

A lawyer conducting a direct examination has been compared to a film director: like a director with a script, the lawyer controls the presentation of facts as part of a comprehensible and believable whole. The witnesses are the actors, but the lawyer-director controls the manner, order, and scope of their testimony and how they present themselves in court. The order, pace, tone of the proceedings are all determined by the lawyer, who bears the responsibility for the final product, the image that unfolds in the factfinders' minds as the trial progresses.

C. Planning and Organizing the Direct Examination

Direct examination must be planned and organized with several considerations in mind. These include:

Impact of the testimony. The examination should be planned and structured so that the witness's testimony makes a strong impression on the factfinders.

Understandability of the testimony. The presentation must be organized so that the testimony is easy to understand and generates clear and unambiguous images in the consciousnesses of the factfinders.

Integration of the testimony with other elements of the presentation. Each witness's contribution should harmonize with and complement the other presentations in the interest of a convincing whole.

It is the lawyer's task to plan how the testimony will take form and to develop the cues and frames of the direct examination questions to make sure that the testimony as given follows the plan.

1. Simplicity and Brevity

Simplicity and brevity are important ingredients in any witness presentation. No matter how resourceful the lawyer, the subject matter of many trials is not likely to be inherently interesting to the factfinders. Assimilation of information transmitted orally, even with the help of visual aids, can be tiring. There is always the risk of boredom, inattention, or distraction. For these reasons a successful trial lawyer will attempt to simplify the material being presented and keep the length of any single examination relatively brief. In pruning a witness's potential narrative into an effective direct examination, the lawyer should scrutinize each detail and ask, "How does this add to my case? Do I really need it?"

2. Selection of Details

In real life, even the simplest happening has an infinity of unique details. Re-creation of a completely accurate image of any real-life event or circumstance would require the capture and communication of possibly millions of individual facts. Suppose, for instance, a lawyer wanted to replicate with complete fidelity the image of someone making a peanut butter sandwich. An accurate description of just the knife used to spread the peanut butter, for example, would involve a large number of details — its color, size, length, apparent age, type, and so on — and then would go on and try to describe accurately how the knife was held! — And how the lump of peanut butter looked on the knife before it was smeared on the bread — And how the bread looked and how it was held. — Not to speak of the jelly, (or was it jam?). One could spend all day just trying to think of all the varying elements in such a picture, let alone trying to capture and communicate them.

Even the most rigorous of trial presentations makes no pretense of accuracy and completeness in every detail. Many details are simply ignored or are left to the imaginations of the factfinders. Other details are communicated crudely, even in cartoon fashion, in the interest of conservation of time. On the other hand, the key elements may be presented with every detail that can be captured in order to facilitate an accurate re-creation of that element as it existed in the lawyer's version of real life. In the final analysis, a picture with a bold and simple outline is usually easier to sell than one with many nuances and shadings and a host of tricky details.

In planning the direct examination, the important task is to determine which details can be omitted or communicated in sketchy fashion and which merit more expansive treatment. While most witnesses have some idea of what is significant, it is up to the lawyer to structure the witnesses' individual testimonies so that the cumulative presentation of all who testify gives due emphasis to the details that are important and does not dwell on the many, many facts that are not.

Usually the trial lawyer needs to present with greatest clarity and authority those portions of the picture that are 1) important to the potential legal consequences, and 2) vigorously contested by the other side. Thus, in the murder prosecution for running the decedent down with the car, the portion of the defendant's picture that is most important in terms of legal consequences is his state of mind as he drove the car down the street, up on the sidewalk, and over the decedent's body. Since most of the other elements of a fact picture associated with murder are incontestable, it is of extreme importance to the defendant that his version of his state of mind be conveyed as powerfully and clearly as possible.

In selecting details for trial presentation, the defendant's lawyer will present as many details as she can that bear on this aspect of the picture because of its vital importance to the result in her case. Other areas of the picture that do not illuminate the defendant's intent are of considerably less importance, and the lawyer should not waste her time and energy and the attention of the factfinders on these details.

Another reason to focus the presentation on the defendant's state of mind is the fact that the prosecution, aware of the burden of proving its case beyond a reasonable doubt, will be focusing on state of mind as well. Because the prosecution will be doing its best to fill in its own very clear and detailed picture of the defendant, it is incumbent on the defense to rebut the prosecution's efforts.

Once the area of detailed focus is identified, those details that bear the most powerful association in common experience with the desired fact image will be the first selected for presentation. For instance, in the murder prosecution, the defendant will be sure to present and emphasize the detail that as he re-entered the house after the confrontation on the porch, he heard his companion calling the police. Why would this be an important detail to include? Because common experience teaches that it is unlikely that a person who knows the police are on the way would then intentionally go out in a car to try to run someone down.

By the same token, the prosecution might emphasize the detail that the brake lights of defendant's car did not come on as his car left the pavement and rolled over the victim. Again, common experience teaches that people who accidentally leave the travelled pavement try to apply their brakes. The failure to brake suggests that the action may have been purposeful.

The process of analyzing the available details in light of consistency, logic, and, above all, common experience, and then selecting the right details for presentation starts early in case preparation and continues right up to the examination itself. The idea is to project the best, clearest, and most significant images of those parts of the picture that really matter.

3.   Sequence of Direct Testimony

The lawyer usually organizes the testimony of the witness to an event by first accrediting the witness, then orienting the factfinders to the scene of the witness's observations and, last, having the witness describe the observed event or action. The theory behind this sequence is that if the witness feels comfortable testifying and appears interesting and credible to the factfinders, the factfinders will pay more attention to the testimony and give it greater credit as it is delivered.

Most action takes place in some spatial context. If the factfinders are oriented to the scene where an event takes place, they will find that it is easier to understand and visualize the action as it is described. Once the witness has described the scene itself, often with the use of a visual aid or exhibit, the description of the event or action follows.

Most oral testimony is presented chronologically. People are accustomed to organizing and remembering images and information in their normal sequence. The lawyer elicits testimony placing the witness at the beginning of the sequence and then guides the witness through an ordered chronological presentation. This gives all parties, witnesses, lawyers, and factfinders a common frame of reference so that the picture can be presented in an orderly manner and easily assimilated and understood.

While the time line is the most common mode of presentation, it is not the only one. Sometimes it is more effective to organize the data on a spatial basis. For example, a case involving claimed defects to a complicated machine might be organized on a defect-by-defect basis rather than chronologically.

4. Repetition of Important Facts

Classroom teachers and trial lawyers know well the value of repetition to get a point across and make it stick. Although the court can and will limit excessively repetitive presentations, a lawyer who is presenting important testimony will want to communicate the key facts more than once in hopes that they will sink in the second time, if not the first. At the same time, merely having the witness repeat the key testimony in more or less the same terms is likely to bore those factfinders who did understand the first time. It is up to the trial lawyer to organize the examination so that the witness describes the key action twice, but in different ways.

The first description could be a summary given as a "run on" answer to a "what happened" question:

Q. Mr. Cluney, what happened after you left the Blue Goose?

A. Well, we drove up Wood Street in Arthur's car and as we came up to the intersection of Wood and Vale Street this green car came right out into the intersection in front of us. I yelled, "Look Out!" but it was too late and we couldn't stop before we hit it. It was a terrific crash and I was thrown forward into the front seat and then back again. . . .

Later, the lawyer might plan to "take the witness back" to go through the description of the event again. An illustrative aid might be used, and the questions would be more controlling, with further corroborative and explanatory details added.

Q. Okay, Mr. Cluney, let's go back to when you left the Blue Goose. Whose car were you riding in?

A. It was Arthur Clark's Camaro.

Q. Who was in the car with you?

A. Arthur Clark was driving. The others were Bill Hooper,
Ernie Bragg, George Hartwell, and me.

Q. Where were you going from the Blue Goose?

A. We were headed back to the Bates campus.

Q. What route did you take?

A. We were headed right up Wood Street, which runs into
College. . . .

The run-on narrative the first time through can be helpful to
capture the tone and pace of the actual event, even though many of
the details are lacking. The later repetition will reinforce the earlier
image and fill in the details. The repetition helps the factfinders
understand and remember the information conveyed by the witness. If certain facts and details are thematic, the repetition of
those facts increases the power of the theme.

5. Thematic Words and Phrases

Especially on direct examination, the lawyer should consider the
use of thematic words and phrases, and repeat these words or
phrases in the presentations of more than one witness and also in
opening or closing. Even a simple word like "crash" can be used
thematically to describe an incident from the plaintiff's point of
view. Correspondingly, the defense would use "accident."
Usually the thematic word is introduced in the opening:

Counsel. And within a split second the defendant's car
crashed into the Clark Camaro, throwing Ray Cluney from
the back seat into the front seat, and then back again.

It next appears in the examination of the plaintiff:

Q. What happened next?

A. The car crashed into us.

Once the witness has used the word "crashed," it is permissible for the lawyer to use the same word in the predicate of later questions,

> Q: When the defendant's car crashed into your car, what happened to you?

Repetition of key words reinforces the images created in the fact-finders' consciousness. Such themes are often extended into the cross-examination of the other side's witnesses and ultimately reappear in the closing.

6. Anticipating Unfavorable Matters

The primary purpose of a direct examination is to contribute positive elements to the lawyer's overall presentation. However, it also offers the lawyer an opportunity to present unfavorable matters in a way that is least damaging to the presentation. Sometimes there is material that would tend to discredit the witness's testimony if presented by the other side in cross or through the testimony of another witness. The lawyer should present the unfavorable matter on direct examination of the witness in the best context, accompanied by appropriate explanation. Such a presentation can defuse the otherwise unfavorable impact of the material. For instance, if a witness involved in a fight had been drinking before the incident, that fact should be brought out on the witness's direct examination. A series of questions such as

> Q. Before you arrived at Jackson Street, had you and Mr. Savage had something to drink?
>
> A. Yes, we had.
>
> Q. What did you have to drink?
>
> A. Some beer and some scotch and soda.
>
> Q. How were you feeling, then?
>
> A. We were feeling pretty good.

introduces the subject of drinking less destructively than will be the case if it first comes up on cross-examination.

Q. Now, before you arrived at Jackson Street, Sir, you and Mr. Savage had been drinking, hadn't you?

A. Yes, we had.

Q. You had been drinking beer?

A. Yes.

Q. And you had been drinking scotch and soda as well?

A. Yes.

Q. You and your buddy were feeling pretty good, weren't you?

A. Well, I suppose we were. . . .

If the direct examiner omits the unfavorable material in the initial presentation, the appearance of it as new material during the opponent's presentation on cross will require the factfinders to revise negatively an image that they have already formed, and doubt will be cast in their minds as to the reliability of the image as initially presented. On the other hand, if an issue such as drinking has already been raised on the direct, an opposing lawyer's later harping on that issue on cross-examination will not be bringing in any destructive surprises.

D.   Introduction of the Witness and Accreditation

Because direct examination usually conveys most of the lawyer's fact image, the presentation should be organized to present information efficiently and in such a manner that it can be easily assimilated and accepted by the factfinders. Usually the precious first few minutes of factfinder attentiveness are best spent in accrediting the witness. As soon as the factfinders are introduced to a witness, they will want to know something about that person so that they can assess the quality and believability of the testimony. They will want to sense if they like the person whom they will be asked to believe and perhaps to help. The lawyer should not scant this important part of the presentation.

The lawyer's introduction of the witness provides an important first impression. The lawyer should express respect and sensitivity for the witness as well as her confidence and authority in the courtroom.

The time-honored

Q. Please state your name for the record.

is not necessarily the best way to orient the witness to relate to the jury in a confident and natural manner. The record will pick up the witness's name no matter how she expresses it. A better introduction is,

Q. Please tell us your name.

or

Q. Please introduce yourself to the jury.

The witness is thus oriented toward the jury rather than to the record. By using the word "us," the lawyer is putting herself in a group with the judge and jury, not bad company during a difficult trial.

Background information that will tend to make the witness be accepted by the jurors should usually be laid out at the beginning of the testimony. Such accrediting background often consists of the usual details of residence, age, and family relationship:

Q. Please tell us, Sir, where you live.

A. I live here in Springfield.

Q. How long have you lived here in the town of Springfield?

A. All my life.

Q. Are you married, Mr. Maxfield?

A. No, I am divorced.

Q. How long have you been divorced?

A. About four years now.

Q. Do you have any children, Sir?

A. Yes; three boys and a girl.

Q. Can you tell us their names and ages?

A. Billy, the oldest, is 14. Then there is Clara, who is 12, and John and Joseph, the twins, who are 10.

Q. And how often are you able to be with your children?

A. I have them with me every other weekend and on Wednesday nights for dinner.

These seemingly insignificant details are important to the fact-finders' acceptance of the witness. They demonstrate that the witness is a real person, like them. If, for instance, one of the factfinders is a twin, or has twins of his or her own, a common bond has been established. The factfinders might be more likely to believe the witness or want to help if they feel some sense of community or kinship with him.

A second purpose of the accreditation is to give the witness an opportunity to "warm up." Most witnesses find testifying a difficult and intimidating experience. It helps the person on the stand to be able to respond to questions that are easy to answer and are positive and familiar.

Although the court may permit counsel to guide a witness through background matters by asking leading questions in order to "move things along,"

Q. You've lived here in Springfield your whole life?

A. Yes.

Q. And you were divorced about four years ago?

A. That's right.

Q. And you have four children, aged 9 through 14, right?

A. Yes, that's right.

such an approach neither provides direct exposure of the witness nor gives the witness much practice in testifying. In fact, the use of such questions to provide background may set up a mesmerizing pattern of leading questions that is hard to break out of when the more controverted areas are reached. The better practice is to start out with open questions that permit the witness to introduce himself as an individual to other peers who are going to be his judges. The bottom line is that the accreditation should bring out facts about the witness that will make the jury like him and want to believe his testimony.

The accreditation of expert witnesses is an important foundation for the testimony itself. That process is discussed in greater detail in Chapter 12.

E. Transition Questions

Following the accreditation is the substantive portion of the witness's testimony. Usually the lawyer will provide a transition from the background details elicited during accreditation to the testimony that is directly relevant to the case. Also, when a witness's testimony covers more than one event or circumstance, it is necessary from time to time to refocus the witness's attention and the factfinders' frame of referenece.

Traditionally, transitions during testimony have tended to be awkward and formulaic:

> Q. On the 12th day of October, 1994, did you have occasion to be on Jackson Street?

However, they need not be:

> Q. Last October 12, were you on Jackson Street?

The transition should be designed to bring the witness smoothly from the accreditation to the chronological or geographic point where the witness's substantive testimony is to commence.

Another form of transition that has found favor in recent years is a simple statement by the lawyer alerting the witness and the factfinders to the subject matter of the next series of questions.

> Q. Now, let's talk about what happened on the night of October 12th, 1994. Would you tell us where you had dinner that evening?

or

> Q. I'm going to ask you a few questions about what you
>   saw on the evening of October 12th. Where were you
>   sitting at about 9:00 P.M. that night?

Such "headnotes" serve to alert the witness and the jury in a
more natural way as to the subject matter of the next question.

On the other hand, such headnotes may be open to challenge if
they add too much factual content that is not already supported by
evidence:

> Q. Now, I would like to take you back to the night when
>   you saw the defendant run over the victim. Where were
>   you at 9 P.M.?

This phraseology is improper if there has not yet been testimony
that the witness had seen the defendant run over the victim. Also,
the too frequent use of such statements by counsel may be a subconscious reminder to the factfinders that it is the lawyer who is
pulling the strings in the presentation.

Sometimes it is necessary to phrase a transition question in a
slightly leading fashion in order to focus the witness on a particular time and place:

> Q. Officer Anderson, at about 5 P.M. on September 14, did
>   you receive a call to investigate an accident?

The leading form of the question permits an economical transition to the matter that counts. As long as none of the subject
matter that is at issue is included, such a question is proper.

F.   Exercising Control
on Direct Examination

While the word "control" is more associated with cross-examination, the exercise of control by the examiner is equally important
on direct. The direct examiner's control of the witness's presenta-

tion, however, is more subtle than that of the cross-examiner, who often must use strong leading questions and intimidation to extract the desired answers from a reluctant and resisting witness.

1. Pretrial Preparation

The direct examiner's control is exercised in a number of ways and at various times. One that instantly springs to mind is during pretrial preparation of the witness. The idea of witness control through pretrial examination evokes the image of the lawyer meeting with the witness before the trial and going through a rehearsed scenario:

Q. Now when I ask "A," you answer "B." When I ask "C," you say "D," and when I ask "E," you say "F."

A. Okay, let's try it.

Q. "A"? . . .

A. "B."

Q. "C"? . . .

A. "D"?

The question mark after the last answer represents a rising tone in the witness's voice as he answers the rehearsed question. While the answer is correct, the tone of voice gives away the witness's hesitation. It is clear to all who are listening that the witness is not testifying from his own knowledge but rather is responding to stimuli like a trained seal. The value of the witness's testimony is immediately and irreparably compromised. Or the witness may respond "F" when asked "C"?. Memory is often unreliable in a pinch. If the only means of controlling the witness is to use a rehearsed script, it is very hard for the lawyer to rescue the situation if the witness gets it wrong.

Without diminishing the importance of pretrial preparation, it is clear that the trial lawyer cannot rely on pretrial preparation alone to provide sufficient control of and guidance to the witness in direct examination.

2. The Witness's Own Understanding of the Case

A witness's preparation on direct examination is also controlled and guided by his own understanding of the issues and the significance of his contribution to the picture. Most parties and witnesses have at least some idea of what is important about what they have to say and at least some ability to say it. If the witness is aware of the reason he is testifying to particular facts and the importance of these facts in the overall picture, it is more likely that his testimony will be informed and will provide the details expected.

At one extreme there are some witnesses, usually doctors or other experts, who could be asked the following question on direct examination:

Q. Doctor, would you please tell the members of the jury exactly what they need to know about this case?

Such witnesses have sufficient knowledge of their subject matter, enough understanding of the issues in the case, and enough experience in testifying to present the facts and create the desired image without further guidance from the lawyer. Their terminology, emphasis, and effect could not be improved on by any amount of external control.

Witnesses who have the knowledge and capability to give their testimony without the guidance and control of the lawyer are rare, however. While possessing some knowledge of the significance of their testimony, most witnesses are not in a position to appreciate the particular inferences that would be apparent to the lawyer. Many witnesses are involved in only parts of the picture and thus are not oriented to the whole. Witnesses are often inexperienced at storytelling, and are often nervous. No matter how much out-of-court preparation there has been, no matter how well the witness has learned to appreciate the significance of his testimony, the lawyer must use in-court control techniques to guide the witness through direct examination as effectively and yet unobtrusively as possible.

3. Cues on Direct Examination

The primary control techniques used by the lawyer in an effective direct examination are the verbal and nonverbal cues directing the witness's testimony and presentation in the order, terms, emphases, and particulars selected by the lawyer. The verbal cues consist of the form and substance of the questions used; the nonverbal cues include the examiner's tone of voice, body position, eye contact, and tempo of questioning.

Although the verbal cues are referred to as questions, effective direct examination is not an interrogation. The lawyer is not seeking to learn information from the witness; she already knows what the witness is going to say. The lawyer merely wants her witness to say it to the factfinders. The purposes of the questions are (1) to cue the witness to provide the next fact or element of testimony and (2) to give the judge and opposing counsel notice of the upcoming testimony in order to permit objection.

The tone of questioning is declarative rather than interrogative. Questions end on a downbeat. For instance,

> Q.   What did you see when you arrived at 33 Jackson Street?

sounds more like a statement than a question. The lawyer does not betray any uncertainty about what the witness saw. She is telling the witness what the witness should next present to the jury. While occasionally a more questioning tone may be inserted for emphasis, the lawyer usually wishes to express confidence and support by a smooth directive examination using questions ending in a downbeat.

Often questions asked on direct examination are worded as directives.

> Q.   Please tell us where you were when you first saw the men.

This form of question turns the witness into the storyteller, but the examiner still controls the presentation by limiting the scope of the requested reply to "where you were when . . .". As mentioned before, the reference to "us" combines the lawyer and the jury into one group of listeners. On the other hand, the common formulation

> Q.   Can you tell us where you were when you first saw the men?

is an ambiguous combination of a question and a cue. It is not clear whether the lawyer is asking the witness whether he *can* tell where he was or to actually say where he was. Such formulations should be avoided.

The tone of direct examination should be encouraging but nonintrusive. The lawyer's role is to maximize the impact and presentation of the witness. The tone and pacing of follow-up questions indicate satisfaction with the preceding responses and confident expectation of the next bit of information.

The lawyer's task on direct is to craft questions or cues that will prompt the witness to provide exactly the information and presentation desired by the lawyer, no more and no less. By its wording and tone, the question should be designed so that the witness will give a fair and predictable response in ordinary parlance. In a sense, the lawyer's question frames the witness's answer. The lawyer says, in essence, "please provide this bit of information and then wait for the next cue."

G.   Form of Questions — Leading and Nonleading

1.   The Spectrum of Witnesses and Issues

In a certain sense, all questions used by a lawyer at trial are leading. Even on direct examination, the lawyer's job is to lead or guide the lawyer to present the testimony in the most precise and authoritative way possible. When the lawyer poses a question to the witness, it should be designed so that the lawyer can confidently expect a particular response.

The trial lawyer has a wide spectrum of questions or cues available, depending on 1) the witness's degree of cooperativeness, 2) the amount of the witness's shared knowledge and orientation, 3) the nature of the subject matter, and 4) the details to be elicited.

At one extreme, a witness who is well oriented to the purpose of the testimony and who is able to articulate the right details may need relatively few cues to give an effective presentation. At the other extreme, the lawyer may need to use strong and direct control to compel a reluctant or adverse witness to concede even minor details. Between these extremes can be found the well-intentioned witness who is flustered or relatively inarticulate, the witness who is mildly adverse and does not really know what the case is all about, the garrulous witness who goes overboard in trying to sell his story, and a host of other variations. Such witnesses need substantial direction from the lawyer in order to make effective presentations.

If the subject matter of a witness's testimony is a sudden event, bound in space and time so that the story "tells itself," less lawyer control and focusing are needed. The events themselves are contained within a small area and a small amount of time, so it is relatively easy to focus on the details that matter and recount the information in such a way that it can be placed in proper context and understood by the factfinders. On the other hand, if the subject matter spans a large period of time or deals with a number of incidents or events or an ongoing condition, more control and focusing are usually needed to extract the more relevant details from a mass of less relevant or extraneous matter. It can be argued that the difference between leading and nonleading questions is merely a matter of degree and that the trial lawyer should employ leading or directive questioning as necessary to provide maximum exposure of the witness's testimony consistent with reasonable control of the presentation.

2. Improper Leading Questions

For centuries the law of evidence and trial advocacy has found it convenient to define a subset of directive cues as "leading" and subject to special treatment. The general rule is codified in Federal Rule of Evidence 611(c):

> Leading questions should not be used on direct examination of a witness except as may be necessary to develop the witness's testimony.

For the purpose of the traditional rule, a leading question has been defined as a "question which suggests the answer." Another way of looking at it is that in a leading question the lawyer *supplies* the information to be conveyed, while in a nonleading question the lawyer *describes* the kind of information expected, but the actual information is provided by the witness.

Thus the question

Q. Did you see two men in the street when you returned to your home?

is a leading question: the lawyer is providing all the information— namely, that the witness saw two men in the street. The witness merely acknowledges or denies this information by answering "yes" or "no." The question

Q. What did you see in the street when you returned to your home?

is an open or nonleading question: the witness is expected to provide the information sought, "two men." The question sets forth with precision the nature of the information desired: the witness is being asked only what he observed in a particular place at a particular time. Although the frame has been drawn, the picture within the frame is to be provided by the witness.

The question

Q. Did you see anyone in the street when you returned to your home?

is, according to this definition, both leading and nonleading. It is leading because the information about seeing anyone is suggested by the lawyer. On the other hand, it can be argued that the question is nonleading because "anyone" is not really specific information but rather is more an indication of the subject matter of the testimony. Questions of this construction are frequently used as "focusing" questions to make a transition, introduce new subject matter, or focus the witness on a particular detail. If the witness responds "yes" to the focusing question

Q. Did you see anyone in the street when you returned to your home?

the next question would be

    Q. Who did you see?

and the witness would be expected to supply the words

    A. Two men.

A slightly less explicit focusing question would be

    Q. Did you see anything in the street when you returned to your home?

Using "anything" in place of "anyone" avoids the leading suggestion of the presence of persons.

The rule against leading questions reflects a policy that, ordinarily, on direct examination the witness is expected to provide the information. The lawyer's role is limited to guiding the witness by indicating the nature of the information that is to be provided. This policy is based on considerations of fairness and accuracy. If the witness is able to give the details directly, without being transmitted through the lawyer, it is more likely that the information will be accurate and authoritative. Factfinders are aware of the effects of a retelling of information. The most accurate information comes "from the horse's mouth."

For the same reason, asking nonleading questions on direct is good trial advocacy. Testimony coming from the witness is likely to be better received and credited than testimony repackaged and delivered through the friendly lawyer.

The qualification in Rule 611(c), "except as may be necessary to develop the witness's testimony," reflects the fact that in some circumstances it is not feasible or practical to conduct the presentation without the lawyer providing some of the information, either to focus the witness or as a prompt to other testimony.

The rule against leading questions is not absolute. As will be seen, there are many instances when the rule permits, and effective advocacy favors, the use of leading questions on direct examination. On preliminary or background matters, that are not contested, such as "name, date of birth, and serial number," leading questions are ordinarily permitted to move things along.

    Q. Your name is Imogene Farris?

A. Yes.

Q. And you are Bob Maxfield's girlfriend?

A. Yes.

Q. And you live at 33 Jackson Street, right?

A. That's right.

This kind of material is not controversial. It does not matter so much that the information is coming from the lawyer rather than the witness. It is up to the lawyer, however, to decide whether accelerating the presentation is more important than gaining the additional exposure for the witness that would be provided by questions in nonleading form.

As discussed below, leading questions may be used to refresh a witness's recollection once it has been exhausted by open questions. And, as suggested above, certain kinds of leading questions may be used to focus the witness's attention on a particular subject matter of testimony or for transition. The rule is one of practicality and necessity.

Even though the rules of evidence may permit leading questions in particular situations, if sufficient control of the presentation can be maintained with more open questions, it is usually preferable to use the more open questions on direct. Even on routine matters, witness exposure and the building of credibility may favor a somewhat slower presentation using conventional questions rather than rushing through by permitted leading questions. The most elegant trial advocates are so able to cue their witnesses with well-crafted "who," "where," "what," "when," and "why" questions that they seldom need resort to leading the witness, even where legally permissible.

H.   Questions as a Means of Control

1.   *Avoiding Leading Questions*

The rule against leading questions on direct is a rule of courtroom procedure, not a rule of substantive law. It is hard to imagine that any case has been reversed on appeal because the trial judge erroneously permitted or prohibited leading questions on direct. As indicated above, the rule is one of practicality and convenience and has many exceptions.

A judge will often permit and even encourage leading questions on accreditation, preliminary matters and noncontroverted points in order to move the case along. Often it is a lot quicker for the lawyer to state those facts and have the witness merely affirm them "pro forma." In many trials, large parts of the direct examination is carried on by leading questions in order to keep the proceedings focused on the core issues and save time with the peripheral matter.

For the less experienced trial lawyer, however, the habit of leading on preliminary or noncontroverted matters can be hard to break when approaching the important part of the witness's testimony. A common trial scenario from the earlier "sink or swim" days of trial advocacy training involved an older lawyer sitting quietly by while his less experienced opponent posed a series of leading questions on direct. At the opportune moment, when the testimony reached a substantive area, the older lawyer would object. The young lawyer, mentally caught in a pattern of leading questions, would struggle to find the right formulation. The resulting feeling of helplessness and embarrassment would ruin a good presentation.

For inexperienced trial lawyers in particular, it is usually advisable to bend over backward to avoid using leading questions. The lawyer should get into the habit of examining without relying on leading questions.

Moreover, as long as a lawyer is asking leading questions on direct, the lawyer's presentation may be in jeopardy. There is always the chance that there will be an objection and that the objection will be sustained. This vulnerability to the opposing lawyer's objections may affect the lawyer's ability to project the self-confidence necessary to support and guide the witness's testimony and give it maximum credibility.

2.   Overbroad or Narrative Questions

The perfectly appropriate "open" question,

> Q.   What happened on the evening of October 10th?

may not be sufficiently controlling. Such a question asks the witness, in effect,

    Q. What do you think is most significant about the evening of October 10th?

The witness could fairly answer the question by running through the entire narrative of the incident, or could give a one-paragraph capsule version or summary, or could start out with the first few details and then stop and wait for a further prompt. The witness could start at any point and end at any point regarding what happened on the evening of October 10th. Control of the presentation has been abandoned by the lawyer and given over to the witness. Needless to say, the lawyer is not doing her job if she allows the witness to tell it in any way he chooses in responding to the lawyer's excessively wide open questions.

    Such overbroad questions are also subject to an evidentiary objection.

    Opposing Counsel. Objection! Too broad; calls for a narrative.

The vice is that the question gives no delineation of the expected scope of the answer. There is no frame or boundary to limit the witness's response, and the opposing lawyer is not given sufficient warning about upcoming testimony to permit opportunity for objection. The witness might roll on and give inadmissible testimony before the opponent can anticipate what is coming. Unless the context of the question is such that the scope of the anticipated response is obvious to all, the "overbroad" objection is likely to be sustained, and the examiner will be asked to rephrase the question.

3. Control with Open Questions

The "what happened?" question can be narrowed considerably without affecting its open configuration. For instance, a narrower version of the

    Q. What happened on the evening of October 10th?

question could be reframed as

> Q.   What happened *at 9 p.m.* on the evening of October
>   10th?

This question at least has a starting point. The witness knows
that he is supposed to start his testimony concerning what happened at 9 P.M. However, there is still no indication of how far
the witness is to go in answering, and he is not limited in the
subject matter of his testimony other than to tell what "happened." Presumably, the witness will not extend the narrative too
far from the beginning point at 9 P.M. A more precise but still
nonleading question would be

> Q.   What *did you do* at 9 P.M. on the evening of October
>   10th?

This question incorporates not only the time limitation but also
limits the scope of the requested testimony to action by the witness. The witness is not being asked what she saw or heard, but
what she *did* at the relevant time.
   Another format might be

> Q.   What did you *see* at 9 P.M. on the evening of October
>   10th?

The use of "see" further narrows the zone of requested information to visual observations of the witness at the time specified.
   Another version might be

> Q.   What did you *first* see at 9 P.M. on the evening of Octo-
>   ber 10th?

The inclusion of "first" further limits the requested testimony. The
implication is that the witness is to stop after describing the first
thing he saw and is to wait for another question.
   Or

> Q.   What did you see *in the street* at 9 P.M. on the evening of
>   October 10th?

This is also a perfectly proper open question. Even though it specifies the location of the observations that are being sought, the witness is being asked to tell only what he saw at that particular location and only at that location at a particular time.

Sometimes the question relates the information sought to information already given by the witness in answer to previous questions.

Q. What did the man do then?

A. He swung at me.

Q. What did you do [think, feel, say] *when he swung at you?*

Incorporation of a witness's previous answer or part of it as the predicate for a later question is a well known and powerful technique to maintain control and enhance the presentation by the lawyer's repetition of the desirable testimony. The lawyer must be careful, though, that the testimony incorporated actually serves as an appropriate predicate for the later question and is not being used solely for the sake of repetition. The repeated words must also be completely identical with the witness's previous answer. A version of the last question such as

Q. What did you do *when he belted you?*

would not be proper or ethical because it is not an accurate incorporation of the prior testimony. This is an example of where the lawyer either consciously or by mistake seeks to "improve" the prior testimony by inserting a better version in the follow-up question.

Classic direct examination is a process where the lawyer uses open-format questions designed to elicit the precise bits of information sought in the precise order desired by the lawyer to build an overall image. The lawyer asks carefully chosen questions to which the expected answer is the next bit of information sought. Assume, for example, that the witness is testifying about seeing some strange men in the street outside her house at night. If, in developing the image, the trial lawyer next wants the factfinder to form an image of the clothes the men were wearing, she will use questions that will elicit this information.

Q.   What did you see outside your house?

A.   Two strange men.

Q.   How were the men dressed?

A.   One was wearing a leather jacket and the other a denim jacket and hat.

If, on the other hand, the lawyer wanted the men's actions to be the next detail to enter the picture, the follow-up question would be

Q.   What were the men doing?

A smooth direct examination uses a succession of these guiding questions unobtrusively to elicit the witness's testimony in the order and with the details the lawyer wants. Yet it is the witness who appears to be the storyteller to the factfinders.

4.   Direct Questions as "Frames"

Another way of thinking about a lawyer's questions on direct examination is as "frames" for portions of a developing image. Each question is a frame tailored for a particular bit of the overall image being recreated in the consciousnesses of the factfinders. Consider, for instance, the sequence of questions about the two men in the street.

Q.   Ms. Mercer, what did you see in the street when you looked out of your bay window?

Although this question on its face could call for anything, the witness knows that he is not there to tell about the tree he could see on his lawn or the fence across the street. The cue will tell her that she is to describe what she saw that is involved in this case.

A.   I saw two men.

At this point the factfinders acquire an image of two men, but it is indistinct at best. They don't know what the men looked like, what they were wearing, or what they were doing. The next frames enable these images to be filled in.

Q.   What were the men wearing?

A.   One was wearing a blue denim jacket, and the other was wearing a leather jacket.

Q.   What did their faces look like?

A.   One was wearing glasses, and they both had beards.

Now the factfinders can fill in clothes and faces on the previously blank male images, but there is no indication of what they are doing. The lawyer then draws the next frame.

Q.   What were the two men doing when you first saw them?

While people do not usually change their basic appearance over a short period of time, their actions are likely to change frequently. Thus the qualifier of "when you first saw them" is intended to focus and limit the witness's responses to a specific point in time.

A.   The man with the glasses had his hand up in the air and was pointing at something.

Now the image is much more complete. To the factfinders the two men have now acquired certain clothes and features and one, at least, is doing something. Each of the questions has served as a frame for conveying another element to the image.

Obviously, the scene in real life contained many more elements, which the lawyer and witness have not bothered to try to describe or recreate. Only those details that the lawyer has selected as important are being framed for the factfinders.

5.   Reticent and Run-on Witnesses

The degree of control used on direct examination varies with the character of each witness. Many witnesses are not especially articulate and will tend to answer questions briefly and include only the first thoughts that come to mind. For such witnesses, fewer limiting qualifiers are generally needed in the questions. Even a fairly broad "what happened?" question may elicit only the most immediate and salient of available recollections. But because such witnesses may not be well attuned to the more subtle aspects of the presentation, they may need more guidance as to what details are being sought in their testimony.

> Q. What happened after you left the Blue Goose?
>
> A. We got in the car.
>
> Q. Where did you go in the car?
>
> A. We headed back toward the campus.

Perhaps a more articulate and aggressive witness would continue by telling where the group next intended to go after leaving the Blue Goose. The reticent witness, however, might confine his answer only to the next immediate detail, "We got in the car."

Other witnesses, however, tend to "run on" if not kept in check. For such witnesses, each question should contain its own natural boundaries for a fair answer.

One witness might respond to the question

> Q. What happened at 9:00 P.M. on October 10th?

with

> A. I heard a noise on Jackson Street.

Another witness might respond to the same question,

> A. I heard a noise, looked out the window, and saw a fight going on and then the defendant's car came out and ran up on the sidewalk and killed one of the people.

This kind of "running on" rarely does justice to the presentation planned by the lawyer. Particular images might be omitted or provided in the wrong order with the wrong emphasis. For the witness who runs on, the trial lawyer will have to craft the questions with clear boundaries so the witness will be inhibited from compromising the overall presentation by a premature and incomplete recital of the main event. The lawyer's question should clearly indicate how far the witness is expected to go in the answer. A question such as

Q. Would you tell us, Sir, the first thing you did when you heard the noise outside your window?

is designed to restrict a witness who might run on to describe just the first in a series of events that occurred on the night in question.

In extreme cases, a lawyer on direct examination may interrupt a witness who is going too far.

Q. At about 9:00 in the evening of October 10, did you hear anything outside your house?

A. Yes, I did. It was a noise like a gunshot. I turned around . . .

Q. (interrupting). Excuse me, Sir, where was the noise coming from?

This kind of control is a bit more obvious than is usually desirable. However, if necessary to maintain the integrity of the presentation, the lawyer should not hesitate to interrupt in a firm but considerate manner in order to keep the flow of information under control.

Sometimes the problem is that the witness is too concise or even opaque in his responses. In such circumstances the lawyer can ask him to elaborate:

Q. How did you feel when you saw the decedent lying on the grass in front of you?

A. Not good.

Q. What do you mean, Sir, by "not good"?

or, frequently with expert witnesses,

Q. What is your professional specialty, Doctor?

> *A.* Orthopedic surgery.
>
> *Q.* Would you tell the jury, Doctor, what is orthopedic surgery?

6.   Forms of Transition Questions

A common problem on direct examination is providing a smooth transition for the witness from background details to the primary subject matter of the testimony, and from place to place and time to time within that testimony. Usually some degree of focusing is required, for instance, to accomplish the transition from the witness' background and "humanizing" part to his substantive testimony.

> *Q.* Did you have the occasion to be at your home on Jackson Street on the night of October 10th?

To be somewhere or do something at a given time is a common, if somewhat artificial, windup to bring the witness to the scene of the testimony.
  Another more natural approach uses a point in time as an anchor:

> *Q.* What were you doing at 9:00 on the night of October 10th?

Or

> *Q.* Would you tell us where you were at 9:00 on the evening of October 10th?

The witness's response will put him in a position from which the attorney can ask a series of nonleading questions designed to elicit the necessary images.

> *A.* In my living room.
>
> *Q.* What were you doing in your living room?
>
> *A.* Watching TV.
>
> *Q.* Where in your house is your living room?

A. In the front.

Q. What does the front of your house face?

A. Jackson Street.

Q. Where were you looking at that time?

A. Out at Jackson Street.

Q. Why was that?

A. I had heard a sound like a gunshot.

Another somewhat contrived formulation used by some lawyers for minor transitions and introductions is to use the phrase "if any" or "if anything":

Q. What, if anything, did you hear outside your house that evening?

The theory behind this phraseology is that the question

Q. Did you hear anything outside your house that evening?

could be interpreted as an improper leading question. On the other hand, the question

Q. What did you hear outside your house that evening?

by itself could also be objectionable because it assumes that the witness had in fact heard something. "If anything" is added to cure the foundation problem without leading.

The problem with this kind of question is that it is not natural or conversational; it sounds stilted, which can be "off-putting" to the factfinders. The "what, if anything" phrasing is often used as a crutch by lawyers who do not want to sort out the circumstances so as to ask the questions in a normal and nonleading fashion.

With a little sensitivity to circumstance, the direct examiner can move along from detail to detail without resorting to contrived questions. If the witness discloses introductory information that makes it probable that something was heard, for instance, it is proper to ask the "what" question directly:

Q. Where did you go on October 10, 1994?

A. I went to the opera.

Q. What did you hear at the opera?

Because common experience teaches us that when one goes to the opera, one ordinarily hears something, it is not necessary to ask

Q. Did you hear anything at the opera?

or

Q. What, if anything, did you hear at the opera?

On the other hand, if the circumstances do not provide any hint of foundation for the "what" question, then a focusing question is appropriate and permissible.

Q. Where were you at 9:00 P.M. on October 10?

A. I was sitting in my living room.

Q. Did you hear anything in the street outside your house?

A. Yes, I did.

Q. What did you hear?

A. I heard a noise like a gunshot.

Common experience suggests that a person sitting in his living room would not be especially likely to hear something in the street in front of the house, so it is appropriate to ask a focusing question using "anything" or the equivalent. The leading should be kept at the minimum necessary to focus the witness on the subject matter; content should not be supplied. The question,

Q. Did you hear a noise like a gunshot in the street outside your house?

ordinarily would include too much of the information sought from the witness and would be objectionable as leading.

The idea is to make the transition questions natural and conversational so that the witness feels comfortable giving the testimony and so that it is readily accepted and understood by the factfinders.

7. Avoiding Conclusions and Characterizations

An effective presentation on direct tends to be in terms of immediate facts rather than conclusions or characterizations. The factfinders recognize that people can come to different conclusions or opinions from the same set of facts. Both rules of evidence and considerations of effective trial advocacy favor testimony in terms of specific facts. The lawyer's cues to the witness should direct the presentation in the direction of specific facts, where feasible.

Q. What did the two men appear to be doing?

A. They appeared to be harassing the young girls.

Opposing Counsel.   Objection! Conclusion.

The Court.   Sustained; the answer is stricken. Please rephrase your question.

Q. What were the two men actually doing with respect to the young girls?

A. They were talking loudly, yelling, waving their arms, using foul language.

That is not to say that a witness's testimony cannot contain any element of conclusion. Almost all observations embody some degree of inference. Many commonplace conclusions are accepted as shorthand renderings of the underlying facts. "He was drunk"; "she appeared upset"; "we had a good time" are all conclusory formulations that would likely be accepted as shorthand descriptions, particularly if the identified condition is not a central issue in the case.

On the other hand, questions beginning with

Q. What did you conclude about . . . ?

or

    Q.   Would you characterize for us . . . ?

are likely to draw an objection and blunt the factual impact of the testimony.

8. *Pacing*

The pacing of a direct examination can be varied to suit the subject matter. Action can be slowed down or sped up by the manner in which the question cues are posed. For instance, if the direct examiner wishes to make certain actions seem deliberate, several small questions separated by brief pauses will elicit the details and give the impression of deliberation in the action itself.

    Q.   As you approached the intersection of Wood and Vale, Mr. Borak, what is the first thing you remember doing?

    A.   I stopped at the stop sign.

    Q.   Would you show us on the diagram where the stop sign was when you stopped?

    A.   Right here (pointing).

    Q.   After you stopped, what is the next thing you did?

    A.   Looked for traffic.

    Q.   Which way did you look for traffic?

    A.   I looked to the left and looked to the right.

    Q.   Would you show us on the diagram where you looked?

    A.   Yes; here and here (pointing).

    Q.   What did you see when you looked to the left?

    A.   Nothing.

    On the other hand, if the examiner wants to give the opposite impression, a quick "what happened?" to prompt a run-on answer might recapture the whole incident in a breath and give the impression of a sudden event in real life.

> Q.   What did you do on the afternoon of October 10?
>
> A.   We went to the zoo.
>
> Q.   Where did you go at the zoo?
>
> A.   We went to the tiger house.
>
> Q.   (quickly). What happened there?
>
> A.   A tiger jumped over the fence and came running at us. I screamed. A man came out of nowhere and shot him.

Once the event has been recounted at a pace appropriate to the occasion, the lawyer can go back and pick up relevant details.

> Q.   Let's go back to when you entered the tiger house. Where were you when you first went in?
>
> A.   Right by the large door in the end of the building. . . .

I.   Refreshing Recollection

An effective presentation through the testimony of witnesses depends on the ability of those witnesses to remember the material to be presented and to relate the necessary elements in response to the cues in the lawyer's questions. Memory varies from person to person and from situation to situation. Many people find their memories impaired by unfamiliar surroundings, stress, and nervousness. Often a court presentation will require a witness to recall and relate considerable detailed data from an event or condition far in the past. Despite the most assiduous preparation, many witnesses suffer greater or lesser lapses of memory when on the stand. Others will misrecognize cues in the lawyer's questions and will not come up with the expected responses.

A witness's temporary lapses of memory and failure to respond to a question cue does not mean that the omitted material is forever lost. Trial lawyers are equipped with several tools with which to try to retrieve the missing information and include it in the presentation.

Sometimes the glitch may be a minor one that can be cured with a slightly rephrased question:

Q. Where were you on the evening of October 10?

A. I was in Springfield.

Q. Please tell us a bit more precisely where you were in Springfield.

A. At my home on Jackson Street.

In more serious cases of a memory lapse, the lawyer may jog the witness's memory so that the missing or inaccurate information can be properly supplied. The process of assisting the witness to testify despite a partial or complete lack of present memory is referred to as "refreshing the witness's recollection." The lawyer should be conversant with and ready to use several techniques to refresh recollection on both direct and cross-examination.

The fact that a witness's recollection needs refreshing or that the witness has made a mistake and is required to correct it is not the end of the world. People do make mistakes, misremember, and freeze up on the witness stand, and the factfinders know this. A lawyer faced with a witness's mistake or memory failure should not try to disregard it or cover it up because of fear that her presentation will be found fallible. Getting the mistake acknowledged and corrected or prompting the missing memory is much less damaging to the presentation as a whole than trying to cope with a missing element or an outright inaccuracy from one's own witnesses.

1. Foundation for Refreshing Recollection

Before the lawyer can attempt to refresh a witness's recollection, she must show that it is in fact impaired. Both good trial advocacy and the rules of evidence prohibit a lawyer from prompting a witness who has not been shown to need prompting. Sometimes the witness will acknowledge a failure of recollection on his own:

> Q. Doctor, when was the first time you met with Mr. Cluney after he left the hospital?
>
> A. I don't remember the exact date, but I am sure it is in my report.

The foundation has been laid by the witness's statement that he does not remember. It is now up to the lawyer to refresh the witness's recollection so that he does remember and can testify.

If, however, the witness does not acknowledge a lack of memory but merely testifies in a manner other than as expected, then the lawyer must bring out the memory impairment before attempting to refresh recollection.

> Q. Please tell us who was there when you first arrived.
>
> A. Arthur Clark and Dan Bragg.
>
> Q. Do you remember anyone else being there at that time?
>
> A. No, I don't.

The foundation has been laid for refreshing of recollection.

Prefacing ordinary fact questions with "Do you remember . . . ?" is usually to be avoided because it focuses the attention of the witness and the factfinders not on the fact remembered but on the condition of the witness's memory. For that very reason it is the right formulation when the foundation is being laid to refresh recollection.

2. Refreshing Recollection with Questions

The simplest way a lawyer can refresh a witness's missing or impaired recollection is with questions designed to stimulate the memory. All that is necessary is some showing that the witness does not remember the answer to a more open or neutral question.

Frequently a witness will fail to remember and will give one of several facts inquired about.

> Q. Who was present on the evening of October 12?
>
> A. Arthur Clark, Dan Bragg, and Christine Cooper.

If at this point the lawyer realizes that the witness has left someone out of the lineup, she can gently jog the witness's memory:

Q.   Was there any one else present?

In a sense this is a leading question. In the context of the preceding question and answer it suggests that there might have been someone else present. Such a question is universally permitted, because it is premised on the examiner's good-faith belief that the witness should be able to testify that there was someone present in addition to the people named.

Often the reference to "anyone else" will be a sufficient stimulus to the witness's memory that he will recall and supply the missing element of the testimony.

A.   Yes, Michelle Dorsey was also there.

In some cases, however, the witness may respond,

A.   I don't remember whether there was anyone else there.

The words "don't remember" are the key words for the foundation to refresh recollection. If the witness testifies on his own to a lack of memory concerning the subject matter of the question, it is almost always appropriate to refresh the witness's recollection with a leading question.

Q.   Was Michelle Dorsey there as well?

A.   Oh yes; now that I think of it, she was.

If, on the other hand, the witness answers the question

Q.   Was there any one else present?

A.   I don't think that there was anyone else present . . .

the lawyer must show some lack of memory on the part of the witness before the lawyer attempts to refresh his recollection by either a leading question or some other device.

> Q. Well, do you remember whether there was anyone else there?
>
> A. Not really.

Now that the witness has testified to a lack of or impairment of memory, his recollection may be refreshed.

> Q. Was Michelle Dorsey there as well?
>
> A. Oh, yes; now that I think of it, she was.

The leading question is permissible only for the purpose of refreshing impaired recollection. Classically, it is not supposed to be asked until the questioner has shown that the witness's recollection is impaired or has been exhausted, which is usually accomplished by the "anything else?" question. Sometimes it is necessary, however, to ask a "do you remember?" question to establish the lack or impairment of memory before refreshing recollection with a leading question.

As a practical matter, leading questions to refresh a witness's recollection are frequently allowed on a mere showing that the witness may not remember something. There is often no particular requirement that other means to exhaust the witness's recollection have been tried and have failed.

The form of leading question used to refresh witness recollection is the one that asks the minimum necessary to jog the memory. It is phrased in the interrogative rather than the declarative:

> Q. Was Michelle Dorsey there as well?

rather than

> Q. Michelle Dorsey was there as well, wasn't she?

The lawyer should not try to take advantage of refreshing recollection to "put the words in the witness's mouth."

Refreshing witness recollection by permitted leading questions is quick and causes minimal interruption to the presentation. If handled properly, it causes minimal damage to witness credibility. However, if it is necessary to use leading questions again and again to refresh the recollection of one's own witness, the witness's credibility may suffer. Too many leading questions can reinforce the impression that the lawyer is really doing the testifying and the witness is only responding to cues.

3. Refreshing Recollection with Documents and Things

Another way to refresh recollection is by means of a document or object. Once a witness's memory has been shown to be impaired, the trial lawyer may refresh recollection by showing something to the witness that is calculated to prompt his memory so that he can testify from his own recollection.

Q. Officer Anderson, what was the length of the skid marks you measured on Wood Street?

A. Well, I am not sure I can remember exactly.

Q. (handing witness a copy of his police accident report). Officer, take a look at this document and tell us if it will refresh your recollection about the length of the skid marks?

A. (looking at document). Yes, it will.

Q. Well, please look at it to refresh your recollection and then tell us how long the skid marks were when you measured them at the scene of the accident.

A. Seventy-six feet.

There is no requirement that the object used to refresh recollection be admissible in evidence. Nor is there requirement that the object have anything to do with the case. Literally, a piece of toilet paper will do, if looking at the piece of toilet paper will prompt the witness's memory so that he can testify.

A note pad with the answer written on it will also suffice. Any kind of hearsay that would itself be inadmissible may be used to refresh recollection — from a newspaper, to the witness's own prior statement, to a prompt made up by the lawyer in advance of the testimony. In fact, the largest category of commonly used refreshers of recollection are inadmissible.

The safeguard against abuse of the license to refresh recollection lies in the right of the opposing party to see what is shown the witness to refresh recollection. On request, the opposing party may see the object used to refresh recollection at the time it is used. Federal Evidence Rule 612 provides that objects used to refresh recollection must be shown to the opposing attorney on request. While the judge may determine when the object may be seen by the opponent, usually it is examined before the direct examination is completed. If the object is a prompt from the lawyer or similar crib, that fact is fair game on cross-examination.

Because the object or document is not being offered or admitted in evidence but is being used only to jog the witness's memory on the stand, it should not be referred to in a manner that gives it evidentiary significance. It is improper to abuse the device of refreshing recollection to secure the publication to the jury of materials that would otherwise be inadmissible in evidence.

After the lawyer has laid the foundation for refreshing recollection and as she shows the witness his prior statement, the lawyer can say, for example,

Q.   May I show you this document? Please read the bottom of the first page to yourself. Does this refresh your recollection about who was there on October 10th?

A.   Oh, yes, Christine Cooper was there too.

If the object used to refresh recollection has not been admitted in evidence, it should be completely neutral as far as the presentation to the jury is concerned. For instance, suppose the lawyer had said something like

Q.   Let me show you this copy of your police report. Does this refresh your recollection as to who was there?

A.   Oh, yes, Christine Cooper was there.

The clear implication of such a question is that the information is coming from the police report, not from the witness's refreshed memory. Even though the police report has not been offered in evidence, and would not be admitted if it were offered, the fact-finders have been made aware of at least a part of its contents. The more potential prejudice in an object, the more careful the lawyer must be to avoid incidental evidentiary impact by use of the object to refresh recollection.

Sensitivity to incidental evidentiary effect varies from jurisdiction to jurisdiction and from judge to judge. However, sometimes misuse of material used to refresh recollection is so flagrant as to constitute unethical conduct subject to discipline or reproof from the court.

When a document is used to refresh recollection, counsel should make it clear that the witness should read the document to himself, not out loud to the jury.

Q. Let me show you this document to refresh your recollection. Would you please read it to yourself and let us know whether or not it has refreshed your recollection as to who was there that night?

A. Yes, it has.

Q. With your recollection refreshed, would you now tell us who was there on that night?

A. Arthur Clark, Dan Bragg, Christine Cooper, Michelle Dorsey, and Norman Epstein were there.

It is sometimes important to structure the questioning so that the witness does not actually read from the document when he is testifying to his refreshed recollection. If the witness appears to be reading from the document as he testifies, the opponent may object to the testimony as hearsay testimony from a document not in evidence.

Q. Officer, did you measure the distance from Mrs. Mercer's window to where you found the body?

A. Yes, I believe I did.

Q. How far was Mrs. Mercer's window from the place where you found the body?

A. I am not sure right now.

Q. (showing document to witness). Would this refresh your recollection of how far Mrs. Mercer's window was from where you found the body?

A.   (reading from document). It says here "97 feet."

Opposing Counsel.   Objection! He is reading from a document not in evidence.

Q.   Officer, without reading from the document, has your recollection of the distance been refreshed?

A.   Yes, it has.

Q.   What was the distance?

A.   97 feet.

As noted above, if a witness's recollection is refreshed with a document or object, the opponent has the right to examine the item used to refresh recollection at the time. There are few, if any, grounds to object to the proper use of a document or other object to refresh recollection, but the opponent always has the right to cross-examine about the stimulus used.

Opposing Counsel.   During your direct examination, your lawyer showed you something to refresh your recollection of who was present on the night of October 10, didn't she?

A.   Yes.

Opposing Counsel. (showing paper to witness).   Isn't it true that the paper your attorney showed you to refresh your recollection was just a sheet of paper with some names on it?

A.   Yes, that's right.

Opposing Counsel.   Isn't it true that this paper was created by your lawyer's associate while you were testifying?

A.   Yes, I guess so.

J.   Past Recollection Recorded

The use of papers and objects to refresh recollection for witness testimony must be distinguished from offering documents and papers as past recollection recorded. In the case of recollection refreshed, the witness's testimony from present recollection, as jogged by the object used to refresh that recollection, remains the source of the information provided. Past recollection recorded substitutes a document or memorandum made in the past for the witness's testimony.

In most cases it is simpler and more efficient to refresh a witness's faltering or absent recollection rather than attempt to offer a prior memorandum as past recollection recorded. Refreshing recollection is usually a quicker and more natural procedure that does not seriously interrupt the flow of the presentation or change the tone of the proceedings.

It is widely believed that presenting important facts via a document that is placed in evidence can add to the authority of the presentation. For some reason a degree of credibility is afforded almost anything that is "in writing." These considerations would appear to favor the use of past recollection recorded to get the facts before the factfinders in written form. However, most of the evidentiary value in having the testimony in a written document is cancelled by the requirements of Federal Rule of Evidence 803(5) and its state counterparts. Rule 803(5) requires that a document admitted as past recollection recorded will be read in evidence but will not be received as an exhibit unless offered by the opposing party. This restriction is designed to prevent the use of the hearsay rule exception to transform oral testimony into written exhibits. Such testimony might otherwise attain undeserved authority with the factfinders because it would be embodied in a writing physically before the factfinders and available to be referred to during deliberations.

There are some cases, though, where the witness does not respond well to refreshing of recollection. In such cases past recollection recorded may be the only way to get the facts before the factfinders.

As with refreshing recollection, the use of documents and papers as past recollection recorded requires that the witness's actual memory be impaired or exhausted. The lawyer lays the foundation for past recollection recorded by first showing that the witness cannot presently remember the information sought.

Q. Officer, please tell the jury what the man was wearing when you first saw him.

A. I don't remember exactly.

The officer has now testified to a lack of present memory to the fact sought. At this point, the examining lawyer can try to refresh the officer's recollection by, say, showing him a copy of his report and asking him if the paper in his hand refreshes his recollection about what the man was wearing. Or he can continue to lay the foundation to offer the report as past recollection recorded.

Q. Officer, at the time of the incident, did you observe what the man was wearing?

A. I am sure I did.

Q. Did you make any kind of memorandum or notes of your observations?

A. I am sure I did.

Q. I show you Exhibit 16 for identification. Do you recognize it?

A. Yes, that is my report.

Q. How are you able to recognize it?

A. It has my signature on it, here on the second page.

Q. We offer Exhibit 16 as past recollection recorded.

The Court. Admitted.

Q. Would you please read the last three sentences of page 1 to the jury?

A. "One of the men was wearing a leather jacket. The other man was wearing a denim jacket and a hat. Both men had beards."

To a degree, this answer is nonresponsive because it goes beyond the original question asked. Sometimes memoranda of past recollection recorded are not in a form that is precisely the same as that which prompted the use of the memoranda. The problem of nonresponsive answers on direct examination is addressed in Chapter 9.

Although a document admitted as past recollection recorded is not placed before the factfinders in specie, the nature of the document used is disclosed as a part of the foundation for admissibility.

The proponent of the testimony thus gets the advantage of any special authority associated with the source of the recorded information. If the source of the information is important to its acceptance by the factfinders and the court strictly enforces the rule of nondisclosure of media used to refresh recollection, use of past recollection recorded might give more impact to the presentation than using the document to refresh recollection during testimony.

K. Redirect Examination

Redirect examination offers the lawyer the opportunity to adduce new or additional direct testimony on points addressed by the opponent on cross. Mere repetition of direct testimony that has not been the subject of inquiry on cross is not generally considered to be a proper purpose of redirect examination. Nor is it generally permissible to use redirect to introduce a totally new subject matter not touched on during the preceding cross.

Within the constraints of its proper purpose, however, redirect can be a powerful tool to clear up problems caused by the cross-examination. It can also be used to build on and further develop points that the cross has attempted to undermine.

Because the purpose of redirect is limited, the organization of the redirect is much more flexible. There is usually no need to proceed chronologically. As on cross, the redirect examiner can skip around a little for emphasis or to follow the pattern of the preceding examination.

Because the redirect usually touches on only a few points and the structure of a continuous narrative is absent, counsel is usually given some leeway to ask leading questions in focusing and transitions.

> Q. Officer, do you remember on cross-examination when you were asked about not seeing anything when you drove by the tree?
>
> A. Yes, I do.
>
> Q. Why was it, Officer, that you did not see anything when you went by the tree?

> A. Because I didn't look under the tree. I was looking at the car.

The focusing question orients the witness to the subject matter under inquiry without giving the specific answer sought. Otherwise, conduct of redirect follows the same rules as direct. The witness should be given the exposure, even if it is focused on only a few issues. The leeway to use focusing questions should not become a pattern of relying on either soft or hard leading questions on redirect.

Chapter 8 Cross-Examination

A. Purpose and Importance of Cross-Examination

Cross-examination offers the trial lawyer the opportunity to obtain and use information from the opposing party's witnesses either to contribute something helpful to the lawyer's own presentation or to detract from the opponent's. The purpose of cross-examination is to extract from an adverse witness relevant facts that add some element to the image being recreated by the cross-examiner or that compromise or blur some aspect of the opponent's image.

One of the primary purposes of cross-examination is to discredit the testimony of the opposing party or witness. The purpose is not to "have a go at the witness," however. Cross-examination is not used to repeat the witness's unfavorable testimony in skeptical tones or to point out and allow the witness to explain apparent inconsistencies. Nor is it used to pre-argue the relative merits of the two competing pictures with the witness who is on the stand.

In the popular image, the lawyer "takes on" the chief witness of the opposing side and reduces that witness to tatters with a dramatic, often sarcastic and incredulous, cross-examination. A cross-examination where the witness wilts, or at least recants, on the stand is the rare exception rather than the rule. Those who strive for such cross-examinations are often disappointed and frequently humiliated in the process. The witness may be given the opportunity to repeat the adverse testimony and be able to explain away apparent inconsistencies in the process. And sarcasm and incredulity in the cross-examiner's voice often serve only to alienate the factfinders. Such behavior rarely undermines either the credibility or the determination of the witness.

Much more often, an effective cross-examination will succeed in establishing some fact inconsistency in the opponent's presentation that might ultimately cast doubt on some key assertion. Or it may merely supply a fact within the opponent's control that is helpful to the understanding and acceptance of the cross-examiner's overall image. In many cases, the success of a line of cross-examination does not become evident until the summation, long after the witness has left the stand.

Technically, cross-examination includes any examination of a witness by any lawyer other than the lawyer who called the witness in the first place. In many cases, however, what is technically cross-examination is performed very much like direct examination. Sometimes the witness is not adverse. — Or the point may not be contested. — Or the witness being "cross-examined" may be the cross-examiner's own party or witness who has been called as a witness by the opposing party.

Frequently a lawyer is called on to cross-examine an entirely neutral witness who has been called by the other party because that party has the burden of proof of the fact known by that witness. In each of these cases, the kind and degree of control required to develop cross-examination testimony will be more like that exercised on direct than the stringent control usually required to cross-examine a truly adverse witness.

There are also cases where it is necessary for the lawyer to call the opposing party or persons associated with the opposing party as witnesses. These witnesses are unlikely to be sympathetic or helpful to the lawyer who is examining them. Adequate control of such hostile witnesses on what is technically direct examination requires an approach more akin to that used in cross-examination. The Federal Rules of Evidence expressly permit the use of leading questions.

> [w]hen a party calls a hostile witness, an adverse party, or a witness identified with an adverse party. . . . [1]

Ultimately the control needed to develop a presentation will vary from witness to witness and from subject to subject. Supportive and presentational direct examination of the lawyer's own client

---

[1] Fed. R. Evid. 611.

or a friendly witness is at one extreme; confrontational and highly controlling cross-examination of a hostile witness or opposing party is at the other. Within the wide range of possibilities in between, it is the task of the lawyer to exercise that degree of control as will ensure that an image develops in accord with the lawyer's version of the case.

B.   Planning the Cross-Examination

The first issue in cross-examination is always whether the lawyer should cross-examine at all. Before embarking on any cross-examination, the lawyer must be able to identify particular bits of information that the witness can be required to concede in the cross-examiner's favor or in derogation of the witness's side of the case. Otherwise, there is no purpose to cross-examining that witness. Unless the witness has information that contributes to the lawyer's picture or detracts from the opponent's, there is no point in taking the time for the examination and undergoing the risk of further exposure of the opposition's resources.

The lawyer must also find some way to compel the witness to provide the desired information. The circumstance, argument, or thing that gives the cross-examiner some assurance that the adverse witness will provide a particular bit of information, or at least agree with the lawyer's assertion, is referred to in this book as a "control device." If the lawyer seeks to cross-examine without such devices, the quest for additional information is little more than a gamble.

Without specific points to be made and control devices with which to make them, cross-examination is likely to do greater harm than good to the cross-examiner. If the lawyer is not aware of any helpful facts that can be extracted from the witness, the best cross-examination is "no questions." Even if the witness has potentially helpful facts, if the lawyer has no means of ensuring that the witness will give the cross-examination testimony desired, usually the gamble that he may do so unbidden is not worth taking. Again, the best response is "no questions." The likely result of attempting to cross-examine under either of these circumstances is that the witness will use the additional exposure to reinforce the testimony given on direct.

There is often the temptation to cross-examine solely to demonstrate to the factfinders the lawyer's own skepticism over the witness's direct testimony by repeating the challenged portions of that testimony in a skeptical tone of voice. Sometimes the cross-examiner will juxtapose the disbelieved testimony with other inconsistent evidence in an effort to demonstrate on the spot the witness's lack of credibility. This kind of cross-examination is essentially an argument: the cross-examiner is not seeking additional facts; she is putting an argumentative spin on the facts already provided.

Argumentative cross-examination is both improper and dangerous. It is improper because argument is supposed to take place at the end of the presentation, after all of the facts have been disclosed, not while a witness is on the stand. It is dangerous because of the risk that the witness will perceive the argument and meet it or disarm it in his testimony.

Sometimes the lawyer might be tempted to cross-examine to pin down or emphasize favorable testimony given by the opponent's witness on direct, or there might be some ambiguity in the testimony given on direct. If the cross-examiner has a basis for believing that the ambiguity can be clarified in a manner helpful to the cross-examiner it may be worthwhile to attempt to pin the witness down. However, if the favorable testimony is already clear from the direct, having the witness repeat it on cross just for emphasis may not be worth the risk that the witness may appreciate the significance of testimony that is favorable to the opponent and try to change it.

Cross-examination is not an efficient way to get information before the jury. It often takes a large number of controlling questions to develop a few comparatively simple facts from a hostile witness. There is always the risk that the witness will resist or escape the examiner's control and begin to explain or rebut the inferences the lawyer constructs in the cross-examination. Most witnesses have a lot more to say for their own side than for the other side. For these reasons the number of points chosen for attack should be few and should be as simple and unambiguous as possible. There is no reason to keep the adverse witness on the stand any longer than is necessary to make those points. "Get in and get out" is the rule for successful cross-examination.

C.   Maintaining Control on Cross-Examination

One can think of direct examination as the lawyer gently guiding the hand of the witness as he draws a picture with as much accuracy and color as possible. Similarly, one can think of cross-examination as the lawyer firmly requiring the adverse witness who has already drawn his picture for the opposing lawyer to acknowledge and agree to details added by the lawyer to enhance her own picture or to compromise the picture being drawn by the lawyer's opponent.

Control on cross-examination is exercised by the form of the questions, by the tone and manner in which the examination is conducted, and by the possession and use of identified control devices. Hand in hand with the identification of points to be made goes the identification of the control devices that will enable the cross-examiner to make those points.

1.   Control Devices

A control device is a fact or circumstance that enables the lawyer to have a reasonable expectation that the witness can be required to give the desired testimony in response to suitable controlling questions. Examples of control devices include a prior statement of the witness, appropriate testimony by another disinterested witness, physical facts or common experience that support the desired testimony, or logical inferences from established facts.

Assume, for instance, the cross-examiner knows that a witness has testified the following at a prior hearing:

Q.   What did the man with the glasses do then?

A.   Well, I couldn't see him. He kind of fell out of sight in the darkness under the tree. It was dark there.

Q.   What is the next thing you saw?

A.   Well, just about then I caught a flash out of the corner of my eye and turned my head back toward 33-½ Jackson Street.

Q. What was the flash?

A. It was the headlights of a car coming out of the driveway of 33-½ Jackson Street.

The cross-examiner knows that the witness is likely to testify in the same manner at a later hearing. The transcript of the earlier hearing can serve as the control device for cross-examination questions such as

Q. And then the man in the glasses disappeared from your sight, didn't he?

A. Well, I don't know about "disappeared."

Q. He fell out of your sight into the darkness under the tree, didn't he?

A. Yes, he did.

Q. It was dark there, under the tree, wasn't it?

A. Yes, it was.

Q. And he fell out of your sight into the darkness under the tree before you saw the flash of headlights coming out of 33-½, didn't he?

A. Yes, I suppose he did.

If the witness does not testify in accordance with the prior testimony, that testimony can be shown to the witness to "refresh the witness's recollection," and, if necessary, can be disclosed to the factfinders. Unless there is some good reason for the discrepancy, the factfinders are likely to accept the witness's prior testimony as authoritative or discredit the witness's presentation altogether. The prior testimony thus becomes a control device. It enables the lawyer to predict with confidence the witness's present testimony and control it if it does not materialize as expected.

A control device cannot be pushed too far. A prior statement that a person "fell out of sight" might not be enough to force acceptance of the word "disappeared" by a tough opposing witness. Anything beyond the earlier specific words and the logical consequences of uncontrovertible facts is an escalation that can involve some risk.

Control devices usually involve the use of common experience, either as the control device itself or to link the control device with the witness's testimony. Common experience tells us that people are at least a little upset if someone calls them names. That common experience provides the control device for a question such as:

> Q.   When they called you a "chunk," Mr. Maxfield, that upset you, didn't it?
>
> A.   Well, I suppose a little.

Common experience also tells us that a person who relates varying versions of a single event might not be a reliable source of information. It is this common experience that the lawyer can call upon to use a witness's prior statement as a control device. Thus the witness who has testified to a certain fact on one occasion will be reluctant to change his testimony and thereby lose his credibility. With prior statement in hand, the lawyer can examine the witness with some confidence that he will admit the facts found in the prior statement.

The use of control devices on cross-examination is discussed in greater detail below.

2.   Facts and Conclusions

In preparing for a cross-examination, it is important to concentrate on specific and distinct facts as opposed to subjective conclusions, characterization, or anything resembling an argument. Simple, unambiguous, and objective information leaves little room for differing opinions. It is hard for the witness to quibble with clear concrete facts. With subjective conclusions the witness has more room to escape the lawyer's control.

Thus, using appropriate control devices, it is usually easier to compel a witness to acknowledge distinct facts about an observed event than to provide conclusions or characterizations.

> Q.   Mr. Savage called you "pug," didn't he?

A. Yes.

Q. He shook his fist in your girlfriend's face, didn't he?

A. Yes.

Q. And he swung his fist at you, didn't he?

A. Yes.

Q. He knocked your glasses off, didn't he?

A. Yes.

Q. Mr. Savage really harassed you and made you upset, didn't he?

A. Well, I don't know about that.

The specific questions about what Mr. Savage did called for facts that the witness can be held to with suitable control devices. The witness being "harassed" and "upset" are much more subjective characterizations. Unless a witness has used the same language in a prior statement or unless the facts admit of no other response, a lawyer will find that it is much harder to force someone to agree with an unfavorable characterization than to obtain concessions on specific and unambiguous facts.

3. Other Factors Affecting Control

The degree of control that must be incorporated into the questions used on cross-examination depends on 1) how adversarial the witness is and how much strength he has to resist control, 2) the nature of the material to be elicited, and 3) the effectiveness of the available control devices. Some witnesses are easily intimidated by the questioning process itself and are willing to agree with even relatively weak questions on cross-examination. Others will fight any attempt to get them to acknowledge any facts other than their own versions of the case. With such witnesses the cross-examiner can maintain control by asking only the tightest, simplest, and most specific leading questions, supported by strong and clear control devices.

More specific facts require less force and firmness than those that are indefinite or subjective. Thus a question such as

> Q. There was ice in the puddles on the street, wasn't there?
>
> A. Yes, there was.

is more likely to get an affirmative answer than

> Q. It was very cold out, wasn't it?
>
> A. Well, I don't know what you mean by "very cold."

Facts that are imperfectly supported by control devices are harder to develop on cross-examination than those that the witness has to admit because of a device such as his own prior statement. For instance, the testimony of a disinterested third-party witness, commonly used as a control device, is usually not as reliable or effective as the witness's own prior statement:

> Q. Mr. Borak is a friend of yours, isn't he, Officer Anderson?
>
> A. Well, I wouldn't really call him a friend. He is an acquaintance.
>
> Q. Well, didn't you call him "Al" when you spoke to him at the scene of the crash?
>
> A. I don't remember that.
>
> Q. Well, if Mrs. Godard has testified in this case that you went up and called Mr. Borak "Al," you wouldn't say she is wrong.
>
> A. I wouldn't say she was right or wrong.

D. Leading Questions

Traditionally, questions used by trial lawyers to elicit testimony have been grouped into two large categories, "open" or "nonleading" questions on the one hand and "leading" questions on the other. Open or nonleading questions are used to develop the testimony of friendly witnesses on direct examination. On cross-examination, however, the examiner must use leading questions. By using leading questions, the lawyer exercises more stringent control over the witness's responses and can extract key facts from adverse witnesses, who might otherwise be loathe to supply them.

1. Why Leading Questions?

The primary means of maintaining close control during cross-examination is to use strong, controlling, or "leading" questions. Leading questions *ask* the witness nothing. Rather, they incorporate all of the information sought into the questions themselves—the information is presented in such a form that the witness has no choice but to admit or deny it. The question usually is designed to require the witness to give an affirmative response agreeing with the information set forth in the question.

The whole framework of control of witnesses by this method of questioning rests on habits and assumptions of ordinary social intercourse. A lawyer can expect that a friendly witness will attempt to understand and answer questions placed to him as accurately and helpfully as possible. An adverse witness on the other hand has no such motivation. How is it, then, that a lawyer can expect an adverse witness to submit to the control built into the form of cross-examination questions and answer the question placed?

The lawyer's ability to control a witness by questions is supported by two disciplines. The first is obvious: according to the rules of courtroom procedure, the witness is supposed to answer the question put, not some other question he would prefer to answer. If the witness refuses to answer or gives an answer that unfairly goes beyond the scope of the interrogative, the questioner can move that the nonresponsive answer be stricken or that the witness be disciplined. The court rules as enforced by the judge are the final resort in the case of the witness's utter contumacy. Trial lawyers do not and should not rely on the judge as the primary enforcer to require the witness to answer yes or no to every cross-examination question.

The second discipline to which the witness is subject is psychological. A number of considerations beyond the formal rules of procedure maintain witness responsiveness to proper questions. It is easy for factfinders to appreciate when a witness is not responding to the question asked or is going beyond what would fairly be called for in giving the response. Factfinders tend to react negatively to someone who is apparently trying to circumvent the questioning process or who tries to add self-serving material to his answer. If a question is clear, unambiguous, and limited in scope, a witness who tries to evade or goes beyond the question's fair scope is running the risk of being seen as manipulative and tricky by the factfinders.

All questions are controlling to some extent in that they delineate the subject matter and request a response. As has been indicated, on direct examination the lawyer has a whole range of proper "open" questions that provide direction to the witness as to the desired response. While none of these formulations are objectionable as "leading," they vary in the amount of control exerted by the lawyer. The same is true of the leading questions used on cross-examination. Different formulations contain varying amounts of control and involve different degrees of risk.

What is the risk on cross-examination? The risk is if the adverse party or witness is not properly controlled, the cross-examination will be merely another opportunity for the witness to reiterate or reinforce his own picture of the event rather than contributing to that of the examining lawyer. Any question that permits the witness to provide the content of the answer involves the risk that the answer will leave the cross-examiner worse off than she was before asking the question. The leading question minimizes the risk by putting the question to the witness in such a way that the witness's only options are to affirm or deny the information in the question. If the witness affirms, as expected, the question has succeeded. If the witness denies, the harm is minimized. All that has happened is that the witness has not admitted something he was asked to admit. He has not been given the opportunity to add contradictory and damaging information.

By definition, the leading question contains within itself all the factual material sought from the responder. The answer is merely an affirmance or denial of this.

2. "Soft" and "Hard" Leading Questions

The two major subcategories of leading questions vary greatly in the amount of control exercised over the witness. These may be identified for convenience as "soft" or open questions on the one hand and "hard" or closed questions on the other.

The soft or open leading question is in fact a question:

Q. Did you see another man along with the defendant?

Q. Was it cold on the night in question?

Q. Were you speeding down Jackson Street?

Such questions are actual interrogatives. They ask the witness for information. The rigor of the control provided is less than that found in the closed or hard leading questions. It is easy for the witness to answer the soft leading question with "yes, but . . ." or "No, not quite . . ." and then to give an explanation that favors the witness's version of the matter in question.

Usually such questions are asked with a rising tone at the end to signify the question mark. Such a tone of voice discloses the examiner's uncertainty. It may also signal the witness that the examiner is not sure of the answer. The witness may feel that he thus has room to elaborate on or vary from the suggested response.

The open leading question is a weak form of cross-examination. It can be used successfully where the witness is relatively compliant or where the information sought is unambiguous. It can be used where the witness is subject to very strong control devices such as prior statements, inconsistency with physical fact, and the like. In many situations, however, the open leading question is not controlling enough for effective cross-examination of stronger or more adverse witnesses.

The stronger form of leading question is the "closed" or "hard" question, which is actually a declaration of fact by the lawyer, coupled with a demand for affirmance by the witness.

Q. You were home on the night of August 16th, were you not?

Q. You had three drinks before you left the restaurant, didn't you?

> Q. Isn't it true that you were angry when you got into your
>   car that night?

Each one of these questions is actually a statement, ending in a down beat. There is no uncertainty in the examiner's tone of voice. She is seeking confirmation for what she already knows. True closed leading questions leave no room for the witness to do anything but affirm or deny.

A key function of the closed leading question is the demand for affirmance. It should be clear from the question what a "yes" answer means. Usually clarity is aided by starting with the declarative statement and placing the demand for affirmance at the end of the question. For instance, it is clear that a "yes" answer to

> Q. You were home on the night of August 16, were you not?

would mean that the witness was in fact home on that night. On the other hand, if the demand for affirmance is at the beginning of the question, there is the possibility of ambiguity. If the question is phrased

> Q. Isn't it true that you were angry when you got into your
>   car that night?

an affirmative response might be taken to mean that the asserted fact is not in fact true.

Sometimes the demand for affirmance may become dullingly repetitive.

> Q. You went into the house, right?
>
> A. Yes.
>
> Q. You picked up the phone, right?
>
> A. Yes.
>
> Q. You dialed the police, right?
>
> A. Yes.
>
> Q. You told the police about the two men, right?

The power of the repetitive pattern may overwhelm the content of the examination and become a significant distraction to the factfinders.

Sometimes an express demand for affirmance may be omitted entirely. The cross-examiner depends on tone, relationship, pace, and momentum to elicit the affirmative responses.

Q. You went into the house?

A. Yes.

Q. You picked up the phone?

A. Yes.

Q. You dialed the police?

A. Yes.

Q. You told them about the two men?

A. Yes.

The questions are simple statements delivered in a firm confident tone that anticipates that the witness will agree. Each question contains a single indisputable fact. The momentum carries the questioning along. This kind of "soliloquy" or narrative cross makes an elegant presentation. It is truly an aria — sung by the lawyer.

3. Simplicity of Subject Matter of Cross-Examination Questions

A lawyer maintains control on cross-examination not only by the form of the question but by the breadth of the subject matter and the unambiguousness of the terminology. The simpler and more concrete the fact to be established, the more likely it is that a clear concession can be obtained in the response. Complicated facts, multiple facts, the interrelationship of facts, and characterizations are all harder to establish on cross-examination than simple clear facts put one at a time.

Regardless of the hard leading form of the question, it might be difficult to get a clean acknowledgment to the following on cross-examination:

> Q. You were hurrying because it was cold and it was almost eleven o'clock, weren't you?

It is easy for the witness to quarrel with a package of facts presented in some kind of interrelationship. The witness could answer "no" or quibble with the question if he disagreed with any one of the facts presented or even if he disagreed with the way the facts were related to each other in the question. Possible responses could be

> A. No, I was hurrying because I was late.

or

> A. It wasn't that cold.

or simply

> A. No, not really.

Moreover, such a response would not be held against the witness. The factfinders would also appreciate the difficulty of making a clean response to a convoluted compound question.

On the other hand, if the lawyer broke down the subject matter, the same facts could be elicited more safely and efficiently one by one.

> Q. It was cold that night, wasn't it?
>
> A. Yes.
>
> Q. You were hurrying, weren't you?
>
> A. Yes.
>
> Q. It was quarter to eleven at night, wasn't it?
>
> A. Yes, it was.

When presented individually, the witness can scarcely deny the concrete facts of the temperature, what he was doing, and the time. The lawyer can argue the interrelationship of those facts in the summation. Or, once the basic facts have been established with the witness, the lawyer can cautiously escalate her relationing those facts together.

Q. You were hurrying because it was cold, right?

A. Yes, that's right.

Q. And because it was nearly 11 o'clock at night.

A. Yes, a quarter of eleven.

When a lawyer has difficulty in getting clean affirmative responses on cross-examination, the first reaction should be to review the questions to see if they are too long or too complicated. Often a mere simplification of the questions will be all that is required to reestablish and maintain positive control of the cross-examination presentation.

E.   Effective Use of the Control Device

There is a saying among trial lawyers that one should never ask a question on cross-examination unless one already knows the answer. What this saying means is that on cross-examination the lawyer should ask questions containing only those facts that she expects the witness to acknowledge for some good reason that the lawyer can identify. The basis for the lawyer's expectation is the control device for the question.

A "control device" is a fact, circumstance, bit of evidence, or common experience that can be used by the lawyer to prompt the witness into agreeing to a particular fact or that can be used to discipline the witness if the witness refuses to do so. Being able to identify the effective control devices gives substance to the lawyer's expectations of the witness's responses.

Control devices come in many forms. A common one is a prior statement of the same witness. If the witness has stated certain facts before, it is likely that he will acknowledge those facts again.

If he refuses to do so, the lawyer can produce the previous statement and argue that the witness's varying testimony is not worthy of belief.

If the witness previously stated "the automobile backed out of the driveway," if asked on cross-examination in court,

Q. The automobile backed out of the driveway, didn't it?

he probably will agree. If he does not, the lawyer can remind him of his prior statement. If he still refuses to acknowledge the fact sought, the prior statement can be introduced in evidence as prior inconsistent testimony to impeach the witness's testimony. The witness's fear of impeachment tends to make the witness stick to the prior testimony despite his wishes or interest to the contrary.

Other control devices are undisputed physical facts and the testimony of other witnesses. For instance, the fact that Jackson Street has only one small street light at each end can serve as a control device for the following line of cross-examination:

Q. There are only two street lights on Jackson Street, aren't there?

A. Yes.

Q. Those lights are at the ends of the street, aren't they?

A. Yes, they are.

Q. On the night of October 10, those street lights did not give much light on the middle of the block, did they?

A. I guess that's right.

If the witness disagrees with any of the cross-examiner's questions, the cross-examiner can call the factfinder's attention to the undisputed facts concerning the location and size of the street lights. Common experience does the rest.

If one disinterested and credible witness remembers a particular fact in a particular way, a lawyer can ask another witness in a similar position to agree to that fact and have some assurance that the witness will agree. The lawyer knows that even if she does not, she will still have the testimony of the disinterested witness, which can be used to impeach the unexpected refusal to agree on cross-examination.

As explained above, common experience both serves as a control device for many questions and links control devices with the testimony sought. Control on cross-examination can be simply a matter of common sense.

The control device ordinarily is used to control the witness without giving the witness the opportunity to explain why the testimony diverges from the expected. The lawyer may be able to present the information at the time of the witness's unanticipated answer. Or the controlling or impeaching information may be presented at another point in the trial and linked up by the lawyer in her summation.

1. Use of Control Devices to Frame Cross-Examination Questions

Every cross-examination question should be supported by a suitable control device. As the lawyer plans the cross-examination questions, she should also know how to control or discipline the witness if the expected answer is not given.

In a case where a witness's testimony at trial departs from a pretrial statement or deposition, the cross-examiner can use the prior statement to frame questions to reassert control over the witness's testimony. The cross-examination could go something like:

> Q. Isn't it true, Sir, that you then threw a beer bottle at the house?
>
> A. (unexpectedly). No.

The cross-examiner's control device for the above question is a statement made by the witness to the police shortly after the incident. It comes into play in the next question:

> Q. Well, isn't it true that when you spoke to the police officer you told him "when the children called us names we threw a beer bottle at the house."
>
> A. I guess I did.

Q. The interview you gave for the police officer was right after the incident, wasn't it?

A. Yes, it was.

Q. And certainly your memory then was fresher than it is right now.

A. Yes, it was.

The lawyer does not ask the witness why it is that his testimony has diverged from the prior statement. Nor do the lawyer's questions give the witness an easy opportunity to make any explanation. Obviously, the proponent of the witness can later attempt to clear up the apparent discrepancy on redirect.

Usually the simplest way to invoke the control device is the best. Confronted by an unexpected denial, the lawyer can first invoke the device through a simple question:

Q. Well, isn't it true that when you spoke to the police officer you told him, "when the children called us names we threw a beer bottle at the house."?

In many cases the reminder in the leading question will be sufficient to "get the witness back on the leash." He will acknowledge the fact, and the examination can proceed.

A. I suppose I did say that.

If the facts contained in the prior statement are of any consequence, the cross-examiner will want to incorporate that statement in the present testimony.

Q. So you did in fact throw a beer bottle at the house?

A. Yeah, I guess we might have.

Q. Not "might have," Sir; you *did* throw a beer bottle at that house, didn't you?

A. Yeah, I think Roscoe did do that.

If for some reason the witness does not acknowledge the existence of the prior statement, it may be necessary to address it more concretely. Depending on how he seeks to avoid it, the statement can be used to refresh the witness's recollection or it can be offered in evidence as a prior inconsistent statement.

2. Use of Prior Statement to Refresh Recollection on Cross-Examination

Often balky witnesses will "not remember" making prior statements when asked about prior statements on cross-examination or may simply be nervous or genuinely confused. Whenever the witness indicates some uncertainty or lack of memory in response to a question, his memory may be refreshed, whether he likes it or not. From the prior example:

> Q. Well, isn't it true that when you spoke to the police officer you told him, "when the children called us names we threw a beer bottle at the house."?
>
> A. I don't remember that.

Since the witness has indicated a lack of memory, the cross-examiner can show the prior statement to the witness and say

> Q. I show you this document to refresh your recollection. Doesn't this refresh your recollection that in fact you did throw a beer bottle at the house?
>
> A. Yes, I guess so.

In front of the witness is his statement with the actual controlling language. It is not necessary that the document be in evidentiary form or even that it ultimately be admissible in evidence. The idea is to use the prior statement to prod the witness into admitting on the stand what he has already admitted.

If the witness's recollection is refreshed by this method and the witness then agrees with the lawyer's earlier question, the control device will have fulfilled its purpose. The testimony of the witness with memory refreshed, even if his response is only a grunted "yes," becomes the witness's present testimony and can be used for all purposes. Sometimes the lawyer will want to make this clear by underlining the refreshed recollection:

> Q. So in fact you and your buddy did throw a beer bottle at the house?
>
> A. Yeah, I guess we did.

On cross-examination it is not necessary or in many cases even desirable for the lawyer to identify the object used to refresh the witness's unwilling recollection. If the object used on cross is the witness's prior statement or report, it is likely that most of the material in it will be favorable to the opposing side. Ordinarily the cross-examining lawyer will want to minimize unnecessary exposure of the prior statement and its contents. Thus the lawyer will make it a point not to identify in her question what is being shown to the witness. If the cross-examining lawyer does give evidentiary significance to a statement used to refresh recollection, there is a chance that she might thereby open the door to allow the entire statement to be admitted in evidence, even if it were otherwise not admissible.

> A. Here, let me show you your statement. Doesn't it say right here, "We threw a beer bottle at the house"?
>
> A. Yes, it does.
>
> *Opposing Counsel.*   At this point, Your Honor, we move for the admission of the entire statement as Exhibit 12. Counsel for the defendant has opened the door.
>
> *The Court.*   Agreed; the statement is admitted.

If this happens, the jury has in front of it not only the favorable material used to refresh recollection but the rest of the statement, which is likely to be unfavorable to the cross-examiner and his client.

Use of a control device to refresh a witness's recollection on cross may be subject to abuse if the cross-examiner unfairly implies that the statement or other paper supports the assertions with which the witness is expected to agree.

> Q. Let me show you this document. Doesn't this refresh your recollection that you told the police that you threw beer bottles at the children in the Farris house?

> *Opposing Counsel.*   Your Honor, may we see what Counsel is showing the witness in an effort to refresh recollection?

> *The Court.*   Please show her the document.

> *Opposing Counsel* (after looking at the document).   Your Honor, may we approach?

> The Court.   Counsel will approach the bench.

> *Opposing Counsel* (at the bench).   Your Honor, we object to this question. The implication is that somehow this witness has told the police that he threw "beer bottles" at the "children" in the Farris house. All this statement says, and I quote, is "We threw a beer bottle at the house."

> Q. Your Honor, we are just using the statement to refresh recollection.

> The Court.   Counsel, do you have any other good-faith basis for that question?

> Q.   Well, the children were in the house . . .

> The Court.   Objection sustained. Counsel, you be careful how you use documents to refresh recollection in this court.

The Federal Rules of Evidence entitle the opposing counsel to see anything that is being used to refresh a witness's recollection while testifying. [2] Unless counsel is aware of what the statement is, she should ask to see the statement when it is first referred to on cross in order to curb the possibility of this kind of abuse.

---

[2] Fed. R. Evid. 612.

3. Offering the Control Device in Evidence

If the control device is a prior statement by the witness and if the witness denies unequivocally making the statement or refuses to acknowledge it when shown it is to him in an effort to refresh his recollection, the cross-examiner can use the prior statement directly by offering it in evidence. In some jurisdictions, a party is not permitted to offer exhibits in evidence during cross-examination. In these jurisdictions, the cross-examining lawyer should lay the foundation for offering the statement while the witness is still on the stand. At the next permissible opportunity, the lawyer can then offer the statement in evidence as an admission if the witness is a party or, in any event, as a prior inconsistent statement of the witness. In jurisdictions that permit the offering of exhibits on cross-examination, the control device can be authenticated and offered immediately.

A.   I show you a document marked as Exhibit 12 for identification. Is this not a copy of your statement to the police as signed by you on October 12?

A.   I guess so.

Q.   And you can say that because that is your signature at the end of the statement?

A.   Yes, it is.

Q.   We offer Exhibit 12 for identification.

The Court.   Admitted.

Q.   Now, Mr. Ralston, would you please read to the jury starting with the line marked number 23 of page 12 of Exhibit number 12?

A.   (reading). "When the children called us names, we threw a beer bottle at the house."

Q.   That was your statement to the police the day after the accident, wasn't it?

A.   I guess it was.

Usually offering the prior inconsistent statement in evidence is used as the last resort after other efforts to elicit the statement by leading questions and refreshing recollection have failed. If the prior statement is in evidence, even if for the limited purpose of impeaching the witness's in-court testimony, the jury will be able to read not only the impeaching portions, but also the rest of the statement, which is likely to be favorable to the opposing side and damaging to the position of the cross-examiner.

4.   Using Prior Statements for Impeachment and as Substantive Evidence

A prior statement by a party witness is an admission and is substantive evidence of the facts contained in the statement. Under Federal Rule of Evidence 801(d)(1), the same is true of a prior inconsistent statement given under oath in certain prior judicial proceedings. As substantive evidence, such prior statements can support arguments and inferences about the actual fact issues on trial. Thus, in the above examples, if the prior statement of the witness Ralston had been given under oath at a prior hearing or at a deposition, it would serve as proof of the fact that he and Savage had thrown a beer bottle at the house, regardless of whether Ralston could be brought to admit at the trial throwing the beer bottle.

On the other hand, prior inconsistent statements by witnesses that do not comply with Federal Rule of Evidence 801 are admitted not for the truth of the facts contained in the statements but for the fact that they were made as bearing on the credibility of the witness. The inference is that a person who testifies to two different versions of the same incident is not to be believed. Counsel would be permitted to use the statement as evidence that the jury should not believe Ralston's testimony (including his denial) but not as evidence that he did in fact throw the beer bottle.

Mere impeachment of witnesses by use of prior inconsistent statements is an important function of cross-examination and is discussed in greater detail below. However, if the facts in the prior inconsistent statement are important and the prior statement is not admissible as substantive evidence under Rule 801, it is important to attempt to get the witness's present testimony to conform to the statement. After the statement has been admitted and the witness has been confronted with it, the lawyer will seek to make that statement the witness's present testimony.

Q.   So it is true, then, is it not, that you and Roscoe did throw a beer bottle at the house?

A.   Yes, we did.

Once again, when offering the prior statement either as substantive evidence or to impeach, the cross-examining lawyer ordinarily should not give the witness room to explain the discrepancy or why he would not acknowledge the statement earlier in the cross-examination. Nor should the lawyer allow the witness opportunity to add any qualifications that he might wish to include. Both by tight leading questions and by firm tone and demeanor, the cross-examiner makes the witness pay the penalty for straying from the path laid out by the lawyer.

Of course, the lawyer who called the witness on direct might well seek to explain the discrepancy on redirect:

Q.   Can you tell the jury why during cross-examination you were unwilling to agree that you threw a beer bottle at the house, even though you said that in the police report that is Exhibit 12?

A.   Because I didn't actually throw any beer bottle. I think Roscoe did.

F.   Choosing Between Control and Impeachment

Where a witness's testimony as given on either direct or cross-examination is at variance with a control device available to the cross-examiner, the cross-examiner must decide whether the control device should be used to modify the witness's testimony or to impeach the witness as unreliable.

If the truth of any witness's testimony is important to a party's picture before the factfinders, it does not make sense to try to undermine the believability of that witness. With some witnesses and some facts the cross-examiner will use the available control devices to make sure that the witness remembers and relays accurately the favorable facts the cross-examiner is hoping to extract. With other witnesses and other facts, when there is an inconsistency between the testimony given and an available control device, the cross-examiner's primary use of the control device is to establish the inconsistency and thus to reduce the factfinders' belief in certain or all of the assertions of the witness. In some cases the cross-examiner may achieve both goals.

In deciding whether to stress control or impeachment on cross-examination, both the importance of the favorable facts about which the witness can testify and the role of the witness should be considered. If the favorable facts are important and the witness does not have otherwise seriously adverse testimony, the emphasis should be on establishing the important facts rather than destroying the credibility of the source of those facts. If the favorable facts available from use of the control device to bring the witness's testimony back in line are unimportant and the witness's testimony is seriously adverse in other matters, the cross-examiner might prefer to emphasize the inconsistency of the testimony as casting doubt on the witness's other assertions.

Even if the favorable facts are important, if the witness is strongly identified with the other side, it is possible to validate those facts and attack the credibility of the witness on other matters as well. This is so because the factfinder perceptions

(1) that a seriously adverse witness would not admit facts favorable to the cross-examiner unless they were true; and

(2) that a witness who testified inconsistently on one matter might also have done so on others

are not necessarily inconsistent. Factfinders can fully credit a concession dragged from a reluctant adverse witness while at the same time questioning the overall credibility of the witness.

Suppose the witness had been asked on direct examination

Q. Did you throw anything at the house?

A. No.

The cross-examiner has a police report that includes a statement by the witness that "we threw a beer bottle at the house." The lawyer can use the prior statement to try to get this testimony modified, or she can use the statement to impeach the witness as unreliable. If the fact that the witness and his companion threw a beer bottle at the house is an important element of the cross-examiner's own picture, it may be more important to get the witness to acknowledge that fact than it is to merely undermine the credibility of the witness. On the other hand, if the issue of the beer bottle is of less direct significance, the cross-examiner might use the discrepancy primarily to impeach the witness's overall reliability on other disputed matters.

If the cross-examiner is seeking to control or modify the witness's direct testimony, she would simply ask,

> Q.   Isn't it true that when the children called you names, you and your companion threw a beer bottle at the house?

The question would follow as closely as possible the language of the prior statement. It would leave the least possible room for quibbling or ambiguity. If the witness reconsiders his prior testimony and says,

> A.   Yes, we did.

then the task is accomplished.

If the point is important, the cross-examiner might hammer the new fact home by repeating the question or asking

> Q.   We should disregard anything to the contrary you might have said in your direct examination, isn't that right?

If the witness resists the initial effort to obtain the concession on cross-examination, the control device can be used in the same manner as if the discrepancy had first emerged on cross-examination. The whole thrust of the examination is to use the control device to bring the present testimony in line with the testimony expected from the control device.

The use of a control device such as a witness's prior statement to establish a discrepancy with the witness's direct testimony primarily for impeachment proceeds along a somewhat different route. It is the discrepancy rather than the truth of the statement that becomes the emphasis of the cross-examination. The cross-examiner wishes to heighten and dramatize the discrepancy, not erase it. The technique for accomplishing this is discussed in greater detail below.

G. Impeachment

1. *Purpose and Importance of Witness Impeachment*

Witness impeachment is an important tool by which the lawyer can seek to discredit the image being presented by her opponent and to give the factfinders reasons to prefer her own presentation. In most cases the two parties present competing versions of a single incident or circumstance that occurred in real life. The factfinders must select between these two versions and determine which one more accurately reflects reality. Since there was only the one incident in real life, one or both of the versions being presented must be inaccurate. How do the factfinders determine which is and which is not?

Throughout the trial, the lawyer seeks to accredit the image she is presenting. She hopes to show that the picture she proposes is internally consistent and is also in accord with the factfinders' experience and that the image being generated by her witnesses comes from sources that have been accurately preserved and transmitted. She attempts to make her witnesses real and interesting to the factfinder and to use communications media that are authoritative and credible.

At the same time, she seeks to show that the image being presented by the other side is not accurate or believable. She can argue that elements of the opponent's picture are not internally consistent and do not hang together. She can compare the opposition's version with common experience. And she can point out that the opponent's witnesses and media are not reliable or trustworthy.

If, for instance, the lawyer can show that the testimony of one of the opponent's key witnesses is not accurate or that the witness is not truthful with respect to one or more details of consequence, the factfinders' confidence in that witness's contribution to the opponent's picture will be shaken. The factfinders' confidence in other elements of the opponent's picture might thereby also be undermined. The factfinders will tend to rely on the image presented by the impeaching lawyer rather than that presented by those whose testimony has been impeached. Impeachment of the other party's witnesses and evidentiary media is therefore a key function of the trial process. This does not mean that the lawyer must automatically try to impeach and discredit every witness called by her opponent. The testimony of many witnesses is uncontroverted. There is no point in trying to discredit an opposition witness who does not say anything with which the lawyer disagrees.

There are other witnesses who cannot be impeached because there are no grounds for doing so. Attempts to impeach honest, disinterested witnesses who testify accurately often backfire. The factfinders might tend to identify with the witness whose credibility seems to be unfairly assailed.

Merely because a witness has testified adversely does not mean that he can or should be attacked on the stand. If the lawyer has no means for impeaching the witness, expressing skepticism about the testimony will accomplish nothing. The adverse information will have to be dealt with by contradictory testimony from authoritative witnesses or in argument.

There are many witnesses, however, who are subject to some degree of impeachment. Their testimony may be affected by their own failure to accurately recall and relate. Their testimony may be colored by bias or interest or they may be consciously prevaricating. Witness impeachment consists of effectively bringing out these reasons as to why the opposition's witnesses should not be wholly credited.

While impeachment often starts on the cross-examination of the witness, the witness can be impeached (subject to certain limitations) by contradictory evidence from other witnesses, by prior statements proved by extrinsic evidence, by physical evidence that makes the witness's assertion hard to credit, and by argument from the evidence and from human experience. While the temptation is great to show the witness up as a liar while he is still on the stand, prudence suggests that the chain of inferences proving his unreliability should be pointed out in argument rather than while he is still testifying. This is for the same reason that other argumentative points are saved for summation — the witness will not have the opportunity to perceive and defuse the effect of the potential conclusion.

At the same time, some court rules[3] require that a witness be confronted while testifying so that he has an opportunity to give an explanation if there is one. Even if not required by court rule, sometimes witness impeachment is most effective if it comes right away.

2. Impeachment by Proof of Prior Inconsistent Statement

One of the most common forms of witness impeachment is by proof of a prior inconsistent statement. If a witness testifies at trial in a manner inconsistent with his prior statement on the same subject matter, the lack of consistency can support the inference that the trial testimony is inaccurate.

The dimming of memories gives added authority to the statement closest in time to the event. The prior statement may have been made at a time or under circumstances when the witness may have had less motivation to present a particular version of the event. The inference is that either the witness's present memory is inaccurate or that the witness has deliberately changed his testimony. Setting up either such inference can be a powerful assault on the opponent's presentation.

Cross-examination impeachment by prior inconsistent statement follows a logical pattern. With a little experience, the trial lawyer can become sufficiently familiar with this pattern so that she can move into the impeachment whenever she becomes aware that a witness has testified inconsistently with a known prior statement.

This does not mean that the lawyer should always do so. Sometimes the witness should not be impeached at all. More often it is more important for the lawyer to get the witness to testify authoritatively to the gist of the prior statement than to destroy his overall credibility. In such circumstances the lawyer will use the prior statement to control the witness rather than to support arguments that the witness should not be believed. It should be remembered that the value of a prior witness statement as a control device

---

[3] For example, Fed. R. Evid. 613.

derives in part from the witness's fear of being impeached if she testifies inconsistently with that statement.

Assume that a witness has testified in a manner inconsistent with the witness's prior recorded statement taken immediately after the incident in question. The process of impeaching the witness with that statement has three steps. In the usual sequence these are

(1) committing the witness to the statement to be impeached or "setting the hook,"

(2) accrediting the circumstances of the prior statement, and

(3) proving the prior inconsistent statement.

a. Committing the Witness to the Statement to Be Impeached

The cross-examiner's first task is to get the witness committed to the present testimony that is to be impeached. Trial lawyers refer to this process as "setting the hook." The idea is to put the witness in a position so that the witness's present testimony is definite enough so that the prior statement is clearly inconsistent.

If the in-court testimony is ambiguous or susceptible of different interpretations, an apparent inconsistency with a prior statement may be explained away by the witness. The witness may "wiggle off the hook."

Because the present testimony the lawyer is seeking to impeach is usually unfavorable to the impeaching lawyer, the lawyer does not want to appear to adopt that testimony by asking the witness to agree with her statement as a fact.

Typically, the cross-examiner sets the hook by asking

Q. On direct examination you told us that you did not throw any beer bottle at the house, didn't you?

A. Yes, that's right.

The cross-examiner distances herself from the unfavorable and impeachable testimony by referring to the direct examination testimony as what the witness said, not as substantive fact. The difference is between the indirect or "distancing" formulation:

> Q. On direct examination *you told us* that you didn't throw
>   any bottles at the house, didn't you?

and the direct formulation:

> Q. You didn't throw any bottles at the house, did you?

The latter is preferred where the trial lawyer is attempting to
establish the fact itself. The "you testified" or "you said that"
language is used in the relatively few instances where the matter
to be established is not a fact believed by the cross-examining
lawyer but is what the witness testified to so that testimony can
then be impeached.

When the testimony to be impeached has been given clearly and
unambiguously on direct, it is sometimes not necessary to commit
the witness to that testimony on cross-examination. There is always
some risk that to do so will cue the witness into an explanation or
qualification that will compromise the effect of the impeachment.

> Q. Now, on your direct examination, Officer, you said that
>   the car backed out of the driveway before driving east on
>   Jackson Street, didn't you?
>
> A. Yes. Well, I *think* that it backed out, but it could have
>   gone out forwards.

The potential impeachment by anticipated contradictory evidence that the car drove out of the driveway forward has been
deflated.

If the vulnerable in-court testimony is given on cross-examination, the hook can also be set.

> Q. Now, Mr. Ralston, you and your buddy yelled at those
>   boys in the window and threw a beer bottle at the house,
>   didn't you?
>
> A. No, we didn't.

Because this question is compound and hence potentially ambiguous, it would be wise to commit the witness to an answer that can
be clearly impeached.

Q. So, you are telling us that you and your buddy did not throw a beer bottle at the house?

A. That's right.

Now the witness is committed, and any possible ambiguity is removed.

Sometimes an impeachable answer given during cross-examination is clear enough when given to permit immediate impeachment.

Q. And then you threw a beer bottle at the house, didn't you?

A. No, we didn't.

Here there is no need to set the hook. The witness has done so by answering the question in a manner inconsistent with his prior statement.

b. Accrediting the Circumstances of the Prior Statement

Once the witness is clearly committed to the testimony to be impeached, the lawyer can go to the next step of the impeachment, setting up and accrediting the prior inconsistent statement. The idea is to give the prior statement as much definiteness and circumstantial credibility as possible.

Q. You were interviewed by the police right after the accident, weren't you?

A. Yes.

Q. And you gave the police a statement, didn't you?

A. Yes.

Q. That statement was tape recorded, wasn't it?

A. Yes.

Q. There was a transcript made of the tape recording, wasn't there?

A.   Yes.

Q.   You then signed the transcript, didn't you, Sir?

A.   Yes.

The lawyer tries to bring out facts about the circumstances of the prior statement that will lend it credibility. If the statement was made close in time to the events described, was made to a police officer or other authoritative figure, was under oath, or was recorded at the time, these circumstances would be established to accredit the prior statement, so that the factfinders would tend to accept its likely accuracy and truthfulness.

Usually the accreditation of the prior statement is accomplished without disclosure of its contents. In that way the witness will not have the chance to discredit or qualify the prior statement before the impeaching confrontation can take place. The idea is to accredit the prior statement circumstantially before disclosing the inconsistency to the witness.

c.   Proving the Prior Statement

Once the impeachable present testimony has been reaffirmed and the prior impeaching statement has been accredited, the lawyer can proceed to the impeachment. As a matter of logic, it is not always necessary for the lawyer to perform the impeachment with the witness on the stand. All of the facts have been established. Instead, the lawyer can simply lay the foundation and offer the inconsistent statement in evidence at some later time and then argue the discrepancy to the jury.

> *Counsel.*   You heard Mr. Ralston testify on direct. He told us that he and his companion did not throw any beer bottle at that house. On cross-examination I asked him again about that testimony, just to make sure that we understood him correctly. But we also know from Exhibit 7, page 23, that he told an entirely different story to the police. During his police interview he admitted that when the children called them names they threw a beer bottle at the house. It is obvious that Mr. Ralston is not telling us the truth. If he

isn't telling the truth about the beer bottle what else isn't he telling the truth about?

Under the rules of most jurisdictions, including Federal Rule of Evidence 613(b), extrinsic evidence of a nonparty witness's prior inconsistent statement cannot be introduced unless the witness is first confronted with the statement and given the opportunity to explain it. This requirement means that as a practical matter the impeachment must be pursued with the witness on the stand.

The most common way to confront the witness and prove a prior inconsistent statement is with a strong leading question:

> Q. In your statement to the police officer you stated, "When the children yelled we threw a beer bottle at the house," didn't you?

Often such a question will develop the inconsistency immediately.

> A. Yes, I guess so.

However, if the witness pleads lack of memory:

> A. I don't remember that.

the lawyer can refresh recollection by showing the statement to the witness:

> Q. Doesn't this document refresh your recollection that in the police interview you said "We threw a beer bottle at the house"?

If the witness denies the statement initially or refuses to acknowledge it after recollection has been refreshed, the document containing the prior statement can be authenticated and offered in evidence either on the spot or at the next opportunity presented by local court rule or practice.

When the document is offered, the prior inconsistent statement can be read by the lawyer or the witness.

> A. (in response to the previous question).   No, it doesn't.

Q. Your Honor, may this be marked as Exhibit 12 for identification?

The Court.   So marked.

Q. I show you Exhibit 12 for identification. That is your signature there on the bottom of page 3, isn't it?

A. Yes.

Q. And Exhibit 12 for identification is the statement that you gave to the police and that you signed there on page 3, isn't it?

A. I guess so.

Q. We offer Exhibit 12 in evidence.

The Court.   Is there objection?

Opposing Lawyer.   No objection.

The Court.   Admitted.

Q. Now, Mr. Ralston, would you please read from Exhibit 12, your statement to the police, the third line from the bottom on page 2.

A. I don't know which one you mean.

Q. The third line from the bottom — the one that begins "When the children yelled . . .".

A. (reading). "When the children yelled, we threw a beer bottle at the house.".

or

Q. And, Mr. Ralston, Exhibit 12, your statement to the police right after the accident, says here, on page 2 [showing the document to the witness and pointing] "When the children yelled, we threw a beer bottle at the house," doesn't it?

A. Yes, I guess it does.

or

> Q. Your Honor, at this point may I read from Exhibit 12?
>
> A. You may.
>
> Q. Page 2, third line from the bottom — "When the children yelled, we threw a beer bottle at the house.".

The efficacy of this kind of control and impeachment depends in large part on the clarity and unambiguousness of both the present testimony and the control device. The clearer the contrast, the greater the impact of the impeachment. Where either the prior statement or the present testimony is ambiguous or unclear, there is always the potential that an apparent discrepancy might be easily explained during either cross-examination or redirect. Any discussion of the implications of the discrepancy on the credibility of the witness should not be brought up with the witness; it should be reserved for argument. Once having shown the discrepancy, the lawyer should resist the temptation to ask the witness a question such as

> Q. So now you say that you were not throwing any beer bottles at the house, whereas before, right after the incident, you said that you did?

Even though this question may be posed in strong leading form practically demanding a simple affirmance, it is the psychological equivalent of

> Q. How can you say now that you did not throw a beer bottle at the house when you said that you did throw a beer bottle at the house right after the incident?

Although in form such a question demands an affirmance, it actually requests an explanation. It is argumentative and suggests an inference or deduction about the credibility of the witness.

By the same token, counsel should resist the temptation to lace her voice with sarcasm or incredulity when confronting a witness with a prior inconsistent statement. Such tones have the same effect as explicit argument in the language of the question. The witness will be impelled to try to explain the inconsistency.

Such an argumentative question as that in the example will

usually be excluded if objection is made. But the potential loss of control over the witness and the opportunity of the witness to undo the impeachment are the real risks with such a question. There is no way the lawyer can restrict the witness to a yes-or-no answer. Common parlance and understanding recognizes that a fair answer to such a question cannot be restricted to a "yes" or "no." Fairness requires that the witness be permitted to answer and explain or rebut the argument inherent in the question. Many a lawyer has seen an entire impeachment evaporate in the witness's response to the "one question too many."

A.   Well, I didn't throw any beer bottle — I think Roscoe did.

Impeachment by prior inconsistent statement or inconsistent factual circumstance seeks to establish the unreliability of the testimony without directly addressing the reason for it. If the prior statement is accepted as accurate, unless the discrepancy is explained, the logical inference is that the present testimony is not. A further inference is that perhaps other testimony the witness has given may not be accurate. But the conclusion drawn from the inconsistency alone does not necessarily go to the reason the testimony might be inaccurate. Prior inconsistent statements are weighed, however, in the context of human experience. The factfinders' natural desire for consistency and understandability in the pictures being presented will assign to a proven inconsistency the reasons associated with that kind of inconsistency in real life. Thus the factfinders may accept an inconsistency in a number as mere forgetfulness in rote memory, which would not seriously discredit the testimony on other matters. On the other hand, the factfinders might associate an inconsistency on some detail that ordinarily would be remembered with a degree of bias or untruthfulness that seriously infects the credibility of the witness.

3.   *Other Forms of Impeachment*

Other forms of impeachment may not show that any particular testimony is actually inaccurate but may establish reasons why the jury might infer that the testimony could be inaccurate. These forms of impeachment address both the witness's opportunity and ability to render accurate testimony and the witness's motive to do so. For instance, cross-examination showing that an eyewitness was in a location where he would have difficulty seeing what he reports assails the reliability of the witness's testimony by under-cutting his ability to see and recount. The witness may be in per-fectly good faith, but if he was not in a position to see what he thought he saw, then his testimony should not be believed.

Q. At the time you saw the fight it was about 9:00 P.M., wasn't it?

A. Yes, it was.

Q. It was nighttime, right?

A. Yes, that's right.

Q. You were at least half a block away from where the men were fighting?

A. About that far.

Q. There were no lights in the vicinity, were there?

A. That's right, there weren't.

Q. And it was dark out, wasn't it?

A. Not really.

Q. What do you mean, not really?

Oops! This last question is actually a risky question for cross-examination. Why? Because it is not a leading question. Control has been relaxed, giving the witness the opportunity to supply the information. The cross-examiner has not supplied the fact and asked the witness to agree; instead she has asked the witness, in effect, to explain the apparent inconsistency of her testimony with the physical facts as developed by the preceding questions. This was the "one question too many," and should not have been asked. In this case, though, the amount of damage the witness can do is limited. The distance the witness was from the scene has already been established. There is not much room for him to come up with an explanation of why it was not dark out at 9:00 P.M. on an autumn night.

A.   Because there was a bright moon out.

Enough said.

4. Impeachment by Proof of Bias

Impeachment by proof of bias seeks to show that the witness has an unusually strong reason for wishing the trial picture to come out in a certain way. The argument is that the witness is influenced in her portrayal by this strong interest so that her version cannot be totally relied upon. Relationships to the parties, interest in the outcome, or strong emotional feelings are all appropriate grounds for the inference that the witness's testimony may be influenced by bias.

Usually impeachment by bias relates not to an individual observation but to the witness's overall testimony. Thus there is no need to set up the statements to be impeached unless the bias would tend to relate to only one particular aspect of the witness's testimony.

The procedure is simple. Using appropriate control devices, the cross-examiner brings out the relevant facts with strong leading questions.

Q.   You are the decedent's brother-in-law, aren't you?

A.   Yes.

Q.   And you have been friends for many years?

A.   Yes.

Or

Q.   Doctor, you are getting paid for your testimony in this case, aren't you?

A.   Yes.

Q.   Now the amount of your payment has not been established between you and the plaintiff, has it?

A.   Yes, that's right.

Q. And you won't determine how much you're going to charge the plaintiff for your testimony in this case until this case has been decided, will you?

A. I guess that's true.

Or,

Q. Doctor, you are appearing as a witness in behalf of your colleague voluntarily, are you not?

A. Yes.

Q. Didn't you say on March 12th at the County Medical Society meeting that "we must all band together to protect each other from the threat of medical malpractice exposure."?

A. Well, yes; I guess I did.

Once again, the inference of bias itself is usually not made the subject of cross-examination. A question such as

Q. You can't expect this jury to accept your testimony if you have so much bias?

although leading in form, would be argumentative and draw objection — or worse, the witness's explanation.

5. *Impeachment by Proof of Bad Character*

Evidence law and trial advocacy permit a witness's testimony to be impeached by certain kinds of evidence of bad character. A lawyer attacking the credibility of a witness is permitted to prove in various ways that the witness's character is such that his testimony should not be believed. Impeachment by proof of bad character can take three forms:

(1) proof during cross-examination of the witness of prior bad acts,

(2) proof of bad character for truthfulness by opinion or reputation, and

(3) proof of conviction of a crime.

Because human experience tends to link identified character traits with the conduct associated with those traits, the use of character evidence to impeach credibility is subject to abuse. Federal Rule of Evidence 403 and its state counterparts can be frequently invoked where the probative value of character evidence on witness credibility is outweighed by other available inferences relating to the substantive issues on trial. For these reasons the lawyer should proceed with caution and be sure of her evidentiary ground when attacking a witness's character to prove lack of credibility. Often issues of admissibility and the use of this kind of evidence are raised by motions *in limine* to avoid the risk of tainting the trial with prejudicial material that is ultimately ruled inadmissible. At the same time, because of the power of this kind of impeachment, the lawyer should be familiar with the procedure to impeach by each one of these methods and ready to use it in an appropriate situation.

a. Proof of Prior Bad Acts

During cross-examination, the cross-examining lawyer is generally permitted to ask the witness about prior conduct or misconduct that might lead to a reasonable inference concerning the witness's credibility.

Federal Rule of Evidence 608(b) provides:

> Specific instances of conduct. Specific instances of the conduct of a witness, for the purpose of attacking or supporting the witness' credibility . . . may not be proved by extrinsic evidence. They may, however, in the discretion of the court, if probative of truthfulness or untruthfulness, be inquired into on cross-examination of the witness (1) concerning the witness' character for truthfulness or untruthfulness, or (2) concerning the character for truthfulness or untruthfulness of another witness as to which character the witness being cross-examined has testified.

The opportunity to impeach by specific instances of prior conduct is limited to the cross-examination of the witness whose conduct is at issue or who has testified to the character of another witness. The witness can be asked about any kind of prior act so long as the judge agrees that the prior act provides a fair inference as to the witness's truthfulness.

> Q. For the last three years you have failed to file any federal income taxes, haven't you?

or

> Q. So isn't it true that in your speech to the Bar Association you plagiarized two whole pages of the 1987 article on impeachment?

or

> Q. Isn't it true that when you were twelve years old you used to pull the wings off flies?
>
> *Opposing Counsel.* Objection, Your Honor. This kind of questioning does not go to truthfulness. The danger of unfair prejudice and remoteness of this evidence outweighs any probative value on credibility.
>
> *The Court.* Sustained. The jury is admonished to disregard the last question.

Since this form of impeachment must by definition take place during the cross-examination, any control devices must be such that they can be used during the cross-examination to extract the desired response. If the witness will not admit to the instances of conduct asserted by the cross-examiner, the cross-examiner is not generally allowed to prove them by extrinsic evidence. An exact acknowledgment of the prior instance and firm control techniques used by the lawyer during the examination are usually necessary for this kind of impeachment.

Impeachment by proof of prior bad acts, like all cross-examination, can be subject to abuse. The cross-examiner must be prepared to show a good-faith basis in order to present a question of prior instances of misconduct. Even if the witness denies such a question, merely asking it may lead to the inference that the witness did what is alleged. Thus, if the lawyer is going to charge

> Q.   You have failed to file any income tax returns for the last three years, haven't you?

she should have reasonably firm knowledge that the allegation is in fact true before posing such a potentially prejudicial question. If challenged, the lawyer must be able to demonstrate the source of the good-faith basis and its support for the question. While the ability to prove the prior act, if permitted, would certainly qualify as a good-faith basis, it is not necessarily required. At the same time, if challenged the lawyer cannot merely assert the good-faith basis without something to satisfy the judge that it exists.

Thus, in the preceding example,

> *Opposing Counsel.*   Objection, Your Honor. May we be heard at sidebar?
>
> *The Court.*   Counsel, approach sidebar.
>
> *Opposing Counsel.*   We object on the ground that there is absolutely no basis for this question and the intimation that my client is a tax dodger. Even if he denies it, the smear will be there.
>
> *The Court* (to the cross-examiner).   What do you have to indicate that the witness has not filed his income tax returns?
>
> *A.*   Well, Your Honor, my client tells me that she heard from some of her friends that he has not filed his taxes.
>
> *The Court.*   Counsel, you will have to have a better foundation for such a question than that. The objection is sustained. [to the jury:] Members of the Jury, you are to disregard that last question. There is nothing whatsoever to indicate that Dr. Evans has not filed his income taxes and any inference on your part from this question would be improper.

If a witness testifies under Rule 608(a) to the character of another witness for truthfulness, the attesting witness is subject to similar cross-examination concerning prior instances of conduct of the witness to whose character he has attested. The typical form of such a cross-examination is

Q. Have you heard that Dr. X didn't file his income tax returns for the last three years?

A better formulation of this question would be

Q. Ms. Witness, isn't it true that Dr. X did not file his income tax returns for the last three years?

If the witness believes the fact to be true for any reason, the second formulation will obtain the positive response. In some circumstances the first form of the question might enable the witness to deny or evade because she hasn't "heard" exactly what the lawyer stated.

b. Impeachment by Opinion or Reputation Evidence of Untruthful Character

The Federal Rules of Evidence[4] and the evidence rules of most American jurisdictions allow evidence of the bad reputation of a witness for truth and veracity for purposes of impeaching the credibility of the witness. Rule 608(a) also allows a witness who has some knowledge of another witness to give an opinion of the truthfulness and veracity of the other witness for the purpose of attacking the credibility of that witness. Once a witness's credibility has been attacked in this manner, similar rehabilitating evidence of good character for truth and veracity is generally admissible.

As foundation for reputation evidence of bad character for truthfulness, the character witness's familiarity with the other witness's reputation in some defined community must be shown.

Q. Are you acquainted with Mr. Jerry Ralston?

[4] Rule 608(a).

    A. Yes, I am.

    Q. In what way are you acquainted with Mr. Ralston?

    A. We have both lived in the same part of Springfield since
        we were children.

Ordinarily the examination would proceed to develop further facts
from which it could be inferred that the witness being questioned
and the other witnesses were both members of the same small
community for a period of time. Once it is shown that the witness
has a basis for knowing the reputation of the other witness, the
reputation question can be asked.

    Q. Are you familiar with Mr. Ralston's reputation in the
        Springfield community for truth and veracity?

    A. Yes, I am.

    Q. What is that reputation?

    A. It is not good.

If permitted by the judge, it is usually helpful to get the witness to
expand a little.

    Q. What do you mean, "not good"?

    A. He does not have the reputation of always telling the
        truth.

c. Impeachment by Evidence of Conviction of Crime

    The evidence rules of most jurisdictions, including the Federal
Rules of Evidence,[5] permit impeachment of a witness by proof
that the witness has been convicted of crime. The theory is that a
person who has been convicted of certain types of criminal behavior has shown a degree of dishonesty and disregard for social
requirements that his testimony under oath might not be all that
reliable. Obviously not all conduct that has been made criminal
involves the same degree of active dishonesty. And there is always

---

[5] See Fed. R. Evid. 609.

the possibility that the factfinders might have an adverse reaction to a jailbird that goes beyond a proper inference based on the crime of which that person was convicted. Moreover, if the witness whose credibility is being attacked is the criminal defendant, there is the possibility that the factfinder will infer that "if he did it once, he must have done it again" and decide against the defendant based on the prior conviction rather than on the actual evidence in support of the pending charge.

Because of these considerations, under the Federal Rules of Evidence as well as the evidence codes of the states, there are elaborate protective provisions that govern when and how a prior conviction can be used. These provisions vary from jurisdiction to jurisdiction. Compliance is mandatory.

Proving and arguing prior criminal convictions as affecting the credibility of the opposition's witnesses calls for restraint and professionalism of a high order. It is very easy to overplay a past conviction. Even a hint of a sarcastic or sneering tone in referring to a prior conviction or arguing it is likely to turn the factfinders against the impeaching lawyer and her client. As with all direct attacks on a person's honesty and integrity, it is almost always best to understate and allow the factfinders to come to the adverse conclusions on their own.

6. *Impeachment by Contradiction*

Another common form of witness impeachment is contradiction of the witness's testimony by that of other witnesses or by other reliable evidence. The effectiveness of this form of impeachment depends largely on the authority of the impeaching testimony or evidence. A partisan witness may be effectively impeached by contradictory testimony from a disinterested witness or by physical evidence inconsistent with the witness's assertions. On the other hand, equally partisan testimony or ambiguous physical evidence is rarely effective to impeach a witness who has given contradictory testimony.

Generally the safest and the most effective way to accomplish impeachment by contradiction is to commit the witness to the testimony to be impeached and then, as soon as convenient, elicit the contradictory testimony or evidence. The lawyer can argue the effect of the evidence to impeach the witness in summation.

With impeachment by contradiction the witness is usually not confronted with the impeaching testimony. However, the witness to be impeached should be committed to the subject testimony the same as with any other form of impeachment.

> Q. Now, Officer Groves, you said on direct examination that the car backed out of the driveway at 33½ Jackson Street, right?

would be an appropriate question to commit the witness to testimony to be later impeached by authoritative testimony from other witnesses and physical evidence that the car drove out of the driveway frontwards. The "you said on direct examination" formulation is better than

> Q. Now, Officer Groves, the car backed out of the driveway at 33½ Jackson Street, right?

because the impeaching lawyer does not want to be implicitly vouching for the statement that is to be impeached by wording it as a positive statement in her question.

Because impeachment by contradiction usually relies on the testimony of another witness or on some other evidence offered for its effect, frequently the impeachment is not obvious to the witness on the stand. Sometimes the lawyer is tempted to "make the point" of the impeachment while the witness is on the stand. However:

> Q. Officer, would it surprise you to know that Mrs. Mercer testified yesterday afternoon that the car drove out of the driveway forward and headed east down Jackson Street?

or

> Q. Would it change your testimony if you knew that Mrs. Mercer saw the car drive out of the driveway forward before turning east down Jackson Street?

are both argumentative questions. Although this kind of "phantom" impeachment is frequently permitted, it is risky at best and is likely to provoke an explanation from the witness of the apparent inconsistency.

Any formulation of a question designed to drive home an impeachment by contradiction is likely to incorporate facts not in evidence or to argue facts that are, or both. Thus, to ask whether or not the witness is aware of the testimony of another witness that contradicts his testimony is not calculated to elicit additional relevant evidence; it is calculated to make the point to the factfinders that another disinterested witness has contradicted this witness's testimony so that this witness's testimony should not be believed. By the same token, when the reference is to facts that have not yet been proven, such a question runs the risk of improperly incorporating facts not in evidence at the time the question is asked. In any event, just the mention of the contradictory testimony creates a strong incentive for the witness to attempt to explain or justify her own version in such a manner as to undercut the impeachment.

> A.   Well, if that is what Mrs. Mercer said, I am sure she is right. Although my best memory was that the car backed out, it may have come out forward. In any event, it did turn right and headed down Jackson Street.

An explanation by the witness reconciling the two apparently contradictory versions is the best way to combat impeachment by contradiction.

H.   Discipline on Cross-Examination

The kind and amount of witness control needed for effective cross-examination will vary depending on the nature of the witness and the subject matter of the testimony. Weak or nonconfrontive witnesses will often yield the desired concessions under only moderately firm control. Such witnesses might often respond affirmatively to soft leading questions, such as

> Q.   Did you throw a beer bottle at the house that night?
>
> A.   Yes, we did.

It is also sometimes possible to get a weak witness to accept characterizations or conclusions posed:

Q. You were angry, weren't you, Mr. Maxfield?

A. Yes, I guess so.

With tougher, more resistant witnesses the lawyer must use the
most firm control techniques available to elicit the desired concessions given without qualifying or damaging explanations or denials. Soft leading questions are not tight enough.

Q. Did you throw a beer bottle at the house that night?

A. No, I didn't throw any beer bottle at the house.

Conclusions, characterizations, and soft leading questions are out
of the question.

Q. You were angry, weren't you, Mr. Maxfield?

A. Well, I wouldn't say "angry," more like "upset."

With the strong or confrontational witness, the cross-examiner
will have to be content with specific facts that are uncontrovertible
or are established by valid control devices and are presented in
hard, closed leading questions.

Ultimately, control over a witness is exercised through fairness
and fear. Ordinarily the witness's sense of fairness will lead him to
respond fairly to the cross-examiner's questioning. Most people are
conditioned to some extent to try to answer fairly and accurately.

Fear, however, also plays an important part. A primary weapon
of the cross-examiner is the witness's fear that if he does not agree
with the lawyer she will punish or discipline him. The discipline or
punishment most to be feared by the witness is that the witness's
testimony will be shown to be false, unreliable, or incapable of
belief. The witness knows that if he does not acknowledge a fact
that is obviously true, the factfinders will know that he is being
unfair. The credibility of his case will be damaged. The fear of the
attendant embarrassment, humiliation, and substantive damage to
the case will force the witness to admit what he has to admit and to

submit to the use of valid control devices by the cross-examining lawyer.

In order to control the witness effectively on cross-examination, the form and manner of the lawyer's questioning must hold the witness fully accountable for the response. As indicated above, the tone of cross-examination questions is the confident declarative. The manner in which the questions are delivered makes it clear to the witness that the lawyer is expecting the witness fairly and honestly to affirm the lawyer's declaration. The implication is that if the witness does not do so her unfairness or dishonesty will be instantly exposed. By tone and inflection of voice the lawyer can sometimes convey the sense of impending discipline if the witness does not acknowledge the truth of what the lawyer is saying.

It is usually considered important on cross-examination for the lawyer to look directly at the witness as the question is being delivered and to watch the witness through the response, to express to the witness that the lawyer is listening, cares very much, and will hold the witness responsible for his response. Some lawyers pose cross-examination questions dramatically while in motion, and even walk away from the witness! Invariably, though, they will fix their gaze on the witness before the final down beat in the question and while the answer is being given.

If the lawyer stops looking at the witness before the witness has completed the answer, the witness may feel relieved to some extent of the obligation to respond fairly and accurately. The witness may even feel able to expatiate or explain. Looking at the witness is a way for the lawyer to maintain some control even after she has yielded the speaking role to the witness. If the witness does not affirm the lawyer's question in the terms posed, it is a sign to the lawyer that either the question was insufficiently clear, simple, and unambiguous or that the control technique was not sufficiently firm.

Of course, some extremely intransigent witnesses will make positive assertions and will give explanations no matter how clear and simple the cross-examiner's question or how firm the control. However, at this extreme both the judge and the factfinders will quickly realize that the witness is not being fair and will tend to discount the explanations. The judge may also admonish a witness who is obviously running wild.

Q. Mr. Ralston, you saw Mr. Savage take a swing at Mr. Maxfield, didn't you?

A. Yeah, but that doesn't mean that he had the right to go and mow Roscoe down with his car, does it?

The Court. Now, now, Mr. Ralston; please confine yourself to answering Counsel's questions! The gratuitous comment may go out.

I. Maintaining Control Through Questions

1. *Short Questions, Simple Facts*

In the great majority of instances, effective cross-examination control can be achieved by breaking down the questions to the least controvertible components and by using firmer techniques of delivery. If the lawyer is having difficulty maintaining verbal control, the form of the questions should be examined. Each question should be pared down to one simple, unambiguous fact. This may result in many more questions, but it is almost always easier to obtain an affirmative response to a question that asks the witness to acknowledge one simple fact rather than a more complex formulation. The lawyer should combine the simplified question with firmness in delivery. The "hard" leading question should be used throughout.

Q. Then you went into the house?

Q. After you went into the house you got your car keys, didn't you?

Q. You then went out the back door?

Q. You got in your car, didn't you?

Q. You drove out of the driveway?

Q. As you drove out of the driveway you turned right?

The use of short unambiguous questions also establishes a rhythm that tends to compel the witness to give affirmative responses.

More colorful words that give "spin" to the questions are likely to provoke resistance in the witness and make it harder for the lawyer to maintain control. For instance, the question

> Q. You jumped into your car, didn't you?

or

> Q. You tore out of your driveway?

would be less likely to get an affirmation from the witness than using "got" for "jumped" or "drove" for "tore out." The witness may respond:

> A. Not really. A Mustang is pretty low to the ground. I had to bend down to get into the car.

or

> A. No, I drove out of the driveway.

The lawyer should also look to the manner and delivery of the questions to make sure that the tone is confident and that the witness is being held accountable.

2. Repeating the Question to Reassert Control

When a witness goes beyond a fair response, the lawyer can often reestablish control by merely repeating the question.

> Q. When you left the driveway, you turned to the right, didn't you?
>
> A. I looked both ways and I didn't see anything but it was dark down there to the right.
>
> Q. When you left the driveway, Sir, you turned to the right, didn't you?
>
> A. Yes, I did.

By repeating the question, the lawyer reminds the witness of the scope of the question asked. The lawyer is also reminding the factfinders that the first answer was not responsive to the question. This kind of discipline tends to keep the witness under control.

3. Moving to Strike Nonresponsive Answers

If a witness persists in going beyond the fair scope of the question in his answers, the cross-examining lawyer may move that the answer be stricken as nonresponsive.

    Q.   It was dark that night, wasn't it?

    A.   I could see perfectly well by the light of the headlights.

    Q.   (to the Court).   Your Honor, we move that the last answer be stricken as nonresponsive.

    The Court.   The last answer will be stricken as nonresponsive.

The motion to strike for nonresponsiveness is frequently confused with the motion to strike for inadmissibility. The motion to strike for nonresponsiveness is made by the lawyer who asked the question to which the nonresponsive anwer was given. It is almost always used on cross-examination or on direct examination of an unwilling or hostile witness. If the answer does not fairly respond to the question asked, it does not matter that the response would be admissible otherwise. The motion to strike is solely directed at the witness's lack of cooperation with the examination process. It is the lawyer's effort to invoke the rules of the court to assist in control of the witness.

    Q.   Mr. Ralston, you had been smoking marijuana that day, hadn't you?

    A.   So what if we had; that doesn't mean that he had any right to run Roscoe down like that, does it?

    Q.   Your Honor, may the last portion of that answer go out as nonresponsive?

> The Court.   The last part of the answer will be stricken, and
> the jury will be instructed to disregard it. Mr. Ralston,
> please try to answer the question just as it is asked.

On the other hand, sometimes a lawyer will move to strike the
answer to one of her opponent's questions and refer to the answer
as nonresponsive.

> Q.   Was there anyone else lying on the grass besides you, Mr.
> Borak?

> A.   Yes, one of the college kids in the other car was there. He
> told me, "I'm sorry, we were going too fast."

> Opposing Counsel.   Objection! We move to strike the aswer
> as nonresponsive and hearsay!

Under these circumstances, the nonresponsiveness of the answer is
not the grounds for striking it. As a matter of evidence law, the
answer should be stricken only if the nonresponsive testimony is
also inadmissible.

> The Court.   Counsel?

> Q.   Your Honor, the Court may remember the testimony of
> the plaintiff to the effect that he was the only passenger
> of the Clark car who was lying on the ground. His state-
> ment to the defendant was an admission.

> The Court.   Motion to strike denied. The testimony may
> stand.

The purpose of striking the answer is not to discipline the witness
for failing to follow the cues of the examiner. The answer will be
stricken if it is in fact not admissible. The nonresponsiveness is
relevant because it justifies the objectant's failure to anticipate the
potentially inadmissible evidence in time to object before the testimony was given so that the objection will not be deemed to have
been waived.

4.   *Chastening the Witness*

Generally, the cross-examining lawyer should not try to tell the witness how to anwer the cross-examination questions. Trying to maintain control over witnesses by chastening them usually fails.

> Q. Professor Haven, you can't say for sure that the defendant didn't see the body of Roscoe Savage, before he ran him down, can you?
>
> A. Well, my own opinion is that it was extremely unlikely that he could have seen him.
>
> Q. Professor Haven, you answer my questions "yes" or "no"! Now, you can't say for sure whether he saw him or not, can you — yes or no?
>
> *The Court.*   The witness may respond in any way he thinks fair and is not required to answer "yes" or "no" if "yes" or "no" would not be a fair answer to the question.

While the factfinders might look askance at a witness who is obviously stonewalling or trying to evade cross-examination questions, if the lawyer starts to berate the witness, the factfinders' sympathy will quickly switch to the witness and against the lawyer. Any excessive intimidation of a witness is likely to backfire.

5.   *The Varying Power of Control Devices*

As has been shown, the power and precision of control devices vary greatly. Some, such as prior statements of the witness, are accurate and reliable. With such devices a lawyer can usually extract the substance of the expected testimony even if the witness wishes to depart from it on the stand.

Other control devices, such as the anticipated testimony of other witnesses, are much less powerful and precise. Here the strength of the device will depend on the authority and credibility of the other witnesses. Some are nothing more than arguments that the cross-examination witness's testimony is contrary to proven facts or human experience. In planning a cross-examination, the lawyer assesses the power of the control devices against the importance of the expected testimony and the amount of resistance anticipated from the witness.

Some points of the anticipated testimony will be so crucial that one can expect a considerable amount of resistance from the witness. Such points will require accurate and powerful control devices to get the expected affirmative responses or concessions. On other points of less import, it might be reasonable to expect the witness to give the expected acknowledgments with less potent control devices.

The effectiveness of control devices in obtaining cross-examination concessions can sometimes be increased if the witness does not fully appreciate the significance of the concessions sought. If the device is weak, the lawyer need not try to make her point while the witness is on the stand. If the lawyer can obtain a concession in a context of apparent innocuousness, the concession's true import can be argued later when the witness is not on the stand.

6. Varying Control Techniques to Suit the Need

Even where the lawyer possesses strong and specific control devices, the technique needed to effectively cross-examine a witness depends in large part on the witness. When the lawyer finds that the witness is not responding as requested, the lawyer needs to intensify the examination technique as necessary to "get the witness back on the leash." This can be accomplished by use of a modulated series of techniques each of increasing power until control is gained or regained and the witness is responding properly to the questions.

If a witness does not answer a leading question with a simple "yes" or "no," before the lawyer tries to punish the witness, she should look again at the question. Was it really a leading question? If the form of the question is not a closed and leading one, no lawyer can reliably expect a "yes" or "no" anwer.

Before blaming the witness, the lawyer should also look at the subject matter of the question. Did it call for affirmance of more than one specific fact? Did it attempt to link two facts together or ask the witness to agree with some kind of conclusion or characterization? Did it have an argumentative content or tone? In most cases, an apparently nonresponsive witness is merely taking advantage of the latitude afforded by an imprecise, subjective, or compound question. The lawyer should rephrase the question in more specific terms.

Assuming that the question is an appropriate one, simple repetition is often the trial lawyer's resort in the event of a nonresponsive answer the first time around. If the witness persists, sometimes a second repetition of the question will make the question clear to all concerned, including the witness. If the circumstances indicate, the lawyer might add a little more emphasis in tone, volume, and energy to convey without words the message "this time, I mean it!"

If the witness still refuses to answer a specific and firmly delivered cross-examination question, it should be obvious to all that the witness is indeed recalcitrant. The lawyer is then, and only then, justified in using more forceful techniques. These may include approaching the witness and more obviously increasing the volume or pitch of the lawyer's voice when asking the question for the third time. It must be emphasized that these more intimidating forms of witness control may be resorted to only once it is obvious that the witness is unfairly refusing to answer a truly proper question. The lawyer should exhaust all resources of tightened question form and repetition before increasing the force.

If the lawyer is unable to obtain an appropriate answer by applying the standard techniques with escalating intensity, it may be time to involve the court. Moving to strike a nonresponsive answer can be effective if the lawyer's own efforts are not enough to obtain responsive answers. Before such a motion is made, the lawyer must be sure that the question was unambiguous and fair and that the answer was not.

The last resort for gaining control of an adverse witness is a simple appeal to the judge.

Q. Your Honor, this question clearly calls for a simple "yes" or "no" answer. Would the Court kindly instruct the witness to answer the question "yes" or "no"?

In cross-examination as well as in direct, it should be always the lawyer's goal to exert the least obtrusive control technique to achieve the necessary control. The declarative form of a leading question should be considered at minimum. From there, the lawyer can exert more obvious forms of control only to the extent that the witness's responses make them necessary in the eyes of the judge and factfinders as well as the lawyer. Bullying a witness almost always causes the factfinders to empathize with the witness and to penalize the lawyer.

J. Physical Intimidation and Sarcasm

In the past, physical intimidation was considered by many as an important feature of cross-examination. Large stature, a booming voice, and an aggressive courtroom approach were considered potent tools to control an obstinate witness. Now it is recognized that proper question form and delivery are more effective than physical attributes in keeping a witness under control. The more precisely and strongly the lawyer formulates the question, the less "freight" is required in the delivery.

Using physical intimidation can backfire. The factfinders can readily appreciate when a question is fair and unambiguous and requires a clean concession. If the concession is not forthcoming, the factfinders will tend to hold it against the witness. But the factfinders can also appreciate when a question is not totally fair and the answer is sought by physical threat rather than factual accuracy of the question. If the factfinders get the impression that a lawyer is using physical intimidation to obtain concessions to which she is not really entitled, their sympathies will usually lodge with the witness, and the lawyer's all-important credibility will suffer. While there are still instances where a lawyer can take advantage by physical intimidation, there is little that physical intimidation can accomplish that cannot be better accomplished by other means.

Sometimes a lawyer will use sarcasm or skepticism in the tone of her questions in an effort to heighten the effect of the cross-examination questioning or to increase accountability of the witness. The tone adds an element of argumentativeness as the question is being put and says something about the credibility of the witness's assertion.

Q. So, Mr. Maxfield, you're trying to tell us that you really couldn't see *anything* under that tree when you turned your car and drove up on that sidewalk, right!?

    A. Well, now it may seem incredible to you, but I really
        couldn't see anything. I just did the best I could.

The lawyer is saying, by the tone of her question, "How can you
say that?" or "I don't believe you . . ." Both of these implications
have the same drawbacks as the argumentative question. Sarcasm
and skepticism tend to arouse resentment on the part of the witness
or the factfinders because of the implicit personal affront. Questions laden with sarcasm or skepticism are subject to objection as
argumentative. Regardless of how closed such questions may be in
form, often the court will not restrict the witness to a "yes" or "no"
answer, but instead will permit him to explain the apparent inconsistency. Thus it is usually advised that the lawyer not inject sarcasm or skepticism in the tone of her cross-examination questions
unless she has a very good reason.

K.   Escalation

The working rule for cross-examination — that one does not ask a
question unless one has a control device calculated to extract an
expected answer — is no more absolute than any of the other rules
for trial advocacy. Sometimes the lawyer may suspect that the
witness may be willing to agree to a fact favorable to the cross-
examiner's case, but the lawyer has no control device to support
that suspicion. Under these circumstances the lawyer might try to
approach the desired fact somewhat indirectly. The purpose of
using such an approach is so the lawyer can get an inkling of the
answer to the crucial question and can ultimately ask it with some
confidence of the answer. This process of cautiously departing
from facts supported by good control devices into areas where the
cross-examiner does not have a real control device is called "escalation." Escalation requires a high degree of precision, control, and
sensitivity by the examining lawyer.

    A cross-examining lawyer would consider escalation if she has
some reason to hope that the witness might agree to certain facts
favorable to the cross-examiner but where she has no adequate
control device. Posing the key question to the witness directly would
risk a denial and might undermine other inferences that the lawyer is
trying to establish. Rather than risk damage from a head-on assault,

the lawyer might escalate carefully and gradually in the desired direction to see if the helpful testimony can be obtained even without a control device. For example, assume that the prosecutor, cross-examining a criminal defendant, hopes that the defendant will admit that he was angry after a confrontation with the decedent. The prosecutor may risk asking the defendant straight on:

> Q. After that confrontation you were angry at Mr. Savage, weren't you?

The control device for this question would be the argument to the jury that they shouldn't take a denial seriously since their human experience tells them that people usually are angry after confrontations. A convincing denial from the defendant might undermine this argument and the whole motive relied on by the prosecution.

> A. Well, I was upset, of course, but mainly concerned, concerned that these men would come back and harass Ms. Farris and the children at a time when I was not around to protect them.

Under these circumstances, the prosecutor might elect to escalate toward the desired testimony by a series of small questions aimed at getting an inkling of the defendant's state of mind.

> Q. Now, Sir, these two men came up on your porch, didn't they?
>
> A. Yes, Sir.
>
> Q. They called you names, didn't they?
>
> A. Yes.
>
> Q. They put their fingers in your girlfriend's face, didn't they?
>
> A. Yes, they did.
>
> Q. And after she went in the house, one of them took a swing at you, didn't he, Sir?
>
> A. Yes.

> Q. This got you a little upset, didn't it, Mr. Maxfield?
>
> A. Yes.

At this point the lawyer is listening carefully to the witness's acknowledgments to the questions. Do they come willingly or reluctantly? If they come willingly, the lawyer is likely to be on the right track. The next question will be a slight escalation.

> Q. In fact, you were more than a little upset, weren't you, Mr. Maxfield?
>
> A. Yes, I suppose I was.

Again the lawyer listens carefully. How readily did the witness admit that last description? If the witness is still going along with the lawyer's questions freely and easily, maybe it would be worth the risk to try another step:

> Q. In fact, Mr. Maxfield, wouldn't you agree that you were angry after what those men had done up there on the porch?

The risk is minimized by the small size of the progressive steps. If the witness, impelled by the momentum of the examination, says "yes," the escalation has been successful. If the witness is not prepared to go any further and says "no," the lawyer can retreat to firm ground by repeating the last, most favorable answer.

> A. Well, I wouldn't really say "angry."
>
> Q. But is it fair to say, Mr. Maxfield, that you were more than a little upset as a result of these events, right?
>
> A. Yes, it is.

The key to successful escalation is small questions under tight control, venturing from the known territory (in this case the already attested facts of the confrontation) toward the unknown but desired goal (the defendant's anger after the confrontation). As the question is put, the lawyer must carefully appraise the witness's response. At all times the lawyer should be ready to drop the escalation if the witness becomes reluctant. The examiner should retreat to firm ground if the witness gives a denial and should resist the temptation to try to overcome a denial by arguing with the witness.

Q. Well, Mr. Maxfield, are you saying that you weren't angry after all that?!

Or, even worse,

Q. Mr. Maxfield, how can you say that you weren't angry after all these things happened to you!?

Such argumentative questions merely permit the witness to explain away the desired inference. Cross-examining lawyers are better off saving the argument for the summation.

L.   Open Questions on Cross-Examination

The basic cross-examination technique here outlined relies heavily on a closed declarative question to maintain consistent control and to obtain from the witness concessions or acknowledgments to specific facts supplied by the lawyer's question. This technique gives the lawyer the most precise control possible. Once the declarative question technique has been mastered, the lawyer may wish to experiment with questions in which control is maintained by other techniques.

An open question can be used on cross-examination when the examining lawyer wishes the witness to be the direct source of the facts *and* when all conceivable answers to the open question are within the lawyer's ability to handle with appropriate control devices or argument.

Situations in which the use of an open question on cross-examination is safe and appropriate are much rarer than one might at first imagine. There are very few questions as to which all possible answers are equally satisfactory to the examining lawyer. In most cases, one potential answer will be better than the others. That is the answer that should be favored by the form of the question. If it is incorporated into the question, the lawyer will have the best chance of obtaining an affirmative response.

With the preceding example, the prosecutor as cross-examiner can take the position that all conceivable answers to the following question will equally serve the prosecution's case.

> *Q.* What was your state of mind after the confrontation?

If the witness says that he was angry, the prosecutor can argue anger as a motive for the subsequent killing. If the witness says that he was cool and collected, the prosecutor can argue deliberation. Under this circumstance the prosecutor might decide that an open question can be used without danger.

This approach, however, assumes that both the deliberation and the anger theories are equally plausible and provable at the trial. That is seldom the case. Usually, the lawyer will have picked a particular fact scenario as the preferred one, even if another scenario would not be a total disaster. Thus, if the prosecutor's theory of the case was that the defendant was angry and went after the decedent in a rage, the question should be put

> *Q.* After the confrontation, you were angry, weren't you?

rather than

> *Q.* What was your state of mind after the confrontation?

One instance in which an open form of cross-examination can provide considerable impact is when the witness has authenticated a prior inconsistent statement and is then asked to read the statement to the factfinders.

> *Q.* Officer Groves, a few minutes ago you testified that Mr. Maxfield had said something when you were both standing by the body of Roscoe Savage in front of 37 Jackson Street, didn't you?
>
> *A.* That's right.
>
> *Q.* Officer Groves, Exhibit 12 for Identification is a copy of your report, is it not?
>
> *A.* Yes, it is.

Q.   You recognize Exhibit 12 as your report because you see your signature on it, right at the bottom of the second page, don't you?

A.   Yes, that's right.

Q.   You made out Exhibit 12 within hours of the events about which you are testifying today, didn't you?

A.   Yes, I did.

Q.   You tried to include in that report everything about this incident that you could remember at the time, right?

A.   Yes, I suppose so.

Q.   Your Honor, we offer Exhibit 12 for identification.

Opposing Counsel.   No objection, Your Honor.

Q.   Officer Groves, please look now at your report, which has been admitted in evidence as Exhibit 12, and tell us if there is mention anywhere in that report of any statement by Mr. Maxfield when you were standing by the body of Mr. Savage.

A.   (pauses, reading.) No, there isn't.

This is an example of impeachment by omission from a prior statement. The last question invites the witness to look at the report and tell the factfinders if there is any mention of the statement to which the witness just testified. The last question is not a closed, tight declarative question. But the power of having the witness "eat his words" on the witness stand may justify the risk that the witness will take advantage of the latitude of the more open question to explain.

A.   Well, there are some things that I did not remember to write down at the time, but that have come back since.

A safer if less dramatic way to accomplish the confrontation would be another closed leading question:

Q. Isn't it true, Officer, that nowhere in Exhibit 12 is there
    any mention of any statement similar to the one you just
    attributed to Mr. Maxfield as you were standing to-
    gether in front of 37 Jackson Street?

A. Yes, that's right.

The circumstances in which satisfactory control can be maintained on cross-examination without the use of hard leading questions are rare. In most cases where the cross-examiner expects a
particular answer to a particular question, the hard leading kind of
question is the most effective. It should be used for all cross-
examination questions unless there is a commanding reason to the
contrary.

9 Evidentiary
         Objections

A.   The Role of Evidentiary Objections

Trial advocacy is a competitive process. Each party has its own version of the relevant facts, which its advocate is attempting to recreate at the trial. The lawyer must not only formulate and accredit her own picture of the events at issue, she must also attempt to impede or discredit the image that is being developed by the other side.

The trial lawyer can assess what kind of picture her opponent will be able to portray based on her own knowledge of the available information. Both parties are subject to a common set of rules regulating evidence and other aspects of the trial presentation. These rules limit the kinds of information the parties may present and the manner in which it can be presented.

As the lawyer plans her own case and tries to predict what the opponent's case will look like, she does so on the assumption that the rules of evidence and procedure will apply to the opponent as well and that they will be enforced. If they are not enforced, the opponent may gain and exercise unwarranted advantages in the content of the presentation or in the manner in which it is made.

Most of the procedural and evidentiary rules are not enforced automatically by the judge: the threatened or actual violation of a rule must be called to the judge's attention by an objection.

Thus, when the lawyer apprehends that her opponent's presentation is about to violate a rule of evidence or procedure or a rule of ethical conduct, the immediate remedy is a prompt objection to call the violation to the attention of the court so that it might be prevented. The remedy is the same if the lawyer believes that a violation has already occurred. The violation must be called to the attention of the court so that remedial action can be taken.

B.   To Object or Not to Object

The lawyer is not required to object to every violation of the rules of evidence or procedure. Most improprieties committed by the opponent are not worth objecting to and can be either ignored or waived. Whether or not to object is a tactical, if not strategic, decision for the trial lawyer. When should a breach of the rules be ignored, and when should an objection be raised?

Much has been written about the effect of objections on the patience and interest of factfinders. Many commentators have argued that a lawyer who insists on punctilious enforcement of the rules by frequent objections will give the impression that she is trying to play lawyers' games or even hide the full story from the factfinders. Interviews with jurors have confirmed their disgruntlement with frequent bench conferences from which they are excluded. Judges who are required to rule "on horseback" sometimes express impatience with repeated objections. These considerations are cited by many lawyers as reasons why many apparently sound objections to elements of the opponent's presentation are simply not made.

There is no question that meaningless or picayune objections, even if technically sound, may be counterproductive. Factfinders become aware of what the real issues are in the competitive presentations. They are quick to sense whether a lawyer is trying to advance the state of their knowledge or whether procedural gambits are being used to muddy the waters or harass the opponent.

On the other hand, if a sound objection is quickly made and sustained, the objecting lawyer is effectively asserting some control over the opponent and requiring her to conform to the rules. Moreover the soundness of the objector's position is publicly affirmed by the judge. The interplay of counsel on objections is often a welcome diversion to the factfinders.

The failure of counsel to assert more evidentiary objections may be more properly attributable to inertia and risk aversion than to conscious tactical considerations. When a lawyer objects, usually she is interrupting the other's presentation. The spotlight is on the objector. Usually the objector has to be prepared to defend the objection within seconds. If the objection is overruled she feels admonished on the spot. Many lawyers will continue to object as long as they consistently seem to win but will stop if they have lost even one or two of these procedural skirmishes.

While there are many legal grounds for objections, the issue of whether to object or not usually depends on whether a favorable ruling on the objection will make a difference. Will sustaining the objection affect the picture being portrayed by the opponent and his witnesses or the manner in which that portrayal is being made? Thus, for example, if an objection to a leading question is made and sustained, the examining counsel is required to rephrase the question. Presumably, the rephrased question will be less familiar to the witness and less comfortable to the examiner than the one initially chosen. Possibly the witness will not choose the same words as those anticipated by the lawyer. The examiner will be restricted to the degree of freedom allowed by the rules. To some small extent, the opponent's presentation will suffer. All of these factors bear on whether to object to the leading question, and many of them suggest that the objection should be made.

There are some objections that go to the admissibility of potential evidence or witness testimony. If such objections are sustained, the opponent might be deprived of an important element of her fact picture. The lawyer's failure to make an objection may give the opponent an unfair advantage in the information presented to the factfinders.

Many objections are not likely to lead to exclusion of important evidence but may affect the form in which the evidence presented, the power and momentum of the presentation, the words chosen, or the degree of control exercised by the opposing lawyer. One or more of these factors may justify such objections. The potential advantage to be gained may seem marginal at the time. But even under these circumstances, successful use of objections can contribute to an overall edge with the factfinders.

A lawyer who has confidence in her ability to assert objections to her opponent's violations of the rules of evidence or procedure enjoys a feeling of power and control over the proceedings that is not felt by a lawyer who is inhibited or tentative about objecting. Conversely, a lawyer who is always in fear that her opponent may raise valid objections to her presentation may be subject to a feeling of insecurity that infects and undermines her whole presentation.

C.   Techniques for Making Objections

When a lawyer objects to a question seeking oral testimony or to tangible or visual evidence proffered by the other side, the lawyer's first task is to seize the attention of the court and stop further proceedings. Using whatever formula is accepted in the jurisdiction, the lawyer firmly and definitely makes it known that she has an objection:

"We object!"

"May it please the Court!"

"Objection!"

The objection is not phrased as a question but as a strong declaration. Counsel's voice does not trail off as she rises to announce her position. The tone of the objection must be firm and confident. The phrase ends on a downbeat.

In most jurisdictions the lawyer is expected to stand to make an objection. In fact, it has been said that to be an effective objector one must first train the muscles of the legs to stand up instinctively when something objectionable is sensed. On the way up comes the "Objection!" Once the lawyer is on her feet and has stopped the proceedings, presumably she will quickly think of the rationale for the objection. Usually, the pace of trial proceedings is such that if the lawyer tries to think of the reason for the objection before making it, it will be too late. The objection will be waived or made ineffective by the witness's answer.

Once having stood to make the objection, the lawyer should remain standing throughout any argument or colloquy on the objection and until the court has ruled. The objector has challenged the examiner. Sitting down before the ruling sends a message that the challenge is being withdrawn or abandoned.

Expressing the objection itself arrests the attention of the trial judge. Everything comes to a halt in the courtroom. The witness doesn't answer or stops her answer if he has started one.

Often counsel is tempted to lace the objection with indignation or sarcasm. The hope is that the factfinders will thereby better appreciate the degree to which the opponent is out of line and penalize him for it. Usually though, excessive indignation works against the objector. If it is not echoed by the tone and effect of the court's ruling it begins to appear hollow very quickly. Overplaying objections can very quickly undermine the personal credibility of the objecting lawyer and lead the factfinders to put very little weight on her presentation in general. Indignation and sarcasm should therefore be used very sparingly, if at all. Much more effective is a firm, professional objection. If it invokes some indignation from the judge who then directs it at the opponent, so much the better.

How to handle an objection once the objecting lawyer is on her feet must be attuned to the style of the judge who is being asked to make the ruling. Some judges will tend to sustain or overrule evidentiary objections without waiting for grounds to be stated by either side. Others will usually give the objector an opportunity to state the grounds for objection or even ask for the grounds before ruling.

> *Counsel.*   Objection!
>
> *The Court.*   The grounds, Counsel?
>
> *Counsel.*   Hearsay, Your Honor.

The trial lawyer needs to get a feeling for the style and tempo of the particular presiding judge and then tailor her objections accordingly. If the judge is likely to rule quickly without waiting for counsel to state the grounds or to ask for them, the lawyer might wish to blurt out the grounds along with the objection.

> *Counsel.*   Objection, Your Honor! That's hearsay.

On the other hand, if the judge is likely to ask for the grounds, the lawyer might prefer to wait for the judge to ask before asserting the grounds.

> *Counsel.*   We object!
>
> *The Court.*   The grounds?
>
> *Counsel.*   The question called for a conclusion of a lay witness, Your Honor.

Similar considerations apply to the lawyer whose question or evidence is objected to. Sometimes in order to be heard before the judge rules, the examiner must respond immediately to the objection.

> *Counsel.* Objection, Your Honor; hearsay.
>
> *Opposing Counsel.* Not for the truth of the matter, Your Honor — it goes to the defendant's state of mind.
>
> *The Court.* Objection overruled.

Sometimes the judge will proceed more deliberately and give each lawyer a separate opportunity to address the issue.

> *Counsel.* Objection, Your Honor!
>
> *The Court.* The basis for your objection, Counsel?
>
> *Counsel.* That is hearsay, Your Honor.
>
> *The Court* (to the other lawyer). What do you say to that, Counsel?
>
> *Opposing Counsel.* Your Honor, it is not being offered for its truth, it goes to the defendant's state of mind.
>
> *The Court.* Objection overruled. It may be admitted for the limited purpose of showing the defendant's state of mind at the time he heard the statement.

D.   Making Objections Under Difficult Circumstances

1. *Quick Rulings by the Judge*

Many trial judges feel under some pressure to keep the presentation moving. Usually this is because they feel that the lawyers are not moving it along quickly enough. A dynamic pace that keeps the factfinders and judge interested and engaged is very important to all trial presentations. Maintaining the right pace to retain interest and color while making a complete presentation of the relevant details is the responsibility of the lawyer in any trial. Sometimes the pace chosen to inform and educate the factfinders is slower than suits the judge. While the lawyer should be sensitive to the judge's reaction to the pace of the proceedings, it is a mistake to permit the judge to unduly hurry the lawyer. What may quickly appear clear to the judge may take some time and require some repetition for the factfinders to completely understand.

Judicial impatience or a particular judge's personal style can sometimes lead to overly hasty rulings on evidentiary and procedural objections. The lawyer might lose the skirmish before she has a chance to fight. If the point is at all important, the lawyer should not accept an adverse ruling without requesting an opportunity to be heard. Unless the grounds for the objection have been placed on the record at the time the objection is made, the trial court's ruling, whether "sustained" or "overruled," is likely to be immune from appeal.

Federal Rule of Evidence 103 provides that the overruling of a generalized objection without more preserves no issue for appeal. The same is true with general offers of proof that may be admissible for some limited purpose. Objections that are sustained to evidence that is admissible for some limited purpose cannot be attacked on appeal unless that limited purpose is made known to the court at the time of the objection. What is more, an objection that is sustained without either argument of counsel or an explanation from the court does not give the opponent much guidance on what was wrong with the question or the proof offered so that the infirmity can be cured.

The lawyer must keep in mind that she, not the judge, is responsible for the presentation. The judge enforces the rules by which the lawyer must work, but that is the limit of his role. The lawyer can and should insist on the right to be heard on evidentiary and procedural objections. Thus, if an objection is overruled before the lawyer has any opportunity to support it, she can very properly request a hearing.

    Counsel.   Objection!

    The Court.   Overruled.

    Counsel.   Your Honor, may we be heard?

The Court.   Go ahead, Counsel.

The lawyer's request to be heard is made immediately, in confident and firm tones. The lawyer expects that the court will accede to the request. When specifically asked, the judge will almost always hear counsel on an objection. The lawyer may be able to convince the judge that the earlier ruling should be modified. At least the point is preserved for appeal. If the court does not permit the lawyer to address the point when asked, the failure to point out the grounds for the objection will not be considered a waiver on appeal.

2.   *Offers of Proof*

When an objection is raised to the examiner's question or to the offer of some other kind of evidence, the lawyer seeking admission of the evidence must be ready to make an offer of proof. If the objection is sustained, unless the nature of the evidence is obvious from the circumstances under which it is offered, the proponent of the evidence must make a timely offer of proof in order to attack the ruling on appeal. [1] In many instances the trial judge has to know the nature of the evidence in order to make an informed ruling.

Q.   What did the children tell you when you found them upstairs?

Opposing Counsel.   Objection; hearsay.

Q.   Your Honor, may we approach the bench?

The Court.   Counsel will approach.

Q.   (at the bench). Your Honor, if permitted, the witness will testify that the children told them that the men in the street had called the children names and thrown a beer bottle at the house. This is being offered not for the truth of the matter, but to show the defendant's state of mind at the time of these events.

---

[1] Fed. R. Evid. 103 and its state counterparts.

> *Opposing Counsel.* Your Honor, may we have a limiting instruction?
>
> *The Court.* The objection is overruled. [to the jury:] Members of the jury, you are to consider the evidence that you are about to hear not for the truth of what was said, but for the effect of these statements on the defendant's state of mind at the time. [to the lawyers:] Please proceed, Counsel.

If the court has already ruled to exclude the evidence, the offer of proof must still be made at the earliest opportunity to preserve the point for appeal. Usually this is on the spot.

> Q. What did the children tell you when you found them upstairs?
>
> *Opposing Counsel.* Objection; hearsay.
>
> *The Court.* Sustained.
>
> Q. Your Honor, may we make an offer of proof?
>
> *The Court.* Counsel may approach.
>
> Q. (at the bench). Your Honor, if permitted, the witness would have testified that the children told them that the men in the street had called the children names and thrown a beer bottle at the house. This is not hearsay because it is offered not for the truth of the matter but to show the defendant's state of mind at the time of these events.

Sometimes the offer of proof may lead the judge to see things in a different light and reconsider his earlier exclusionary ruling.

> *The Court.* I see, Counsel. Well, for the limited purpose of showing the defendant's state of mind, I'll admit it. [to the other lawyer:] Do you want a limiting instruction?

Offers of proof can be made informally by the lawyer merely stating to the court what she expects the witness will say. In some instances it is necessary or advisable to make the offer of proof more formally, by having the testimony given for the record in the same question-and-answer form as it would have been given for the fact-finders. For such offers of proof the factfinders are excused and leave the courtroom, and the witness is then asked the questions to which the objection has been made. The answers are heard by the judge and recorded for the record on appeal. Sometimes, where the effect of the ruling is to exclude a witness's entire testimony, counsel will be allowed to make an offer of proof by submitting a written statement of what the witness would have said if allowed to testify.

> *The Court.*   After giving the arguments of counsel due con-
> sideration, the Court sustains the prosecution's objection
> to the testimony of Dr. Haven on the ground that such
> testimony would not be helpful to the factfinders as re-
> quired by Rule 702.
>
> *Q.*   Your Honor, may we submit an offer of proof in writing?
>
> *The Court.*   Counsel may submit an offer of proof in writing
> at any time before the evidence is closed.

Needless to say, counsel is bound by an obligation of good faith in making informal or written offers of proof. The offer of proof must fairly and accurately reflect what the testimony would have been had it been permitted. Misuse of informal offers of proof to "improve" excluded evidence for the sake of a better record on appeal is improper and unethical.

Offers of proof must be made outside the presence of the factfinders. Making an offer of proof at sidebar in a stage whisper that is audible to the factfinders is a serious ethical breach. In bench trials as well, the judge has the right to require that an offer of proof be made in writing if he believes there is a risk that it would taint his ability to decide the case on the evidence that was admitted.

3. *Objections Sustained Without Stated Reasons*

Almost every young lawyer has experienced a situation in which the opponent's objection was sustained without any grounds being stated by the objector or any reason being given by the court. Sometimes, with a moment's thought, the likely reason for the objection and ruling is obvious, but sometimes it is not.

If the lawyer has a particular argument that can support the question, she should ask to be heard and then make the argument.

> Q. Tell us, please, what the children told you when you first came home that night?
>
> *Opposing Counsel.* Objection!
>
> *The Court.* Sustained.
>
> Q. Your Honor, this is not being offered for the truth of the matter, but for the effect of the statement on the defendant's state of mind.
>
> *The Court.* For that limited purpose, then, it may be received.

If the lawyer does not understand the reason for the objection or for the judge's ruling, she may be in a quandary—how is she going to be able to cure the objection or rephrase the question if she does not know what was wrong with the first one? Again, the lawyer should not quit the field without trying to get the matter clarified. The obvious choice, merely asking the other lawyer for the reasons for his objection or asking the judge his reasons for the ruling, is not the best one. Court rules and etiquette usually bar colloquy directly between counsel. The judge is subject to no procedural rule that requires him to disclose to counsel the reasons for his evidentiary rulings. Moreover, by asking either the opposing lawyer or the court the reasons for an objection or ruling, the lawyer essentially surrenders control of the presentation in order to gain the necessary information.

On the other hand, if it is otherwise impossible to go forward, then one has no alternative. Maybe the judge will be kind:

> *Opposing Counsel.* Objection!
>
> *The Court.* Sustained.
>
> Q. Through the Court, would Counsel be willing to state the ground on which the objection was made?

Or

> Q.   Would the Court be so kind as to indicate the reasons for
> its ruling?

Sometimes it is better to risk the reply:

> *The Court.*   Counsel, if you can't see the reason for my rul-
> ing, then you shouldn't be practicing in this court.

rather than forgo some important piece of the evidentiary
presentation.

Another way to try to ferret out the problem is to repeat the
question or evidentiary proffer to which the objection was made.
Sometimes just repeating the question alone will make clear what
was wrong with it so the objection can be cured. And there is some
likelihood that the reason for the objection or ruling will come out
the second time around.

Where the objection is to a lack of foundation, it can often be
cured by starting at the beginning and repeating the complete
prepared foundation. Chances are that the lawyer merely forgot
to touch one of the bases required to establish the necessary
foundation.

4. *Objections During Opening Statement or Summation*

Objections to opposing counsel's presentation are less common
during opening statement or summation than during witness testimony. That does not mean that they should not be made where
necessary to enforce the rules and to prevent undue prejudice. The
most common ground for an objection during opening statement is
that the opening is being misused as an opportunity for argument.

> *Prosecution opening.*   And when he was taken back to that
> tree, Mr. Maxfield said, "You bastards got what you de-
> served." That will be the proof of his guilty intent. If Mr.
> Maxfield had not intended to kill Mr. Savage, who had just
> harassed and even assaulted him and his girlfriend, why
> would he have said, "You bastards got what you *deserved.*"?

> *Opposing Counsel.*   Objection. Your Honor, that's argument.

> *The Court.*   That is a little argumentative, Counsel. Would
> you please refrain from argument in the opening statement.
> You will have a chance for that in summation.

With inexperienced lawyers, a common ground for objection
during the opening is that the lawyer is expressing a personal
conviction or belief.

> *Counsel.*   Ladies and Gentlemen, when all is said and done,
> you will believe, as I do, that Mr. Maxfield is just not the
> kind of person who could possibly form the intent to kill or
> harm another human being.
>
> *Opposing Counsel.*   Objection. Personal belief of Counsel,
> Your Honor.

This objection can be dealt with from the floor. Counsel has
used terms of art rather than discussing the facts. If the objection
involves any discussion of the facts or inferences, or if it includes
any disparagement of the other lawyer, it must be made outside the
hearing of the jury.

> *The Court.*   Sustained. Members of the jury, Defense Coun-
> sel's personal belief in the guilt or innocence of his client
> has nothing to do with this case. You will disregard the last
> sentence of Defense Counsel's opening. [To the lawyer:]
> You may proceed.

Because interruptions in the tone and momentum of an opening
statement or summation can be serious distractions and can throw
the lawyer off stride, they should be made only when substantial
and necessary. It is a serious ethical breach to lodge a poorly founded
objection merely to break the spell of the opponent's presentation.

Objections in summation include some of those applicable
to opening statements. Misstatements of witness testimony and
appeals to emotion or prejudice are also common grounds for
objections.

> *Plaintiff's summation.*   And it is not over. Ladies and Gentle-
> men, you heard what Dr. Swallow said about Mr. Cluney's

future. As he gets older, he is going to have pain, traumatic arthritis, probably even a spinal fusion — all as the result of Mr. Borak's negligence in not stopping for that stop sign, or stopping and not looking . . .

Opposing Counsel.   Objection. May we approach . . .?

The Court.   Counsel approach sidebar.

Opposing Counsel.   Your Honor, that is a plain misstatement of the testimony! The Court will recall the rhubarb we had about even letting Dr. Swallow testify about future problems at all. All she said was that the plaintiff had a *possibility* of traumatic arthritis or spinal fusion, not that they would happen or even probably happen!

Plaintiff's Counsel.   Your Honor, based on all the facts and circumstances, I think the jury . . .

The Court.   Counsel, you think the jury nothing! There is no question that the doctor could only say these things were possibilities. Your argument goes too far.

Opposing Counsel.   Would the Court instruct the jury on that point, Your Honor?

The Court.   Members of the jury, you are instructed that you should disregard anything in that last portion of the plaintiff's counsel's argument that referred to any future consequences of this injury as anything other than possibilities. Dr. Swallow said that these future consequences "are possible"; she did not say that they would happen or that they are even probable.

E.   Objections and Control of the Presentation

1.   *Objections as Interruptions in the Fact Presentation*

An opponent's objections and the rulings on those objections can easily impair and disrupt a lawyer's control of the presentation she is making to the factfinders. The act of objecting is itself a disruption of the portrayal. Some lawyers abuse the objection process solely to break up the opponent's case or to rattle the lawyer. As discussed in Chapter 3, this is a misuse of the objection process and is ethically improper. It is important that the lawyer making a presentation maintain overall control over what is going on during the objection process. Objections should thus be treated for what they are — interruptions of the ongoing process. The examining lawyer ordinarily will seek to minimize the disruption and resume the presentation as soon as possible. In the process of image-building, continuity is important.

If the lawyer has been conducting the examination while standing, she should remain standing during the opposing lawyer's argument of the objection. Any response to the objection should be directed to the judge, not to the opposing counsel. Counsel should resist the temptation to show indignation or exasperation when an opponent objects. A lawyer's indignation brings factfinder condemnation of the indignant lawyer as often as it does for the object of the indignation. The objector should also resist the same temptation.

2. Bench Conferences on Objections

Frequent bench conferences to discuss evidentiary objections are damaging to the ongoing presentation. During the bench conference the attention of the factfinders wanders, whatever image is being formed blurs, and the tone and tension of the presentation are lost. The factfinders being left out and are distanced from what is going on. For these reasons the lawyer asking the questions will usually try to minimize bench conferences. Of course, where argument of the objection requires discussion of matters that the factfinders should not hear, they must be discussed outside the presence of the jury.

Sometimes bench conferences are unavoidable. The objecting party can request to be heard at the bench, and that request will be granted unless there is evidence that bench conferences are being unnecessarily invoked or abused.

Nonetheless, there is much that the examining lawyer can do to make sure that her presentation will not be disrupted by arguments of evidentiary objections outside the presence of the jury. First of all, if serious evidentiary issues are apprehended, they can sometimes be addressed in advance by requesting a ruling *in limine*. The Federal

Rules of Evidence specifically authorize resolution of evidence issues by preliminary advance rulings outside the presence of the
jury. [2] A motion *in limine* can be made either formally or informally,
in writing or orally, depending on the local procedural rules. The
idea is to argue the evidence point in advance so that the potentially
inadmissible material will not slip out before objection and so that
the trial will not be delayed by in-court argument.

Although many evidentiary issues can be resolved in advance, in
some cases the ruling, if not the motion itself, will be deferred until
the judge has a better idea of the context of the presentation in
which the evidence will be appearing.

> *The Court*   The Court will defer ruling on the defendant's
> motion *in limine* for the exclusion of Dr. Swallow's testi-
> mony on future complications and procedures until the
> time such evidence would be offered in the trial. In the
> meantime, though, counsel for the plaintiff will not refer to
> such evidence in opening statement or otherwise until the
> Court has had opportunity to give its ruling.

Less serious evidentiary issues can often be handled from the
courtroom floor without going to the bench and without improper
disclosure of inadmissible facts or improper argument. If the objection is couched solely in lawyers' words of art, the interruption to
the tone and pace of the proceedings will likely be minimized.

> *Q.*   Would you tell us, please, what the children told you
> when you got home that night?
>
> *Opposing Lawyer.*   Objection!
>
> *The Court.*   Yes, Counsel?
>
> *Opposing Lawyer.*   That's hearsay, your Honor.
>
> *Q.*   Your Honor, it is not being offered for the truth of the
> matter but solely for the effect on the defendant's state
> of mind.
>
> *The Court.*   Objection overruled.

[2] Fed. R. Evid. 104.

In the above example, the examining lawyer did not discuss the content of the evidence or argue its effect other than in the most cursory terms. The court was able to determine the admissibility of the evidence based on the shorthand objection and response without the need for extended colloquy at the bench. The objection was dealt with, and the show could go on.

3. Reasserting Control After a Ruling

If the objection is overruled, it is often appropriate for the examining lawyer to repeat the question. The witness will then be reminded of the exact question posed. The lawyer can re-establish the tone and pace by "rewinding" to the point where the presentation was interrupted, preventing an embarrassing silence while all of the participants seek to recall where they were before the objection or bench conference.

> Q. Now, Officer, what did Arthur Clark say about the speed of his car at the time of the accident?
>
> *Opposing Counsel.* Objection! May we be heard at the bench?
>
> *The Court.* Counsel will approach the bench.
>
> *Opposing Counsel.* Your Honor, that's hearsay!
>
> *Counsel.* Your Honor, if permitted to testify, Officer Anderson will state that Arthur Clark told him that they were going 50 miles per hour. That's in a 35-mile-per-hour zone. The parties have stipulated that Mr. Clark is "unavailable" within the meaning of Rule 804(a). We submit that the statement is a statement against interest that is admissible under Rule 804(b) (3).
>
> *The Court.* Objection overruled.
>
> Q. Now, Officer, would you please tell us what did Arthur Clark say about the speed of his car at the time of the accident?
>
> A. He said he was going 50.

On winning an objection, some lawyers will say to the court stenographer:

Q. Please read the last question back.

Such a request can be an unnecessary burden on the stenographer. More important, it surrenders the control of the presentation temporarily to the stenographer. This individual is likely to hunt through his notes for a while and then read back the lawyer's last question in a monotone that adds no interest to the question and no support to the witness. Moreover, when a lawyer asks the court stenographer to read back the lawyer's last question, it may convey the impression that the lawyer has forgotten her own question, that it was not important, or both. Finally, where the stenographer is actually a tape recorder, a playback of the last question may be technologically impossible.

A lawyer who can remember and repeat the last question, with the aid of notes if necessary, will be able to minimize the impact of objections far better than one who has to rely on the court reporter or a tape recorder to resume presentation. By reasserting control promptly and going on with the examination, the lawyer will maximize the wins and minimize the losses, and the pace will be maintained.

4. Thanking the Judge, and Other Cheap Shots

A lawyer who has won an objection should not thank the judge for a favorable ruling. Such a ploy may draw a rebuke if it appears to be an effort to magnify a win on an objection or create an impression of judicial approval. Sometimes the lawyer who has lost an objection will thank the judge in an effort to give the false impression that the ruling was somehow in her favor. This is clearly improper and will subject the lawyer to sanctions in most courtrooms.

The skirmishing that attends the handling of evidentiary and procedural objections offers many opportunities for abuse, as discussed in Chapter 3. Lawyers should shun these practices solely because they are "cheap shots" and are a misuse of the privilege of presenting cases in court. Moreover, a lawyer who indulges in these cheap shots loses her vital credibility with the judge and the factfinders, causing both the lawyer and her client to suffer the punishment.

F. Voir Dire on Objections

1. The Purpose of Voir Dire

In most cases, all of the facts necessary for the court to rule on an evidentiary objection are obvious by the time the question is asked or the proof is offered. In some cases, however, some fact important to determining the admissibility of the evidence at issue has not come out before the objection is lodged. Of course, if an objection is made and the examining lawyer becomes aware that there is something missing in the foundation, the lawyer can cure any ambiguity or lay any additional foundation merely by asking a few more foundation questions to adduce the necessary facts. However, if additional facts are necessary to support the objection rather than the admissibility of the evidence, the objector must obtain these necessary facts by a voir dire.

2. Technique for Voir Dire

A voir dire is, in effect, a limited-purpose cross-examination. It is not used to discredit the witness or the evidence generally. Typically, the questions on voir dire are very tight and controlled leading questions that usually call for affirmance. The idea is to extract the single or few facts necessary to support the objection without giving the witness room to enhance or expand on his testimony.

> Q. Ms. Mercer, how fast was that car going as it came down Jackson Street?
>
> *Opposing Counsel.* Objection! Your Honor, may we have a brief voir dire?
>
> *The Court.* Yes, you may.
>
> Q. (by opposing counsel on voir dire). Ms. Mercer, you have never had any training in estimating the speed of automobiles, have you?

A. No, not other than driver's ed when I got my license.

Q. You were sitting in your chair in front of your TV, weren't you?

A. That's right.

Q. All you could see of this car was its headlights, wasn't it?

A. That's right.

Q. And you only saw it for a very short time as it went by your house — isn't that right?

A. Yes, that's right.

Q. Your Honor, it is clear that there is no foundation for an estimate by this witness of the speed of the defendant's automobile. Under the circumstances of this case any estimate would be a pure guess.

The Court. The Court is inclined to agree. [To the direct examiner:] Do you want to try to lay additional foundation?

Q. We will withdraw the question, Your Honor.

Opposing Counsel. Thank you, Your Honor.

The Court. Counsel, my rulings are based on the rules of evidence as I understand them. They are not given as personal favors. Please do not thank me for my rulings.

One of the most common uses of voir dire is the challenge to the credentials of an expert witness when he is asked an opinion question. A discussion of such voir dire can be found in Chapter 12. Voir dire is also frequently used to challenge the evidentiary foundation to a document or other exhibit. See Chapter 11.

3. Abuse of Voir Dire

Voir dire can be subject to abuse. Sometimes, faced with a long wait before starting cross-examination, opposing counsel may be concerned that the factfinders may get a particularly firm impression that may be difficult to shake when cross-examination comes around. Counsel may be tempted to use voir dire to "get a few licks in" at a proffered exhibit or bit of testimony before the factfinders' impression about the evidence has a chance to jell. If the additional facts go only to the weight or credibility of the evidence and not its admissibility, these facts should not be raised on voir dire, but instead saved for cross-examination. When a lawyer requests the opportunity to conduct a voir dire, she implicitly represents to the court that she has a good-faith belief that she can develop facts that will be relevant to the court's determination of the admissibility of the evidence. Using voir dire to conduct an advance cross-examination is a misuse of the privilege and a breach of lawyer's ethics. This and other ethical considerations of objections are addressed in Chapter 3 above.

Chapter 10 Illustrative Aids

A. Visual Media at Trial

"Make it visual!" — A word to the wise, for almost any kind of presentation, from teaching in the classroom to trying cases in court. The traditional nostalgia that trial advocacy is an oral tradition, dominated by the great wordsmiths and dramatic orators, is no longer valid in the courtroom of today, if it ever was. Successful, accurate, and authoritative presentation of information requires the vigorous use of visual media.

1. The Limitations of Oral Communication

In daily life, the great bulk of information concerning what is going on in our environment comes to us through our eyes. Direct visual images are perceived and transmitted to the brain. Most visual information is observed directly as it happens or in live photographic image, such as on television. Other information is obtained through observing more or less literal representations, such as drawings, cartoons, and the like. Much is learned by reading text, charts, and other symbolic representations. The massive volume of information that we absorb through visual observation dwarfs the quantum of information that comes to us through our ears.

Voice, language, and memory are convenient tools for transmitting limited amounts of information. But in court oral communication alone, whether by lawyer or by witness, is woefully insufficient for the transmission of larger volumes of even moderately complex data.

First of all, oral communication is linear. One word must follow another out of the mouth of the speaker and into the ears of the listener. This means that only one coded bit of information can be transmitted and absorbed at a time. People speak far too slowly to move much information to each other by spoken words.

Second, the words themselves are not images, but have to be translated into images through associations within the listeners' consciousness. This process takes time. There is likely to be some uncertainty in the association of particular words with particular images. People's vocabularies are not all the same. A single misunderstood word can undermine the process of comprehension of an entire idea or sequence of action.

Third, people's ability to absorb and remember orally communicated information is limited. Only a certain amount can be accommodated before the teacup of ready recall overflows, and the overflow may be lost.

If lawyers were limited to oral communication alone in their presentation at trial, it would be literally impossible to develop complex cases, and the presentation of simple ones would be a long and laborious process for all concerned.

2.   *The Power of Visual Media*

A visually communicated image is transmitted directly and immediately via the eyes to the brain, where it remains as a visual image. Information can be extracted from the visual image and translated into verbal communication if needed in that form. But the visual reception of information is infinitely faster, more efficient, and more accurate than by ear.

A person attempting to describe through words alone even the simplest layout of streets, driveways, and buildings may take a considerable time to produce differing images in the minds of a group of listeners. A simple drawing on the blackboard immediately transmits the same image to all.

As the complexity of trial subject matter grows, the importance of visual media to teach and explain generally increases. Diagrams, models, computer simulations, and similar visual media are increasingly used by lawyers to recreate images of complex or unusual materials in the consciousness of untutored lay jurors.

Even where words remain the primary means of communication,

visual displays of the words enhance comprehension and retention of the verbal message. People usually read more rapidly than they speak. Salespeople presenting their pitches by means of flip charts and whiteboards have long used visual depictions of key words to make those words stick with their customers. Teachers have found that writing selected words on the blackboard as they are discussed in class increases student learning of even the most abstract material. Eyes and ears together absorb more than either can alone.

As our knowledge of the communications process increases, the use of visual media in the trial process can do nothing but grow.

B.   Exhibits in Evidence Versus Illustrative Aids to Testimony

Objects used in trial presentations can be grouped into two conceptual classes. One class, which is referred to here as "exhibits in evidence," or "exhibits" for short, includes objects that directly convey relevant information from and of themselves. For example, a weapon used in an alleged criminal assault, a photograph of the scene of an accident, or a business record of a purchase-and-sale transaction all directly teach the factfinders by virtue of their own authority. The factfinders make their inferences directly from the object itself.

The other class, often referred to as illustrative aids, or "chalks," comprises various forms of visual representation of a witness's recollection or testimony. Diagrams of streets used by witnesses to illustrate how an accident took place, charts and graphs used by expert witnesses to make their points, computer simulations used to chart the paths of crashing planes or gas explosions — all are forms of visual embodiment of witness testimony, whether a recollection of facts or an expert opinion. These illustrative aids do not themselves provide the bases for inferences; they merely assist in transmitting or communicating information from the witnesses who are their sources. It is the witness's testimony or opinion, communicated visually or verbally, that is to form the bases of the inferences and determinations by the factfinders.

Generally, exhibits that carry their own factual message must satisfy certain tests of authenticity, relevance, and reliability to be admitted in evidence. Once in evidence, they are ingredients of the fact picture and can be relied on directly by the factfinder. On the other hand, illustrative aids need not be admissible in evidence to be used during a trial presentation by counsel or witness. Authenticity is not an issue. The sole function of the aids is to illustrate or convey the testimony of the witnesses or to demonstrate a point made by counsel in argument. The only concern in using aids is whether the media used may unfairly distort the message to be conveyed.

As will be discussed in Chapter 11, different kinds of exhibits have different kinds of evidentiary significance and require different foundation showings to be admitted in evidence and used at trial. Exhibits in evidence are usually sent to the jury room for use by the jury duing deliberations. An exhibit can be cited as the basis for a factual assertion or finding.

Under most circumstances, however, objects used solely as illustrative aids are not sent to the jury room, but rather are used only in the courtroom during testimony or during counsel's opening or argument. That is not to say that counsel may not agree that a particular illustrative aid can be sent with the jury to assist in the deliberations. But, in the absence of agreement or some special circumstance, the traditional view is that visual representations of witness testimony or argument are not evidence in and of themselves.

It should be stated that the conceptual distinctions between exhibits and illustrative aids are not observed by every court. In some jurisdictions, material used by a witness to illustrate his testimony will be offered in evidence as a "demonstrative exhibit" or as "demonstrative evidence." In some jurisdictions, illustrative aids go with the jury during their deliberations unless there is some reason to withhold them. And, as is discussed in greater detail below, sometimes an exhibit, such as a photograph, which has probative force of its own, will be used by a witness as an illustrative aid during testimony. In these matters, as in many others, the lawyer must learn and follow the local rules and customs.

C.   Laying the Foundation for Use of Illustrative Aids

The foundation required for use of a diagram or other visual aid to illustrate witness testimony is a simple one. The lawyer proposing to use an aid with a witness need merely show that its use will be of assistance in presenting the witness's testimony.

Q. Would the use of this blackboard [diagram, model] help you to illustrate your testimony for the jury?

A. Yes, it would.

Q. With the aid of the blackboard, would you please show the jury where you were when you first heard a noise?

Although customary procedures may vary from jurisdiction to jurisdiction, logically there is no requirement that the witness testify that the illustrative aid "accurately depicts" anything in particular. The issue of distortion is usually left to the opposing party. If the potential is so great that the danger of unfair prejudice would outweigh the value of the illustrative aid to visualize the idea being testified to, the other party can object. The opposing lawyer may request a voir dire to establish the distortion for the court before the damage is done by exposing the illustrative aid to the factfinders.

For most of the incidental distortions found in everyday illustrative aids, cross-examination enables the opposing party to point out the limitations of the media as related to the circumstances of the case.

Q. Ms. Mercer, the diagram that you have just used during your direct examination is not to scale, is it?

A. That's right.

Q. If the diagram were to scale, Jackson Street would be much wider than it appears on the diagram you used?

A. Yes.

Of course, in the simplest kind of situation, where the witness draws on a clean blackboard, there is no preexisting diagram to assess for distortion. As the witness draws the pertinent features, the opposing lawyer must be alert for any distortion the witness creates, whether intentionally or as a result of poor drafting.

Illustrative aids can also come in very elaborate forms, including color computer or laser disk simulations, detailed models, and sophisticated graphics. Sometimes aids that are proffered ostensibly to illustrate a witness's testimony may carry substantial persuasive force in their own right. It is easy for a factfinder to appreciate that a blackboard drawing is not entitled to any more credence than the testimony of the person who drew it. It may not be so easy to keep in mind that an impressive computer simulation is also no more credible than the person who programmed the computer.

The possible unfair prejudice caused by the use of sophisticated illustrative aids can be both subtle and profound. Fairness demands that counsel who propose to use such materials for illustrative purposes show them to opposing counsel sufficiently in advance of use so as to afford a reasonable opportunity to inspect the aids and to object if warranted.

D. Choice of Illustrative Aids

Part of the trial lawyer's job in preparing the case is to choose the most effective available media for the trial presentation. Certain kinds of images lend themselves to visual expression more readily than others. For instance, testimony about any kind of location or scene involving spatial relationships is almost always best presented graphically. Relationships such as directions, distances, and relative positions are very hard to express verbally with any degree of accuracy. No matter how completely and carefully presented, a verbal description of even the simplest scene will produce twelve different images in the consciousnesses of twelve factfinders. A diagram or other depiction presents the material instantly and accurately so that all who see the image will have the same understanding.

Other kinds of fact material, such as abstractions or states of mind, are usually expressed verbally. Modern techniques, however, have expanded the role of graphics in communicating many kinds of information that were traditionally imparted by words alone. For example, it is now common to use survey techniques and graphics to permit vivid presentation of sociological, economic, and demographic comparisons. Diagrams are used to analyze cause and effect, relative merits, and decisions of authority and responsibility. All of these new and evolving forms of graphic communications are potential resources for a case in court.

Some kinds of information can best be shown by dynamic graphic depiction such as is now available through computer simulations. Computer programming can not only generate a graphic image but can make that image move. As long as the witness is able to testify that what is on the video screen is illustrative of his testimony, even this powerful medium may be used in court as an illustrative aid.

E. Dangers and Risks of Illustrative Aids

The use of illustrative aids carries with it the risk that the undeniable power of visual media might be abused in the form of extraneous or intended distortions by the media itself. For instance, even a hand-drawn diagram may engender inferences not supported by the witness's testimony. With any diagram, there is a strong human tendency to draw conclusions based on the positioning of the objects depicted. Yet such conclusions may be spurious if the diagram is not to scale.

Paradoxically, the cruder the diagram, the less likely the risk of prejudicial inferences. The crudeness of the rendition reminds the factfinder that the diagram has no greater dignity than the testimony of the witness who drew it. A more sophisticated diagram, particularly one that looks like an engineering drawing, might increase the tendency of the factfinder subconsciously to rely on the visual scale of the drawing. If the drawing is not true to scale, however, the distortion may result in unfair prejudice by virtue of these subliminal inferences.

By the same token, a computerized reenactment appearing on screen may carry considerably greater persuasive authority than is justified by the testimony and assumptions on which the reenactment is based. For some reason, many people accord a particular measure of credence and respect to things they see on television. The slickness of the medium contributes unwonted authority to a witness's message in the courtroom. It's hard to remember "garbage in, garbage out" if one is awed by the ostensible accuracy of the video playback.

Sometimes illustrative aids may be designed to appeal to the factfinders' emotional or subconscious processes. Colors or symbolic patterns may carry implicit and powerful psychological messages that are wholly different from the ostensible purpose for which the aid is used.

For these reasons, in the development and use of illustrative aids, the lawyer should be cautious about overstepping the legitimate purpose for which they are permitted. And the lawyer faced with a sophisticated multi-media presentation by her opponent must be alert to spot and be able to articulate to the court the potential prejudicial inferences created by the illustrative media used.

Although the Federal Rules of Evidence do not specifically address the in-court use of illustrative aids that are not themselves admitted in evidence, it is generally agreed that the inherent power of the trial court to preserve the fairness of the proceedings extends to restricting the use of media in order to avoid the danger of unfair prejudice from potential extraneous inferences.

> Q.   Doctor Hughes, do you have a video computer simulation that will help illustrate your testimony for the jury?
>
> A.   Yes, this computer video simulation simulates the movements of the two vehicles in the crash as they approached the intersection.
>
> *Opposing Counsel.*   Objection. May we be heard at sidebar, Your Honor?
>
> *The Court.*   Counsel will approach sidebar.
>
> *Opposing Counsel* (at sidebar).   Your Honor, that video recreation is based on a number of assumptions, such as a constant speed of both vehicles, uniform reaction times of the drivers, standardized factors for friction of tires on pavement, an assumed path of both cars, and assumed speeds of both vehicles. Variance of any of these assumptions would make things entirely different.
>
>   The video gives an artificial sense of exactitude to something that is really based on a number of shaky assumptions. It does not contribute anything except an impressive graphic depiction of the plaintiff's theory of the case.
>
> Q.   Your Honor, there is some evidence to back up each one of those assumptions. It is helpful to the jury to understand the expert's testimony.
>
> *The Court.*   The Court is inclined to agree that the video does not add much to the expert's testimony but may give

an artificial sense of certainty to something that is a far from certain accident reconstruction. Objection sustained.

The factors a trial judge will likely consider in ruling on objections to the use of illustrative aids are set forth in the Federal Rules of Evidence. [1] These include the danger of unfair prejudice, confusion of the issues, misleading the jury, the likelihood of undue delay, waste of time, or needless presentation of cumulative evidence.

Overall fairness and thoughtful application of these Rule 403 considerations by the trial judge favors the early disclosure of illustrative aids. This gives opposing counsel a reasonable opportunity to review them and analyze their impact, both direct and incidental, before they are produced during the trial. Any appropriate objections can be raised and then ruled on. If a complex illustrative aid is not disclosed to the opposing lawyer until it is to be used at trial, there is a risk that the court will not want the trial to be delayed while opposing counsel studies the aid. The simple solution for the judge is to exclude use of the illustrative aid and let the trial proceed.

On the other hand, the form of the lawyer's presentation, as opposed to its content, traditionally has been viewed as a kind of work product and immune from pretrial discovery. For example, the precise form of a non-expert witness's testimony is generally not discoverable, although the identity of persons having knowledge of the facts at issue and the scope of their knowledge is. Pretrial disclosure of illustrative media would give the other side advance notice of the lawyer's work product and would enable the opponent to challenge the lawyer's presentation more effectively. In addition, there is some reluctance to extending and enlarging the scope of discovery right up to and including pretrial preparation. At present, this issue is resolved on an ad hoc basis, either when the aid is produced or in a pretrial or scheduling order by the court.

In the absence of a formal rule, the trial lawyer is well advised to make disclosure of any potentially controversial illustrative material far enough in advance to permit reasonable time for objection. Counsel should not be expected to reveal illustrative media so far in advance as to unveil the pretrial preparation process, however.

[1] Fed. R. Evid. 403

When and what to disclose should depend on the complexity and importance of the illustrative aid. Relatively simple items, such as diagrams and charts, should be disclosed only a brief time before their use. Little time is required to understand and appreciate the significance of such simple and conventional media. On the other hand, complex aids, such as computer simulations or more elaborate drawings, charts, and graphs, should be disclosed well in advance so as to permit the opposing lawyer the opportunity to investigate the computer program generating the aid, the source of the graphs or charts, or the accuracy of the elaborate model. Advance disclosure of potentially controversial material will also give the proponent of the aid more time to regroup and reorganize the presentation if the court rules that the aid should not be used at the trial.

Finally, it should be noted that the trial judge's rulings on the use of illustrative aids in presenting witness testimony are very unlikely to be overturned on appeal. Only in an egregious case would an appellate court second-guess the trial court's discretion in either allowing or not allowing the use of illustrative aids during the trial presentation.

F. Techniques in Using Illustrative Aids

1. *The Witness as Teacher*

An effective direct examination makes the witness into a teacher. The witness explains the features of the desired image to the factfinders. From their earliest days of formal education, most people have developed habits of receiving information from teacher figures. The presentation of witness testimony in this manner takes advantage of these habits and patterns of learning as subconsciously retained by the factfinders.

The use of illustrative aids enhances the opportunity to work from these old teacher-student patterns and relationships. Teachers using a blackboard or other educational aids are associated in the minds of most people with learning and understanding the truth. The presentation of the witness with the illustrative aid should be managed so as to project the image as effectively as possible and at the same time take advantage of the teacher-student pattern of information transmittal. If the witness uses the aid like a teacher would, the likelihood of the factfinders' acceptance of the image is increased.

2. Positioning the Illustrative Aid

An illustrative aid should be positioned so that the factfinders can see it from about the same orientation and with about the same ease as students in the first few rows of a classroom can see the blackboard or other displays by the teacher at the front of the room. Where possible, the aid should be set up right in front of the factfinders in an open area in the courtroom.

When illustrative aids are used with witness testimony, the lawyer will want to give the witness who is teaching with the aid as much prominence as possible. This means that the lawyer should step back and align herself with the factfinders facing the "teacher" at the illustrative aid. The lawyer should ask the witness something like

> Q. With the assistance of the chart, Ms. Mercer, would you please show us where you were on the night of October 10th at about 9:00 P.M.?

If the lawyer positions herself near the factfinders during the illustrated presentation, the witness, responding to the cues of the lawyer, will tend to focus the presentation toward the factfinders. By the same token, the lawyer will be able to see whether the presentation is reaching the factfinders, whether the drawings are large and clear enough, whether the witness is speaking out and can be heard, and whether the overall effect is as intended.

The lawyer must resist the tendency to become drawn to the illustrative aid. It can have a magnet effect on the attention of everyone in the courtroom, so the examining lawyer may be tempted to go up to the illustrative aid while the witness is using it in his testimony. But if the lawyer goes up to the aid and questions the witness from there, the image of the witness as teacher is destroyed. The flow of energy from the witness to the factfinders is reduced. The factfinders may be left out of a two-way conversation between the lawyer and the witness with the illustrative aid between the two.

The witness's presentation becomes focused on the lawyer instead of on the factfinders, who are further away. The impact of the presentation is diminished, and the lawyer is no longer able to determine whether or what the factfinders can see and hear. In the worst case, the lawyer or witness might even block the factfinders' view of the aid. All of these undesirable developments can be avoided if the lawyer disciplines herself to manage the presentation from the vantage point of the factfinders.

3. Using Illustrative Aids on Direct Examination

Because it is the witness, rather than the illustrative aid, who provides the evidence, the examination should be structured and conducted to make it clear that it is the witness's *testimony* that is being presented, as illustrated by the aid, rather than the information that the illustrative aid provides. Thus the form of questions should be something like

> Q. Ms. Mercer, using the diagram to illustrate your testimony, could you please show us where on Jackson Street you live?
>
> A. (indicating). Here, where it says 28.

rather than

> Q. Now, will you tell us what is depicted on the illustrative aid?
>
> A. It shows my house and some of the other houses on Jackson Street.
>
> Q. Where on the diagram is your house?
>
> A. Here.

Since the illustrative aid is not evidence itself, the examination should not be posed as if the information is coming from that source. If the witness's testimony is formulated in terms of pointing out features shown on a chart or map that has not been admitted in evidence, the information derived from the chart is considered inadmissible hearsay. The form of the questions should make it clear that the information being elicited comes from the witness, not from the aid and that the aid is being used merely to make visual what the witness is conveying.

The use of illustrative aids does not in any way affect the need to comply with the rule against leading questions and the overall policy of giving the witness maximum exposure. Open questions that cue the witness to use the aid in his answer comply with the rules of evidence and guide the witness in using the visual media. For example, questions such as

> Q. Would you show us where you were when you first saw the two men?

or

> Q. Using the illustrative aid, please show us which way you went when you left the driveway.

are proper questions on direct examination. Questions such as

> Q. (lawyer indicating on the diagram). When you first saw the two men, were you here?

or

> Q. (lawyer indicating on the diagram). Is this the way you went when you left the driveway?

are improper leading questions.

The lawyer's pointing to a feature on a visual aid provides information to the jury visually just as a classic leading question does in words. This kind of question accompanied by pointing to the aid is objectionable as leading.

> Opposing Counsel. Objection! Counsel's pointing on the diagram is leading the witness.

> The Court. Sustained. Counsel, please let the witness do the pointing.

The use of an illustrative aid on direct examination enables the witness to magnify the impact of his testimony. The lawyer's role as guide and facilitator is vital to the success of an illustrated presentation.

G.   Illustrative Aids and the Trial Record

In planning the use of illustrative aids and in carrying out the examination, the lawyer must keep in mind the need to provide an intelligible verbal record of the significant references to the aid for purposes of a possible appeal. If important information is conveyed by the illustrative aid, it should be marked or otherwise identified for the sake of the appellate record.

A blackboard is very commonly used in trial presentations. When a crucial fact is presented on the blackboard, counsel may have difficulty in preserving the information for the record. Sometimes counsel will have to photograph a marked-up blackboard to preserve the necessary information for the appellate court. For this reason, it is sometimes easier and safer to use a large white drawing pad: the pages can be marked, identified on the record, and preserved for possible use on appeal.

It is also important to make sure that references to the illustrative aid appear in the trial transcript. For instance, if a witness testifying with a diagram is asked the question,

Q.   Where were the two men when you first saw them?

and the answer is simply

A. (indicating an unmarked spot on the diagram). Here.

someone reading the transcript later will not be able to recapture that portion of the witness's testimony even with the aid of a replica of the diagram. If the information is important, the "Here" with the witness indicating has to be memorialized for later reference.

Sometimes the illustrative aid provides sufficient identification of what is being referred to. For example, if the witness's answer to the question

> Q. Using the diagram on the easel, would you show us where you live?

is

> A. Here, where it says "28,"

a person reading the transcript can glance at the diagram, find the box on the diagram marked "28," and understand what the witness was pointing at during the testimony.

The identification need not be so explicit:

> Q. Are there any trees near your home?
>
> A. Yes, here at this bushy spot in front of my house.

If one looks at the diagram and sees a "bushy spot" between the box identified as number 28 and the line marking the edge of the street, one can infer that the bushy spot is what the witness was referring to.

Where the witness's testimony does not clearly refer to a recognizable feature on the aid, the lawyer should be prepared to provide the reference.

> Q. Sir, is there any vegetation near your house?
>
> A. Yes, right here there is a tree.
>
> Q. And by "right here" are you indicating on the diagram a bushy spot between your house, number 28, and the edge of Jackson Street?
>
> A. That's right.

Although the question used to establish the reference is technically a leading question, it is permissible for this purpose. Such a question, however, must merely identify the point indicated by the witness and must not add additional information.

> Q. And are you indicating a large bushy maple tree at the bushy spot on the diagram between your house and Jackson Street?

is a leading question because it not only identifies the spot indicated by the witness, it adds the extra information "large bushy maple tree."

It is also permissible for the lawyer to have the witness's indications on a diagram recorded by other means. If there is no mark where the witness is pointing, the witness can be asked to place a mark at the indicated spot.

> Q. Would you please place a "T" where you are indicating the tree in front of your house on the diagram?

A self-identifying mark such as "T" for a tree makes it easier for someone reading the record or referring to the aid to understand what the witness has said. The "T" is more readily associated with the image of a tree than is a letter such as "A" or "B" used arbitrarily. A small picture or icon of a tree is better yet.

It should be kept in mind that an illustrative aid may be referred to again and again during the course of a trial. The more unambiguous the information shown initially on the illustrative aid or added by the witnesses, the more useful it will be. In planning the use of an illustrative aid the lawyer should determine in advance what information should be on the aid at the start and what should be added by each witness during the trial. Unless one is selective about adding markings, it is possible that a diagram will become so marked up during the trial as to become useless by the time the lawyer is ready to argue to the jury.

One commonly used oral device by which counsel can identify points on an illustrative aid is the directive "let the record reflect":

> Q. Will you show us please, Ms. Mercer, where the two men were when you first saw them outside your window?
>
> A. (indicating). Right here.
>
> Q. Let the record reflect that the witness is indicating a point on the diagram directly below the box marked 28 and midway between the two lines designating the edges of Jackson Street.

The lawyer's statement describing the witness's indicating should be accurate and should not add any facts beyond an accurate description of what the witness was doing with the illustrative aid.

This formulation, however, has the drawback of the lawyer having to conspicuously interrupt the witness's teaching. Doing this also injects a note of artificiality with the reference to "the record." Usually the leading question is a smoother and less obtrusive way in which the record annotation can be accomplished.

In planning a presentation with diagrams and other aids, the lawyer has to decide which marks and indications need to be identified on the record. Usually it depends on how important the mark or indicated feature is to the overall presentation. There is likely to be some temptation to record as much as possible. This temptation should be resisted. The persuasive power of a diagram can be compromised by too many identifying marks and icons. The power of the presentation can be greatly reduced by interruptions to document witness indications on illustrative aids. For the lawyer, it is a question of planning and judgment. The important points ordinarily should be recorded by unambiguous marks on the diagram itself so that they can be referred to later on in the trial and are easily available on appeal. Unimportant indications can be recorded by a simple verbal reference or not at all.

H.   Using Illustrative Aids
on Cross-Examination

All of the factors that militate in favor of the use of illustrative aids on direct examination apply equally to cross. However, on cross-examination, it is the lawyer, not the witness, who is the teacher with the illustrative aid. Thus, as a matter of courtroom dynamics, the roles are reversed. The lawyer approaches the illustrative aid and positions it so that she can conveniently use it to "teach" the jury. The witness is left on the witness stand in a position where he can see the aid and be expected to acknowledge the lawyer's questions. And the questions are leading.

Nor is the cross-examiner limited to the illustrative aids that have been used on direct. Subject to applicable rules restricting subject matter of cross-examination to that covered in direct,[2] a lawyer on cross-examination can devise and use whatever illustrative aids will

---

[2] See Fed. R. Evid. 611(b).

most effectively depict the points to be made and acknowledged by
the witness.

One purpose of cross-examination is to attack potential inferences from the aid arising out of the direct examination:

Q. Now, this diagram that you used on direct is not to scale,
    is it?

A. That's right.

Q. You can't say that the relationships of these streets and
    houses really are as they are in the diagram, can you?

A. That's right.

Q. That's true of the angles and distances as well, isn't it?

A. That's right.

Q. The angles and distances are not necessarily accurate, are
    they?

A. That's right.

Q. And where you have placed these marks on the aid, these
    are only approximations, aren't they?

A. That's right.

Q. And so, for instance, this mark in the middle of the street
    could be a little bit to either side, isn't that right?

A. Yes.

Q. That's because the diagram isn't that accurate.

A. Right.

The lawyer may want to add features to the illustrative aid
necessary to qualify her opponent's presentation or to contribute
to her own picture.

Q. Now, taking this diagram you used on direct, there
    is a street light in front of 33½ Jackson Street, isn't
    there?

A. Yes.

Q.   That would be right here on the diagram, wouldn't it?

A.   Yes.

Q.   And the place that I have marked "S" is where the street light is, right?

A.   Yes.

As with any kind of cross-examination, there is no point in using the illustrative aid to "go over the direct." Sometimes the magnet effect of an interesting visual aid lures the cross-examiner into giving it even more exposure during the cross-examination. The utility of an illustrative aid on cross-examination is to enable the cross-examiner to make visual points with great power and precision. But those points must either detract from the opponent's picture or enhance the image being developed by the cross-examiner. If the cross-examiner is not able to make any such points, the illustrative aid should be removed so that it does not act as a reminder of the direct and as a distraction to the factfinders.

The cross-examiner must also be mindful of the need for a clear appellate record, meaning that she must make sure that any important indications on the diagram are recorded in some manner.

Q.   The man in the denim jacket was here [indicating] when you saw him begin to fall, wasn't he?

A.   Yes.

Q.   The place where I have marked "F" is where he began to fall, isn't it?

A.   Yes.

or

Q.   And when I say "here," I am indicating a spot between the tree in front of number 37 and what is shown as a front porch there? Is that right?

A.   Yes.

I.   Ownership and Control of Illustrative Aids

Illustrative aids are usually treated as the property of the party who prepares and uses them. At the same time, fairness dictates that if a party has used an illustrative aid during the direct or cross-examination of a witness, the aid should be made available to the opposing party for use in cross-examination or redirect.

The blackboard in the courtroom is usually treated as a facility available to both parties. Either party can mark on it and mark over the other's markings. If a party wishes to preserve something on the blackboard, special arrangements need to be made with the court. Usually, if the blackboard is an important element in a witness presentation, it will be photographed for the record on appeal.

Blackboard markings are highly impermanent. Because neither party has exclusive control over any image in this medium, most lawyers use other media for important visual presentations and use the blackboard for only the most informal depictions.

In planning a presentation with an illustrative aid, one must consider the possibility that the other party may seek to add other features to the aid during cross-examination. An elaborately prepared diagram can be seriously compromised by markings placed on it by the opposing lawyer while cross-examining a witness who has used the aid in her direct presentation. If an illustrative aid is used effectively on direct, however, the cross-examiner ought to be able to use the aid on cross.

How many and what kinds of markings can be made on an opponent's illustrative aid during later examination is left to the sound discretion of the court. It is difficult to set forth any principle on which this discretion is usually exercised. At the present state of the law, the practices of trial judges vary widely. Rulings refereeing the use of illustrative aids are almost never issues on appeal. Under these circumstances, both the proponent of an illustrative aid and the opponent should plan to use the aid effectively during cross-examination. If the proponent of a diagram is concerned that the opponent may add distracting marks during cross-examination, the proponent can provide a mylar overlay so that marks can be made without defacing the original. The marked-up overlay can be removed when the original is being used during the course of later witness testimony or argument.

Likewise, the lawyer who expects to mark on her opponent's aid should also provide her own protective overlay. If there is an objection to the proposed marking, the mylar can be clipped on to the illustrative aid so that unrestrained marking can proceed.

Marking of an illustrative aid with the intent to do nothing but destroy the utility of the opponent's image is an unprofessional abuse of the lawyer's prerogatives.

J.   Use of Aids in Opening Statement and Final Argument

The use of illustrative aids is not limited to making the testimony of witnesses into visual images. In opening statement, the lawyer describes to the factfinders the picture to be recreated by her trial presentation. In many cases the use of illustrative aids can make this introductory portrayal even more exact and powerful.

The same is true of final arguments. A simple diagram that is pre-prepared or even drawn during the opening or closing makes the lawyer into a teacher. A lawyer arguing her case from the blackboard acquires at least some of the remembered credibility of the teachers of the factfinders' student days. The lesson comes to life before their eyes.

By definition the illustrative aid is not evidentiary. Its purpose is to make visual what the lawyer is telling the factfinders in the opening or summation.

K.   Thematic Use of Illustrative Aids

Illustrative aids should be considered, planned, and created in the context of the whole case, not just the testimony of a single witness. The task of the trial lawyer is to create a single image of the event or circumstance in the consciousness of the factfinders. This goal is fostered by the use of coordinated aids that can be used not only in testimony (sometimes of several witnesses) but also in opening and closing.

A powerful presentation can be built around a single important illustrative aid that embodies the theory of the case. This aid, diagram, model, graph, or chart can reappear thematically at various points during the presentation. Typically, the lawyer will use the crucial aid in the opening as showing the picture that will be presented. The aid will reappear during the direct examination of the proponent's witnesses and be used by them to teach the image to the jury. In appropriate cases the aid can be used again during the cross-examination of the opponent's witnesses. The illustrative aid thus builds the proponent's case with the assistance and support of the opponent's testimonial resources.

Finally, the illustrative aid becomes a powerful tool in summation. By that time it is familiar to the factfinders. Its frequent appearances and use by different participants has reinforced its authority and reliability in the eyes of the factfinders. It has created a visual theory of the case.

L. Views

Often when a case involves a particular physical location, at some point in the trial the factfinders will be "taken for a view." For instance, in condemnation cases, for an assessment of damages when property is taken for public use, it is common for the factfinders to go look at the property being taken. A view might also be taken of the scene of a crime or an accident.

1. Purpose and Use of Views

As is the case with opening statements, it has often been said that views are not evidence but rather are taken to assist the factfinders in understanding the evidence. A view is often taken at the outset of the trial in order to give the jury a visual context in which to hear the evidence and to avoid disrupting the trial once the taking of evidence gets underway. To a large extent, thinking of views as not being evidence is a fiction. It is hard to believe that people would generate their mental picture of facts concerning a physical location from information related to them by other people rather than through their own direct observations. There can be no doubt that a view has a powerful effect on the fact images developed in the consciousnesses of the factfinders. For this reason, in planning and organizing a presentation in a case involving a view, the view and the inferences that the factfinders are likely to draw from it must be given serious attention.

2. The Traditional Conduct of Views

In most jurisdictions, the issue of whether a view will be taken is usually settled at a pretrial conference or hearing and is within the sound discretion of the trial court. Will the value of the view as a tool to understanding the evidence outweigh the cost, delay, and inconvenience of transporting the factfinders and other trial participants to the site and conducting the view? Sometimes, if evidence such as photographs and diagrams will give the factfinders sufficient understanding of the relevant location, the costs and delays will not be justified. On the other hand, in a case where the locus is important, there is no substitute to having the factfinders see it with their own eyes.

Those physical features that the factfinders are to view are usually identified before the view is taken. For instance, if the view is to be taken of a curve in a road where an accident took place, those features of the area that are of interest to the case might be identified by both parties in advance. The judge, or some other neutral person such as a clerk or court reporter, is then permitted to call the factfinders' attention to these features as the view proceeds.

> The Court (as the members of the jury are standing in the parking lot).   I call your attention to this telephone pole, the wire running from this fixture on the pole, and the pavement here in this area to the west of the pole.

In some jurisdictions, counsel are permitted to call the factfinders' attention to features deemed relevant. In no event are counsel permitted to use the view as an occasion to argue their cases.

3.   Use of Views in Trial Presentations

Because of the tremendous impact of a view to create an authoritative image of the features that the factfinders are permitted to see
with their own eyes, the lawyer as a part of her strategy should
make sure that the view is positively integrated into her case to
create a favorable fact picture of what happened. Both the timing
and the scope of the view should enhance the power and accuracy
of the trial lawyer's presentation.

Although traditionally views are taken at the outset of the trial,
often it is better to take a view after the opening statements. That
way the lawyers can make clear in their openings the physical
details that are of consequence to the case. The factfinders will
know what to look for and why when they are off at the scene.

Sometimes the view should be taken just before or after the
testimony of a key witness. The opportunity to see for themselves
will enable the factfinders to accept or reject the picture generated
by that witness's version of the facts.

Because the timing of the view is usually within the trial judge's
discretion, the trial lawyer does not have direct control over this
important element of the presentation. This means that she must
either obtain an advance ruling on whether a view will be taken
and, if so, when and of what, or arrange her presentation to accom-
modate various alternate possibilities. The potential power and
prejudice of this kind of first-hand information-gathering cannot
be ignored in trial planning; it should be positively incorporated
into a persuasive re-creation of the fact picture.

Even though what the factfinders see during a view might be the
best proof of some vital aspect of a party's trial picture, traditional
doctrine considers views as nonevidentiary, meaning that one is
not permitted to argue fact inferences directly from the view. Under traditional doctrine, an argument such as

> Counsel.   As we could all see from the view we took of the
> intersection of Wood and Vale Streets at the beginning of
> the trial, if Mr. Borak had really stopped at the stop sign
> and looked to the left and looked to the right, he would
> have had to see the Clark car coming up Wood Street. We
> could see with our own eyes how straight that street was,
> and how far Mr. Borak could see.

would be considered improper because the factfinders are being asked to draw conclusions directly from information acquired during the view. This does not mean that the factfinders do not in fact draw conclusions from what they have seen. However, the image on which they base their decision is supposed to be derived from the evidence received in the courtroom, not from their own observations on the view. For this reason, the astute lawyer will be sure that the relevant details of the physical area covered by the view are proved by other forms of evidence, such as testimony or photographs. This evidence will provide the ostensible basis for her factual argument and also a fact record in the event of an appeal. At trial the lawyer can couch her argument in terms of this evidence, referring to the view only in context or to aid the factfinders' understanding, rather than as the basis for the inferences themselves.

There is some indication that this concept of the view as not being evidence may be yielding to reality. If the goal of a trial is the accurate re-creation of a fact picture in the consciousnesses of the factfinders, the factfinders' actual first-hand observations would appear to be the best basis for such a fact picture. Photographs and video tapes offer means by which those facts that were directly observed can be recorded for an appellate record. It can be predicted with some confidence that the fiction that a view is not evidence will soon yield to the fact that seeing is believing.

Chapter 11 Exhibits in Evidence

A. Objects That Teach

Objects and documents that have probative value in and of themselves are important elements of a trial presentation. It is from such objects that the factfinders make inferences directly. The "smoking gun," the missing document, the "dirt" are sometimes the stars of the trial. But there are also a host of other objects that have relevance to the issues in the case but are far less dramatic in impact. In any case, the "real evidence"—photographs, authentic documents, and other physical objects—tend to have high probative value with most factfinders.

Objects that are used for probative purposes can be contrasted to illustrative aids, which are used to illustrate or make visual the testimony of witnesses. An illustrative aid can be used to assist a witness in communicating a visual image, but the authority of the illustrative aid should rise no higher than the credibility of the witness.

An object or document that itself teaches something about the fact picture must be offered and admitted in evidence before it can be used as a part of the presentation to the factfinders. Its credibility derives from its authenticity and the inferences that common experience will connect with it. Such objects and documents are hereinafter referred to as exhibits in evidence or simply as exhibits.

The rules of evidence provide criteria of reliability and fairness that are applied to any proposed exhibit. Part of the process of the evidentiary presentation is to satisfy these technical rules of admissibility and then use the exhibit to teach the relevant facts as smoothly and persuasively as possible.

B.   The Power of Exhibits

Exhibits as visual and tangible media have immense power in trial presentations. Experience leads factfinders to receive images conveyed by oral testimony with some reservation based on commonsense perceptions of the fallibility of memory, the effects of bias, and the imprecision of words as descriptive media. Illustrative aids can reduce or eliminate problems of verbal communication. However, witness testimony conveyed by diagram or demonstration is still subject to the vagaries of human memory and the influence of witness bias or interest. Exhibits are not subject to these infirmities. The proof provided by exhibits in evidence is usually accorded a high degree of authority by factfinders.

A photograph will be accepted as depicting a scene more readily than the most detailed verbal description or the most intricately drawn diagram. A statement in a business record will be afforded more weight than sworn testimony. Prosecutors know that a murder or drug prosecution gains vital authority if the weapon or the contraband is actually before the jury in the courtroom. For these reasons, the effective trial lawyer seeks out documents and tangible things that can teach relevant facts directly. She then incorporates them into the trial presentation in the manner best calculated to enhance the overall image being created.

C.   Laying the Foundation

Rules regulating exhibits and the procedures for offering exhibits in evidence vary to some extent from jurisdiction to jurisdiction. All jurisdictions require that the court make a threshold determination before an exhibit is used. The trial lawyer must lay a foundation of preliminary facts to support a favorable ruling on admissibility.

The admissibility of an exhibit is usually an issue for the judge. However, in most cases the foundation for admitting the exhibit is laid during the ongoing presentation in the presence of the factfinders. Once the lawyer believes that she has elicited the necessary facts to comply with the rules governing admissibility, she offers the exhibit or moves that the exhibit be admitted in evidence.

The opponent has a right to object at the time the offer is made.

If there are facts to be established that relate to admissibility, the opponent may be given the opportunity to conduct a brief voir dire examination and, in exceptional cases, to call her own witnesses in order to attack the foundation. Once the exhibit has been admitted in evidence, the parties may use it both during witness testimony and in argument. Ordinarily, the jury takes the exhibit to the jury room to scrutinize during their deliberations.

Laying a foundation is a complex exercise in the trial advocacy process. While the lawyer is presenting the fact image, she is simultaneously attempting to comply with sometimes technical legal rules and handle the physical objects in a smooth and confident manner. For this reason, laying the foundation for an exhibit's admissibility and then effectively using the exhibit with the factfinders have often been termed a hallmark of professionalism in trial advocacy.

D. The Process of Offering Exhibits in Evidence

The use of exhibits is a complex part of the trial presentation process. It involves a number of steps, some of which take place even before the trial begins.

1. Planning for Exhibits

The use of exhibits at trial has to be carefully planned. An important part of the process is to determine the purpose for which the exhibit is to be used and at what point in the trial it should be introduced. Usually the purpose is to provide a level of accuracy and authority that can be provided only by "the real thing."

The lawyer can make many points with the use of exhibits, but if the point is not important, the exhibit will sometimes be dispensed with in favor of a narrative or a simple illustrative aid to expedite the presentation. For certain vital points, however, the exhibit may lend a level of authority and accuracy that cannot be attained otherwise.

The timing for the introduction of an exhibit is the point at which it can have the most positive impact in the development of the presentation. This will depend in large part on its purpose. For example, if a photograph of the scene of an event is to be used as an exhibit, it probably should be offered when the factfinders are first beginning to visualize the scene. This maximizes the impact of the photograph in establishing and fixing the scene in the factfinders' consciousnesses before another impression is formed. On the other hand, if the photograph is to be used to impeach the testimony of a witness, the lawyer may choose to withhold it until the witness has clearly given contradictory testimony. Introduction of the impeaching photograph at that point will emphasize the contrast and do maximum damage to the opponent's presentation.

While the lawyer is planning the presentation of the exhibit, she must also make sure that she will be able to lay the requisite foundation for its admissibility in evidence. This requires careful consideration of applicable rules of evidence, including in almost all cases the exhibit's authenticity and relevance. In some cases the lawyer will also have to contend with rules such as the "Best Evidence Rule," rules creating privileges, the hearsay rule, and the residual rule that bars evidence if the risk of unfair prejudice substantially outweighs the probative value. Compliance with the applicable rules and exceptions must be resolved in advance.

2. Marking the Exhibit for Identification

From the time the exhibit is first referred to in the courtroom, it is given a designation for purposes of identification. Typically, it is referred to by an exhibit number or letter — "Exhibit 1 for identification," "Exhibit C for identification." The phrase "for identification" is included to indicate that the item has been referred to as a potential exhibit but has not yet been offered or admitted by the judge.

The identification number or letter provides a means by which the trial transcript can be keyed to the actual exhibits used during the presentation. Referring to exhibits by their appropriate designations may sometimes feel strange and artificial at first. It is worth the effort to develop the habit, however, because calling them by their designations improves the smoothness and professionalism of the presentation. It also shows that the lawyer considers the exhibit an important element. Most of all, referring to exhibits by their courtroom designations greatly increases the understandability of the record in the event of an appeal.

It goes without saying that the lawyer should locate the exhibits in such a way that the continuity of the presentation is disrupted as little as possible by retrieval of the exhibits to show them to the witness.

Delays in the trial are reduced if the exhibits are premarked for identification before the trial. Most courts have rules applicable, at least in civil cases, that require the premarking, disclosure, and filing of lists of exhibits prior to trial.

If the exhibit has not been premarked, it will be marked in the courtroom at the time it is first referred to during the proceedings. Depending on local rules and practices, this marking is usually done by either the attorney or a court official.

> Q. Your Honor, may this be marked as Exhibit 1 for
> identification?

This question is not really a question; it is a polite request. Like most of the requests on matters of formality in the courtroom, it ends on a down beat.

Counsel is responsible for tendering the object to be marked to the appropriate person. Usually the ongoing examination of the witness is suspended until the marking is completed. The disjointed pace of the trial caused by this interruption is a good reason to make sure that the exhibits are marked in advance or at least during recess or at the beginning of the trial day in which they will be offered.

3. Showing the Exhibit to Opposing Counsel

Once the exhibit has been marked for identification, the lawyer proceeds to lay the foundation so that the exhibit can be admitted in evidence. Almost every jurisdiction requires that at some point before the exhibit is offered in evidence the other party's counsel have an opportunity to look at it. Many lawyers show opposing counsel the exhibit to be offered just before or after the time it is marked for identification, thus avoiding a potential interruption later.

Another way to handle this requirement is to give the opponent a copy of the proposed exhibit at the time it is marked so he can study it while the foundation is being laid. If the exhibit has not been shown to the opposing counsel before it is offered, the opponent can ask to see it "close up" when it is being offered. The fact that exhibits have already been marked and exchanged does not mean that this step can be dispensed with. Unless the opponent has seen the actual document in the proponent's hand, he has a right to see it before the court rules on its admissibility.

Usually the proponent of an exhibit will simply walk over to the opponent's counsel table and silently show the proposed exhibit to counsel. Opposing counsel is not required to state at the time whether he has an objection but can merely look at the exhibit and await the laying of the foundation required for its admissibility.

Some lawyers accompany the showing of the proposed exhibit with the statement,

> Q. May the record reflect that I am showing Exhibit 13 for identification to opposing counsel?

This practice is of dubious value because it needlessly injects the artificial presence of "the record" into the presentation. If there is any objection to an exhibit that is waived if it is not made on the spot, it is the objection that the proponent failed to show the exhibit to the other lawyer at the time it was offered in evidence. Hence it is hard to see what possible reason there might be to create an appellate record on the issue.

There is one other advantage in showing the exhibit to the opponent before starting to lay the foundation with the witness. Sometimes the opponent will look at the exhibit and indicate that he has no objection to its admission in evidence. In these cases the proponent of the exhibit may be spared some tedious foundation-laying and can go directly on to offering the exhibit. Counsel should not, however, dispense with any foundation questions that aid in the understanding of the exhibit or add to its authority.

4. Handling Exhibits in the Courtroom

An exhibit may not be used as a part of the evidentiary presentation unless or until it is admitted in evidence. The process of laying the foundation for offering the exhibit usually takes place in the courtoom and in front of the factfinders. Because, in a larger sense, everything that takes place within the sight or hearing of the fact-finders is a part of the presentation, the way exhibits are handled even prior to their admission in evidence has impact on the overall image being created at the trial.

A primary consideration in handling proposed but not admitted exhibits is to avoid unfair prejudice by their premature exposure to the factfinders. Thus, if there is any issue about admissibility, photographs and other items that might create undue speculation should be handled and shown to the witness so that the factfinders cannot easily see them before they are admitted. Objects that will be offered in evidence should not be waved about or left in prominent positions to taint the impressions of the factfinders.

Counsel should also deal with exhibits in a manner appropriate to ordinary human associations and sensibilities. Items that may have emotional impact should be treated especially carefully. Guns and knives should not be needlessly brandished or handled in a cavalier manner. Intimate clothing, body parts, and similar objects should be treated with the sensitivity usually afforded them in real life.

At the same time, it is important that a lawyer who is responsible for using exhibits with emotional connotations not be intimidated by concern about spillover prejudice or other adverse reactions of the factfinder to the way the lawyer handles the exhibits. As with many other aspects of trial advocacy, confidence combined with sensitivity to the factfinders' viewpoints should inform the way the exhibits are handled both before and after they are offered in evidence.

It should be kept in mind that once objects have been marked for identification and referred to on the trial record, they are a part of that record and should be left in the custody of the court. It is usually not appropriate for counsel to keep such exhibits at counsel table except when using them in direct or cross-examination. Exhibits in evidence must never be removed from the custody of the court except with the express permission of the judge.

5. The Basic Foundation of Authenticity and Relevance

Laying the foundation for exhibits is largely a question of complying with certain specific legal rules that are applied by the judge.

Counsel is usually allowed some latitude in focusing or even leading the witness in order to establish the preliminary facts. It is
important to lay the foundation so as to contribute to the authority
of the presentation and to enhance the acceptability of the exhibit.

The basic foundation required for the admission of an exhibit in
evidence is (1) a showing that the exhibit is what it purports to be
(authenticity) and (2) a showing that the exhibit has something to
do with the issues on trial (relevance). Put another way, when an
object is offered to teach in its own right, it must be the genuine
object, not a counterfeit. In addition, that which it teaches must
affect in some appreciable way either one of the competing pictures being presented to the factfinders. The concepts of authenticity and relevance are somewhat intertwined. It has been said that
authenticity is merely a subset of relevance because an object or
document is not relevant to the case unless it is in fact the thing it
purports to be.

The requirements of relevance and authenticity apply to all
exhibits. Relevance, of course, is a threshold requirement for all
elements in the fact presentation, both testimony and exhibits. In
one sense, it is a common-sense concept: does the proffered element affect some significant aspect of either of the competing
images when evaluated in light of the factfinders' common understanding and experience? Does it make a difference? Presumably,
the trial lawyer will not want to waste the factfinders' time and
attention with information that has no impact on the presentations being made in the courtroom.

6. *Limits on Admissibility*

The rules of evidence limit the use of exhibits to those that seem
clearly relevant to the factfinders. These restrictions are based primarily on considerations of fairness and public policy. For instance, the Federal Rules of Evidence, on grounds of public policy,
exclude evidence of remedial measures undertaken after an accident even though such evidence might have considerable relevance
as a matter of common sense. [1] Other rules limiting admissibility of

---

[1] Fed. R. Evid. 407.

evidence, regardless of legal or logical relevance are the hearsay rule, [2] privileges, [3] the Best Evidence Rule, [4] and various policy-based exclusionary rules. [5]

All evidence, be it testimony or exhibit, is also subject to a potential objection based on the avoidance of unfair prejudice and efficient management of the trial. Rule 403, the currently cited basis for this objection, gives the trial judge discretion to exclude the evidence if

> its probative value is substantially outweighed by the danger of unfair prejudice, confusion of the issues, or misleading the jury, or considerations of undue delay, waste of time, or needless presentation of cumulative evidence.

A similar policy of discretion is embedded in the evidence jurisprudence of all state jurisdictions.

If this objection is raised, the court's ruling is based on a comparison of the importance or "probative value" of the exhibit to show or accredit some element of the case as against the danger of some unfair inference or reaction to the exhibit by the factfinders. Other grounds for discretionary exclusion are the likelihood that precious time will be wasted in proving the exhibit and considering it, or that the evidence will cause more confusion than enlightenment. As with most objections, the court can allow a voir dire to permit the opponent to bring out particular facts important to the court in making the determination.

Assume, for example, a gory photograph of a murder victim offered through the pathologist who did the autopsy. On a Rule 403 objection, the court will assess the value of the photograph as a method of showing some fact of consequence against the probable danger of an emotional reaction to seeing a blood-covered body. The proponent might argue that the photograph corroborates the prosecutions's version of the event by showing the bruised and broken body of the deceased after being run over by the defendant's automobile. The opponent might counter to the

[2] Id., R. 802
[3] Id., R. 501
[4] Id., R. 1002.
[5] Id., R. 404-412.

effect that the photograph does not show any particular information about the direction and manner in which the decedent was
crushed by the automobile and that causation of death is not
disputed anyway. The opponent could argue in addition that the
jury could be expected to react emotionally to the sight of the
decedent's bruised and broken body in assessing the real issue of
the case, the defendant's intent in steering his automobile.

In order for the court to perform the necessary balancing, it is
often necessary for the lawyers to articulate to the judge the evidentiary value on the one hand and the potential prejudicial inferences on the other. Objections based on Rule 403 are typically
heard at sidebar so that the exhibit's probative significance and the
potentially prejudical inferences can be discussed without being
heard by the factfinders.

7.   Laying the Basic Foundation

Establishing a foundation is usually straightforward. In order to
establish that an exhibit is authentic, the trial lawyer commonly
uses the testimony of a witness who is able to recognize the object
as genuine and give some basis for that recognition. There is no
requirement that authenticity be proven to a certainty, beyond a
reasonable doubt, or even by a fair preponderance of the evidence.
The threshold requirement is merely that the proponent of the
evidence submit evidence from which the factfinders can find that
the exhibit is what it purports to be.[6] In the absence of a factual
challenge, this degree of proof is sufficient.

The time-honored line of questioning to show authenticity usually follows proof that the authenticating witness has some knowledge of the exhibit. For instance, if the proposed exhibit is a knife
found at the scene of a claimed assault, the proponent of the knife
might call the police officer who picked up the knife shortly after
the event. Usually, the lawyer first presents the witness's testimony
about his arrival on the scene and finding a knife next to the body
of the victim. This testimony creates a visual image to serve as a
context for introduction of the actual knife.

[6] See, e.g., Fed. R. Evid. 104.

Q. Officer, at any time during your visit to the scene did your find anything?

This is a slightly leading or "focusing question." It is generally permitted as an introduction to the foundation for the exhibit.

A. Yes, I did.

Q. What did you find?

A. I found a knife next to the body.

Q. Officer, what did you do with the knife that you found next to the body of the victim?

A. I scratched my initials on it and the date.

Q. What did you do with it then?

A. I put it in the evidence locker at police headquarters.

Now comes the foundation for the exhibit.

Q. Officer, I show you an object that has been marked as Exhibit 1 for identification. Do you recognize Exhibit 1?

A. Yes, I do.

Q. Would you tell the members of the jury what Exhibit 1 is?

A. Yes, that is the knife I found at the scene of the incident.

Q. Officer, how is it that you are able to recognize Exhibit 1 as the knife you found at the scene of the incident?

A. Because it has my initials on it — right here [indicating].

In this simple series of questions, the lawyer has established the foundation for authenticity and relevancy. She has shown that the knife is authentic by eliciting testimony that at the time the officer found the knife, he scratched his initials on it and by showing that these initials appear on Exhibit 1 as proffered in court. This builds a logical basis for inference by the factfinders that the object in front of them is the same one that was found at the scene of the crime.

The lawyer has also shown that Exhibit 1 is relevant. It has been shown to be the knife found next to the victim's body and inferentially was involved in the assault. Presumably, viewing this object will provide some information as to how the crime might have been committed.

Sometimes there will be other potential impediments to admissibility, such as the hearsay rule, the best evidence rule, or the danger of unfair prejudice. These are also usually dealt with as a part of the foundation. The proponent will ask questions designed to elicit facts to deal with each of the potential evidentiary barriers to the use of the exhibit. Some of these lines of questions are discussed below.

The court does not usually rule piecemeal on the various elements of foundations for exhibits. When a lawyer is laying a foundation, she must ask the witnesses those questions that she deems necessary to address whatever evidentiary issues she is aware of. The questions and the answers elicited presumably have dealt with all applicable evidentiary constraints by the time she is finished and ready to offer the exhibit. In any event, she will not know whether the court considers the foundation to be sufficient until the exhibit has been offered.

8. *Offering the Exhibit*

After the lawyer has completed laying the foundation, the next step is to offer the exhibit in evidence.

> Q. We offer Exhibit 1 for identification in evidence.

The offer is set forth as a statement, not a question. The response expected is that the court will admit the exhibit in evidence.

Another formulation for offering a thing in evidence is

> Q. Your Honor, we move for the admission of Exhibit 24 for identification in evidence.

The commonly used phrase,

> Q. Your Honor, I would like to offer Exhibit 1 for identification in evidence.

might draw from the judge the rejoinder,

> The Court. Now that we know what you would *like to do*, please tell us what you *are doing*.

A confident tone and a positive approach in offering an object in evidence go a long way toward success in the use of exhibits. Opponents are frequently not completely sure of their potential evidentiary objections. Judges are sometimes inattentive to lengthy foundations. An offer made in a tone expectant of success will tend to deter opponents from possible objections. On the other hand, a tentative offer may draw objections and alert the judge to real or imagined shortcomings in the foundation.

9. Objections to Exhibits

The proper time to lodge an objection to an exhibit is when the exhibit is offered in evidence. An objection taken to the exhibit while the foundation is being laid is likely to be premature.

> Q. Officer Groves, do you recognize the scene depicted in Exhibit 5 for identification?
>
> A. Yes.
>
> Q. What is the scene depicted by Exhibit 5 for identification?
>
> Opposing Counsel. Objection, Your Honor!
>
> The Court. What are you objecting to, Counsel, the question or the exhibit?
>
> Opposing Counsel. The exhibit, Your Honor.
>
> The Court. Well, your objection is too early. Please wait until the exhibit is offered.
>
> Opposing Counsel. Thank you, Your Honor.

The Court.   I told you once before, Counsel; do not thank the
Court for its rulings, particularly when they are against you!

Frequently an objection to admission of an exhibit will be simply

Opposing Counsel.   Objection! No foundation.

"No foundation" means that the opponent believes that the
lawyer who is offering the exhibit has failed to adduce the necessary proof of authenticity and relevance necessary to sustain admission of the exhibit or has failed to address some obvious rule of
exclusion that would likely apply. Usually the objection can be met
by going back over the foundation elements and making sure that
all of the necessary questions have been asked.
    Sometimes a "no foundation" objection is sustained without
any mention either in the objection or the ruling of what element is
lacking. Sometimes a tactful inquiry,

Q.   Your Honor, may we ask that Counsel state the particular
     element of the foundation that is alleged to be missing?

will cause the missing piece to be identified so that the omission
can be remedied. A lawyer is not entitled to such a "tip" as a
matter of right. If the judge does not cooperate, probably the best
course of action is to go through the entire line of planned foundation questions again. If repetition of the planned foundation questions is successful, chances are that one of the necessary questions
was omitted the first time through inadvertence.

10. Voir Dire on Foundation

At the time the exhibit is offered, the opponent may request the
opportunity to conduct voir dire on issues of foundation. The
purpose of the voir dire is to undermine the sufficiency of
the evidentiary foundation for the exhibit. The idea is to show by
strong leading questions that there is some element of the required
foundation missing or that some exclusionary rule of evidence is
applicable.

Opposing Counsel. Objection! Your Honor, may we voir dire as to foundation?

The Court. Yes, you may.

Q. (by Opposing Counsel on voir dire). Officer, these initials scratched on the knife are just block letters, aren't they?

A. Yes.

Q. Anybody can make block letters, can't they, Officer?

A. Yes.

Q. This is not the same as your signature, is it?

A. That's right.

Q. Your Honor, we object on the ground that the officer's scratched initials are not sufficient for the positive identification of Exhibit 1 for identification as the actual knife found at the scene.

The Court. Objection overruled. Exhibit 1 is admitted in evidence.

Although occasionally an opponent can illuminate an otherwise hidden fatal flaw in the foundation of a proposed exhibit, more often the effect of the voir dire is to improve rather than undermine the foundation. Voir dire should not be attempted unless the lawyer opposing the exhibit is confident of developing discrete facts that will undermine admissibility. Use of voir dire merely to smear a concededly admissible exhibit is professionally improper.

11. Ruling on Admissibility

After the foundation is laid, the exhibit is offered, and any objection is made, the judge will rule on the offer and admit the exhibit in evidence or exclude it from evidence.

The Court. Objection overruled. Exhibit 5 for identification is admitted as Exhibit 5 in evidence.

or simply,

> *The Court.*   Admitted.

In some courts exhibits are "marked" in evidence with a designation different from that used for identification. Sometimes letters are used for identification and numbers are used after the object is in evidence.

> Q. Your Honor, may Exhibit J for identification be marked as Exhibit 5 in evidence?
>
> *Opposing Counsel.*   No objection.
>
> *The Court.*   . . . marked as Exhibit 5 in evidence.

Even if there is no objection by the opposing party, an exhibit may not be used in the evidentiary part of the trial without being admitted in evidence by the judge.

> Q. We offer Exhibit 5 in evidence.
>
> *Opposing Counsel.*   No objection.
>
> Q. Now, Officer Groves, can you please show the members of the jury the tree in front of 37 Jackson Street as it appears on Exhibit 5.
>
> *The Court.*   Counsel, please wait until the Court has admitted the exhibit in evidence before showing it to the jury.

12.   Publication of the Exhibit to the Factfinders

Show the exhibit to the factfinders! The last step in the offering of an exhibit in evidence is, of course, the most important. The exhibit is being offered because its proponent wants to use it in the presentation to the factfinders.

Ordinarily the publication of the exhibit to the factfinders should immediately follow its admission in evidence. The factfinders' curiosity is usually whetted by the process of laying the foundation. They often feel somewhat alienated by the more formal, rules-oriented phases of the process. Usually the impact of the exhibit is maximized by using it immediately.

Effective publication of exhibits is discussed at greater length in section H below.

E.   Proof of Authenticity

Since all exhibits must be shown to be authentic to be admitted in evidence, authentication is potentially a part of every evidentiary foundation. Sometimes, of course, authenticity will be conceded or not insisted on by the opponent. Frequently, routine foundation matters such as authenticity will have been dealt with by stipulation or by pretrial order. But in almost every case there is something that must be offered in evidence on the spot. The trial lawyer who is able to prove authenticity without hesitation, lay the rest of the required foundation, and then offer the exhibit with confidence will add convincing quality and authority to the image she is creating.

The means of authentication must fit the nature of the evidence and the resources at hand. Some objects are self-authenticating pursuant to statute or rule of evidence. In other cases authenticity can be proven by recognition of objects that are unique or that have been made unique by identifying marks. Proof of authenticity of objects that are fungible or that are mass-produced may require that the proponent show some sort of chain of custody linking the "real thing" that figured in the case to the object proffered in the courtroom. In each case the goal is to make a foundation presentation that meets the requirements of the evidence rules and adds to the authority of the proposed exhibit.

1.   Self-Authenticating Exhibits

Some exhibits will be accepted as authentic without the need to produce extrinsic proof of their authenticity. Usually these are documents or things that bear their own indicia of authenticity, such as official signatures or seals. For example, documents of agencies with specified seals or authenticating signatures will be accepted as genuine without the need for formal in-court authentication.

Rule 902 of the Federal Rules of Evidence contains a catalogue of the documents and objects that do not require specific authentication. No extrinsic proof of authenticity is required but relevance must still be shown.

> Q.   Your Honor, Exhibit 2 for identification is a copy of the Ames driving record of the defendant, Robert Maxfield, date of birth, 6/15/43, authenticated pursuant to Federal Rule of Evidence 902 (1) by the signature and seal of the Ames Registrar of Motor Vehicles. We offer it in evidence.

The Court.   Admitted.

Since the proposed exhibit bears on its face the necessary authenticating seal and shows that it relates to the defendant, the requirements of both authenticity and relevance have been met. If there is no further ground for objection, such as hearsay, the document is admissible without more.

2.   *Authenticity by Witness Recognition*

Some objects or documents that are not self-authenticating may be authenticated by witness recognition in court. Of these, there is a category of objects that are presumed to be recognizable by a witness with knowledge without proof of any specific identifying marks.

Some objects are by their nature or by personal association unique, so that a person familiar with them will be able to identify them based on familiarity alone. Such objects usually can be authenticated by witness recognition without more. A person's pets, clothing, personal effects, unusual antiques, or paintings usually fall into this group.

> Q.   I show you Exhibit 1 for identification. Do you recognize it?
>
> A.   Yes, I do.
>
> Q.   What is it?
>
> A.   That is my favorite lobster tie.
>
> Q.   We offer Exhibit 1 in evidence.

When authentication is by witness recognition, the showing of authenticity must include evidence that the witness has some rational basis for recognizing the object and asserting that it is what it purports to be. The ability of the witness to recognize a unique or familiar item is inferred from the nature of the exhibit or from the witness's long familiarity with it. If the exhibit is not recognizable as unique or familiar, the proponent must make a more explicit showing of some rational basis for recognition, otherwise the foundation for admission of the exhibit is incomplete.

Q. Officer Levy, I show you Exhibit 2 for identification. Do you recognize it?

A. Yes.

Q. What is Exhibit 2 for identification?

A. That is the knife I found at the side of Mr. Ramirez on the night of November 15.

Q. The defense offers Exhibit 2 for identification in evidence.

Opposing Counsel. Objection. Insufficient foundation.

Q. Through the Court, may we know in what respect the foundation is lacking?

Opposing Counsel. Your Honor, there is no basis for recognition of the exhibit.

The Court. Objection sustained.

A common way to elicit the basis of recognition of an exhibit is to ask a question such as

Q. How is it that you are able to recognize Exhibit 1 as the knife you picked up at the scene of the incident?

or

Q. How do you recognize Exhibit 1 as the knife you picked up at the scene of the incident?

The witness is thus led to state how he is able to identify the
exhibit:

> A. Because it has my initials and the date scratched on it —
> right here [indicating].

Usually the first three questions pertaining to an exhibit are
designed to establish (1) recognition of the exhibit by the witness,
(2) some rational basis for the witness's ability to recognize the
exhibit, and (3) enough information about what the exhibit is to
connect it to the issues in the case.

Phrasing a question

> Q. Can you identify Exhibit 1 for identification?

tends to lump the witness's recognition of the exhibit with the
description of what it is.

> A. That's the knife I found at the scene of the accident.

The use of the word "identify" sometimes makes it easier for
counsel to forget to ask *how* the witness is able to identify an
exhibit. Thus the term "recognize" is preferable to "identify" in
foundation questions for authenticating exhibits.

A witness may be able to recognize and authenticate an item
that is not unique in itself because, like the knife with the scratched
initials, it has been made unique in some fashion, and is hence
recognizable. Common recognition marks include serial numbers,
signatures, or other identifying marks recognizable by the witness.

> Q. (on cross-examination). I hand you a document marked
> as Exhibit 3 for identification. That's a letter you sent to
> my client on or about October 4, 1990, isn't it?
>
> A. Yes, it is.
>
> Q. That's your signature at the bottom of page two of Ex-
> hibit 3 for identification, isn't it?
>
> A. Yes, it is.
>
> Q. We offer Exhibit 3 in evidence.

Exhibits can be authenticated during both direct and cross-examination. In many jurisdictions they may also be offered in evidence on either direct or cross-examination. In other jurisdictions, although the foundation for the exhibit may be laid on cross-examination, the actual offer must await the proponent's turn at bat.

On direct, open or mildly focused leading questions are generally used to lay the foundation. On cross, however, strong closed leading questions can be, and almost always should be, used to lay the foundation and to offer the exhibit.

3. Circumstantial Authentication — Chain of Custody

Objects and documents that are not recognizable in themselves and are not made recognizable by some kind of authenticating marks are usually authenticated circumstantially. Evidence is produced from which the factfinder can infer that, under all the circumstances, the proffered object is likely to be that which it purports to be.

The most common circumstantial proof of authenticity is through the so-called chain of custody. While the chain of custody comes in several forms, the object of the foundation questioning is to show circumstances under which the factfinders can logically infer that the proposed exhibit is in fact authentic.

Many inexperienced lawyers have traditionally regarded authentication by proof of chain of custody as a difficult and perilous exercise in which one misstep or omission could break the chain and consign the vital exhibit forever to limbo. In fact, however, proof of chain of custody usually follows a common-sense approach. The idea is to keep track of the exhibit from the time it was identified with the facts of the case until the time it is produced in court. A lawyer who follows an exhibit through the elements of the presentation should have no difficulty proving its chain of custody. Proof of chain of custody should usually not only satisfy the formal requirements for proof of authenticity but should contribute to the authority and acceptability of the exhibit by providing a rational basis for the factfinders to determine that it is what it purports to be.

For instance, in the preceding example, if the officer had not

made any marks on the knife when he first found it, authentication
by chain of custody could go something like,

Q.   Officer, what did you do with the knife after you found
     it?

A.   I put it in an evidence envelope and brought it to the
     police station.

Q.   What did you do there?

A.   I logged it in at the police evidence locker.

Q.   Are there procedures at the police evidence locker to
     keep track of evidence deposited there?

A.   Yes, there are. Every item is numbered and tagged and
     logged into the evidence record.

Q.   Was the evidence envelope sealed or unsealed when it
     was logged in at the evidence locker?

A.   Sealed.

Q.   When is the next time you saw the evidence envelope
     with the knife in it?

A.   I reclaimed it at the evidence locker this morning when
     we came to court.

Q.   What condition was the evidence envelope in?

A.   It was still sealed.

Q.   Was there any evidence of the seal having been tampered
     with?

A.   No.

Q.   What did you do with the sealed envelope?

A.   I brought it with me to court here.

Q.   What did you do when you arrived at the court?

A.   I broke the seal and took out the knife.

Q.   I show you Exhibit 1 for identification. Do you recog-
     nize it?

> A.   Yes, I do.
>
> Q.   What is it?
>
> A.   This is the knife I found at the side of the victim.
>
> Q.   How is it that you are able to recognize Exhibit 1 for identification as the knife you found at the side of the victim?
>
> A.   Because that is the knife I brought with me today.

In the foregoing example, the authentication relied on the integrity of the seal of the evidence envelope and of the procedures of the police evidence locker. These furnish a rational basis for inferring that the knife that is proffered as Exhibit 1 for identification is the same knife that was found at the scene of the crime.

Circumstantial proof depends on the nature of the exhibit. The question is, if the factfinders accept the proof offered, would they infer that the proposed exhibit is what it purports to be?

For most exhibits, there is a further requirement for proving authenticity. It is not enough merely to show that the object proffered in court is the same object that was involved in the case; the proponent must also show that it is in the same condition it was in at the time of the events at issue. The common question is, for example,

> Q.   Officer, as you look at Exhibit 1 for identification, is it in the same condition as it was when you picked it up by the body of the victim?
>
> A.   Yes, it is.

For objects that are offered in evidence because they were actually connected to events or persons involved in the case, proof of authenticity and relevance is usually a sufficient foundation. But, as indicated above, such objects may still be subject to exclusion based on the possibility of unfair prejudice, delay, and the like. These considerations apply to all exhibits.

Some exhibits, however, are subject to additional foundation requirements to overcome potential evidentiary objections. These may include business and hospital records, government records, transcripts of testimony or statements, publications, and even old newspaper articles. Exhibits that may not have figured directly in the events in question may record, in one form or another, information that contributes to the images being recreated in court. In each case laying the foundation consists of establishing the authenticity and relevance of the exhibit and then overcoming any potentially applicable rules of exclusion.

This book is not intended to be a treatise on evidence. Volumes have been written on the appropriate evidentiary foundations for all sorts of proof. Included here are discussions of foundation problems for only two groups of trial exhibits, photographs and business records. The commonly encountered foundations for offering these media as exhibits at trial illustrate the kinds of issues that are likely to be encountered in the presentation of any exhibit.

F. Photographs

1. *Why Use Photographs?*

Photographic media are very common and very powerful trial exhibits. The ability of photographic processes to accurately provide information is imbedded in the popular consciousness. In preparing a case for trial, the lawyer should be alert to the potential of photographs, slides, movies, and videos to record and convey information to the factfinders.

At the planning stage, the trial lawyer should consider the image to be portrayed and the availability of photographic representations. Time and money expended in taking helpful photographs will save time, empower the presentation, and avoid the risk of ambiguity at trial. Existing photographs of places and things in issue should always be scrutinized for their potential in showing different perspectives at trial.

Choosing the appropriate photographic media depends on the nature of what is to be shown and how the photographic record is to be used in the trial presentation. A simple accident scene may be economically depicted with 8 x 10 color prints. If a photograph is to be referred to repeatedly or used in witness testimony, it might be well to blow the photo up to poster size so that counsel or the witness can stand by the blowup and effectively teach the relevant details to the factfinders.

On the other hand, more complex issues justify more elaborate photographic media. Sometimes a "day in the life" video can illustrate a plaintiff's disability in a way that words or still photographs never can. A series of colored slides can effectively publish facts that have been photographically recorded in sparkling color and larger than life.

2. Laying the Evidentiary Foundation for Photographs

Laying the foundation for admitting a photograph in evidence is usually a simple matter. Because of our now well-established belief in the accuracy of photography, there is usually no need to prove the authenticity of the photograph itself. Nor is there a requirement that a chain of custody or other authentication be demonstrated for the photograph. As long as the proposed exhibit is recognizable as a photograph, it usually does not matter where it came from, who took it, when it was taken, or what has happened to it in the meantime. *There is no need to have the person who took the photograph testify to authenticate it.*

The only foundation requirements for offering a photograph in evidence are (1) a showing that the witness has some familiarity with what is depicted by the photograph, (2) testimony establishing that what is depicted is of some relevance to the case, and (3) testimony that the photograph shows what is depicted fairly and accurately.

Assume the case on trial involves a collision at the intersection of High and Congress streets on July 10, 1990. The lawyer laying the foundation for admission of a photograph of the scene first shows that the witness was familiar with the scene at the relevant time. This can be done either by showing that the witness was one of the participants in the accident or has independent familiarity with the scene. If the witness was a bystander at the accident, his familiarity with the scene can be inferred from his testimony that he was there at the time. Otherwise, the foundation would include some preliminary questions such as

Q. Are you familiar with the corner of Congress and High streets in Portland, Maine, as it was on July 8, 1990?

A. Yes, I am.

Q. How is it that you are familiar with the corner of Congress and High streets as it was on July 8?

A. I lived in Portland at the time and passed that corner every day on my way to work.

Next, the lawyer asks the witness whether he recognizes the scene depicted in the photograph.

Q. I show you a photograph marked as Exhibit 5 for identification. Do you recognize the scene depicted in the exhibit?

A. Yes, I do.

Q. What scene is that, Sir?

A. That's the corner of High and Congress streets.

Finally, the lawyer asks the witness the typical question,

Q. Does Exhibit 5 for identification fairly and accurately depict the corner of High and Congress streets as that area existed on July 8, 1990?

A. Yes, it does.

Q. We offer Exhibit number 5 in evidence.

With most photographs used as exhibits, it is important that the object or scene is accurately depicted as it was at the relevant time. How something or someone has changed might make a difference. Thus qualifying the time as to how something looked "as it existed then" is usually part of establishing the routine foundation for photographs.

How a scene is depicted depends very much on the vantage point from which a photograph is taken. Despite this fact, usually the witness who authenticates a photograph need not ever have viewed the scene from the perspective from which the photograph was taken. Thus a witness whose only acquaintance with an object has been at ground level can authenticate an aerial photograph of that object. A participant who has viewed a scene from the north can authenticate a picture taken from the south. Only where there is some genuine issue as to the fairness or accuracy of the photograph does the perspective or viewpoint of the authenticating witness become a matter of any importance.

It must be stressed again that is is not necessary to call the photographer as an authenticating witness. Nor is it necessary to document the camera, the film, or the photographic process by which the picture was developed and printed. All that is needed is a person who has personal familiarity with the object or scene at the relevant time. That person can then recognize the scene and attest that the photographic depiction is fair and accurate based on his memory of the object or scene.

3. Distortion and Unfair Prejudice in Photographs

Although photographs are routinely offered and admitted in evidence and used at trial, an opposing attorney should be alert to potential distortion and unfair prejudice from this powerful media. Because of the high degree of acceptance of photographs by factfinders, any prejudice from a photograph is likely to be particularly serious.

Traditionally, photographs have been scrutinized for unfair prejudice in their content. If a photograph depicts something of relevance to the case but also causes extraneous emotional reactions, the value of the depiction must be weighed against the danger of unfair prejudice arising from the emotional reaction. Thus a gory photograph of an accident victim might be subject to exclusion under Federal Rule of Evidence 403 or its state counterparts. The argument would be that viewing the photograph raises the risk of the factfinders having an emotional reaction to all the blood. This could prejudice them against the alleged tortfeasor.

On the other hand, if the photograph teaches something of importance on the disputed issues, it will likely be admitted regardless of the risk of an emotional reaction to the gory aspects. As in any Rule 403 determination, the trial judge has to weigh the value of the photograph on the issues in the case, the availability of alternative forms of proof on those issues, and the likelihood of unfair prejudice.

There is also the possibility of distortion in the photograph itself that may arise from changes in the scene between the time of the events in question and the time the photograph was taken. It may arise from the kind of lens used, which could distort the way the scene is recorded on the film. Moreover, the human eye and a modern camera do not have the same ability to see and record visual information under all conditions. The fact that something appears or does not appear in a photograph does not mean that a person who was on the scene would have seen it the same way or even at all.

Assume, for example, that the events in question took place at night, and that visibility is an issue in the case. Even if taken later the same night of the incident, a flash picture of the scene might well distort the apparent visibility of the objects of the scene. Different objects may appear more visible in the picture taken with the flash than they actually were to the naked eye under the natural lighting conditions at the relevant time.

Under Federal Rule of Evidence 403 the objection is articulated:

> *Opposing Counsel.* Objection! Rule 403. The risk of unfair prejudice from this photograph substantially outweighs its probative value.

If necessary, a voir dire can be requested in order to show the facts supporting the argument against the admissibility of the photograph:

> *Opposing Counsel.* Objection! Your Honor, may we have a brief voir dire?
>
> *The Court.* You may proceed.
>
> *Q.* (on voir dire). Ms. Witness, this photograph, Exhibit 5 for identification, was taken at night wasn't it?
>
> *A.* Yes, it was.
>
> *Q.* It was obviously taken with the use of a flash bulb, wasn't it?

A. Yes, it was.

Q. And certainly the light from the flash bulb as shown in this photograph was not the same as the light at the time the accident occurred, was it?

A. That's right.

Q. Your Honor, may we be heard at sidebar?

The Court. Yes, you may.

Opposing Counsel (at sidebar). Your Honor, the primary issue in this case is whether the defendant saw the decedent's body before his car hit him on the night in question. These photographs, taken with a flash, give a distorted impression of the visibility in the area of the accident. The danger of unfair prejudice from the distortion in the lighting substantially outweighs the probative value of these photographs, especially since we already have a plan of the area that accurately shows the locations of houses, trees, and other objects involved in the case.

The ruling will depend on the trial judge's perception of the importance of the issue, the significance of the distortion, and the importance of the photograph in accurately depicting those elements.

In a situation where the photograph may not be reliable evidence for all that it depicts, it may be offered and admitted for a limited purpose.

Proponent of Exhibit (also at sidebar). Your Honor, we propose to limit the offer of Exhibit 5 for identification to the purpose of showing the general layout of the streets and nearby structures at the time in question, and not for lighting or visibility.

The call is a discretionary one with the court. Because of the power of visual impressions, it is difficult to erase or modify them solely by an oral limiting instruction:

The Court. Ladies and Gentlemen of the Jury, Exhibit 5 has been offered and admitted in evidence for a limited purpose,

namely to show the general layout of the streets and nearby
structures at the time in question, and not for lighting or
visibility. I therefore instruct you that you may consider
Exhibit 5 only for the layout of the street and nearby buildings, and not for the lighting or visibility at the time in
question.

This limiting instruction is probably of little efficacy in remedying
any subconscious impression of the lighting or visibility that a
factfinder might have obtained from looking at the photograph.
Although it is generally believed that factfinders try to follow instructions from the court, it is also believed that it is hard to
convince someone to "unsee" something that he has seen merely
because it has been offered and admitted for a limited purpose.
Counsel should thus be especially alert to unwanted prejudice
from photographs and act vigorously to control or eliminate it.

4. X Rays

Some special classes of photographs do require explicit proof of
authenticity. X rays, which are commonly used in personal injury
cases, usually must be authenticated by chain of custody or recognition based on identifying marks. This is because there is usually no
witness who is personally familiar with the appearance of the
bones and structures inside a person's body. Thus there is not
likely to be anyone who can recognize the body parts depicted in
the X ray as those involved in the case.

The reliability of X rays has become universally accepted. Thus
there is no need for a witness to testify that the X ray offered in
evidence fairly and accurately depicts the bones or body parts
shown. The only foundation that need be established is that it is in
fact an X ray of the relevant patient at a relevant time.

Q. Doctor, I show you an X ray photograph that has been
marked Plaintiff's Exhibit 6 for identification. Do you
recognize Exhibit 6?

A. Yes, I do.

Q. Would you tell us what it is?

A. That is an X ray of the left knee of the plaintiff, Steven Jenks, that was taken at my office on July 23, 1990.

Q. How are you able to recognize Exhibit 6 as an X ray of Mr. Jenks taken at your office on July 23, 1990?

A. Because I brought the X ray with me from my files.

Q. Does your office have some kind of a system to keep track of X rays and to identify them?

A. Yes, it does.

Q. What is that system?

A. At the time we take an X ray we mark it with the name of the patient and file it in an X ray file maintained under the name of that patient.

Q. Was Exhibit 6 for identification taken and maintained according to that practice?

A. Yes, it was.

Q. We offer Exhibit number 6.

Opposing Counsel.   No objection.

The Court.   Exhibit 6 is admitted in evidence.

Q. May the doctor publish Exhibit 6 to the jury with the aid of the lighted viewbox?

The Court.   He may.

G.   Exhibits That Are Records — The Hearsay Rule and Additional Foundations

1.   *The Hearsay Rule Applied to Records*

Most documents or things that contain information in the form of a record or statement are likely to involve an issue of hearsay. The hearsay rule, with its many exceptions, has been ridiculed by some teachers of trial advocacy as a toothless lion. The theory is that a resourceful lawyer can somehow get anything that might technically be hearsay before the factfinders via some exception or for some limited purpose. Although this might be true in many cases, there are enough exclusions of claimed hearsay at trial and enough reversals of rulings on hearsay on appeal to keep the issue very much alive in trial planning and presentation.

In addition to hearsay issues, documents and statements may involve issues of privilege. Copies of documents, films, and the like may also be rendered inadmissible by the Best Evidence Rule. In preparing for the offer and use of exhibits in the presentation, the trial lawyer must determine whether any one of these rules poses a barrier to any proposed exhibits and, if so, how the barrier can be overcome.

For instance, many relevant documents or statements by or adopted by the opposing party are not hearsay because they are admissions under Federal Rule of Evidence 801 and the corresponding rules in every state jurisdiction. Other out-of-court statements by third parties may not be hearsay if their relevance does not depend on acceptance of the statements as true. For instance, a contract or notice is usually relevant not for the truth of the matter set forth but for the words employed and their effect as legal acts. The hearsay rule would not bar such evidence.

Even if it is technically hearsay, an exhibit may very well fall within an exception to the hearsay rule. The facts that establish the exception ordinarily are established during the laying of the foundation by the proponent of the exhibit.

It is not always necessary for the exhibit's proponent initially to undertake proving the hearsay rule exception as a part of the foundation. The lawyer can merely lay the foundation of authenticity and relevancy and offer the exhibit. It would then be up to the opposing party to object based on hearsay. If the other party does not bother to object, there is no need to go through the sometimes wearisome and mechanical process of laying a hearsay exception foundation. If an objection is made, the proponent can then lay a further foundation establishing the exception.

On the other hand, laying the foundation for the applicable hearsay rule exception before any objection is raised maintains uninterrupted control of the proceedings and avoids the appearance of a skirmish victory for the opponent. Establishing the hearsay foundation at that time might also enhance the overall credibility and authority of the exhibit even if it is not ultimately necessary to get it admitted.

Whether to lay a complete foundation at the outset or to lay a minimum foundation subject to possible objection from the opponent is a tactical decision based on the circumstances of the presentation, the importance of the exhibit, the tone and momentum of the proceedings, and the kind of additional foundation that might be needed. In any event, the trial lawyer must be prepared to lay the complete foundation smoothly and effectively as soon as it may be needed. If opposing counsel is aware that the lawyer offering the exhibit is capable of laying the foundation, it is less likely that she will lodge an objection, and the presentation can go forward without interruption.

2. Business Records

One of the most common hearsay exceptions applicable to modern trials covers documents that qualify as "business records." The exception authorizing the admission of business records despite the hearsay rule is found in Federal Rule of Evidence 803 (6). The business-records exception has a counterpart in the evidence law of every jurisdiction.

The typical business-records foundation is provided through the "custodian or other qualified witness" with respect to the records to be offered. In an organization, the "custodian" of a record is any person whose responsibilities include custody of that particular record. Anyone from the company president on down to the assistant records clerk can qualify.

The custodian witness is usually asked a series of questions such as

Q. I show you a document marked as Exhibit 4 for identification. Do you recognize Exhibit 4?

A. Yes, I do.

Q. Would you tell us what it is?

A. This is the payroll record for Robert Simmons.

> Q. How are you able to recognize this as a payroll record for Robert Simmons?
>
> A. Because I brought it with me from the files of Mr. Simmons's employer this morning.

So far, this is the same kind of foundation as one would lay for any other exhibit. The authenticity of the exhibit as a payroll record has been shown in testimony that the witness recognizes the document as the genuine record and has a basis for recognition because she brought it with her from the real source. The relevance of the exhibit has been shown by the testimony that the record pertains to one of the parties in the case. Now we come to the foundation to invoke the business records exception to the hearsay rule:

> Q. In your capacity as personnel officer, do you have knowledge of the manner in which payroll records are kept by Mr. Simmons's employer?
>
> A. Yes, I do.
>
> Q. Was Exhibit 4 kept in the ordinary course of the business of Mr. Simmons's employer?
>
> A. Yes, it was.
>
> Q. Was it in the ordinary course of business of this employer to keep records of this kind?
>
> A. Yes, it was.
>
> Q. Would you tell us, please, was the information contained in Exhibit 4 put down at or near the time of the events that are recorded?
>
> A. Oh, yes.
>
> Q. Was this information recorded by a person with knowledge or from information obtained from a person with knowledge at the time?
>
> A. Yes, it was.
>
> Q. We offer Exhibit 4 in evidence.
>
> The Court.   Admitted.

When laying the more complex foundations that are designed to address specific requirements of the rules of evidence, it is usually wise to stick close to the language of the rule itself in establishing the foundation. Judges are accustomed to hearing the traditional language that appears in the rules. If a lawyer tries to be creative and lay the foundation using other terminology of ostensibly equivalent meaning, there is the risk that the court will be confused or may get the impression that there is something out of the ordinary or wrong with the exhibit.

When laying evidentiary foundations, the proponent of the exhibit is usually permitted to use soft leading questions to focus the witness on the elements of the foundation. Thus the questions in the example above, even though they were all more or less leading, would be acceptable in most jurisdictions for foundation purposes.

While foundation testimony to establish a hearsay rule exception may have some value in accrediting the exhibit, most trial lawyers treat it as a portion of the proceeding to be passed through as quickly as possible in favor of more lively material.

H.   Publication of Exhibits

1.   Show the Exhibit to the Jury!

Once the lawyer has gone through the business of laying the evidentiary foundation and complying with the rules regulating the admission of things in evidence, and the exhibit has been offered and admitted in evidence, it is time to use the exhibit as part of the presentation. The idea is to use the exhibit to create the desired image.

Most people have at least some degree of curiosity about objects and papers that are discussed or waved about in their presence. Factfinders in the courtroom are no exception — regardless of what the exhibit is, they usually want to see it. Thus it behooves the lawyer to plan the presentation so that the exhibit can be shown to the factfinders as soon as possible after it is offered. Effectively laying the foundation will convey the impression that the exhibit is a credible bit of information that will contribute to the presentation. When is a better time to expose the factfinders to this element than right after the foundation has been laid?

For some reason, lawyers are sometimes hesitant to publish exhibits to juries during the case presentation. Perhaps this reluctance arises from a hypersensitivity to wasting time. Perhaps it reflects a subconscious concern about loss of control of the courtroom atmosphere or loss of momentum while the factfinders are considering the exhibit. For whatever reason, in many a trial, after struggling long and hard to lay a foundation for a disputed exhibit and after successfully overcoming the objection and securing admission of the exhibit, the lawyer will triumphantly lay the spoils on the clerk's table without even bothering to show the evidence to the factfinders. Frequently, nothing is seen or heard of the exhibit again until the summation!

Certainly, considerations of delay and case momentum and control affect the publication of exhibits. But they primarily affect the manner of publication, not the decision of whether to publish. As a general principle, a lawyer should plan to publish all exhibits in some way to the jury at the time they are offered. The exhibits will thus make a positive contribution to the trial presentation at the time best calculated to have the strongest effect.

The timing and manner of publication of exhibits to the jury are ultimately under the control of the judge. The lawyer must always ask the court's permission before showing things to the jury. It is the judge who has to make sure that the trial moves along at a reasonable pace and that the proceedings are not unduly delayed by lengthy and distracting publication of exhibits. Needless to say, the personal views of the judge on how the exhibits should be published must be taken into account.

Nonetheless, the ultimate responsibility for making an effective presentation of the fact image is the lawyer's, not the judge's. A trial lawyer should not be timid about asking for permission to publish important exhibits in the manner calculated and at the time most likely to make the best impression on the factfinders.

2. Methods of Publication of Exhibits

Exhibits should be published to the factfinders in a way that will generate the most appreciation for the exhibit and its significance with a minimum of delay, disruption, or loss of control of the presentation. The time-honored method of having the object, document, or photograph passed from one juror to another is in many cases a very inefficient means of publication. It is akin to a teacher giving out some explanatory material to be passed from student to student while the remaining members of the class wait and fidget. The lawyer's control over the factfinders' learning processes is largely given up during the time they are waiting for, looking at, or have looked at an exhibit, thus promoting delay and losing focus. While exhibits are being passed along, the lawyer is often left in a dilemma: should she wait to continue her presentation until all of the factfinders have finished examining the exhibit? Waiting will surely dissipate the momentum of the presentation. On the other hand, if she continues the witness examination while the factfinders are passing the exhibit, there is the risk that not all of them will be paying attention to her presentation.

The image of jurors squinting at small photographs, often passed in packs, is a familiar one to most trial lawyers. Familiar also is the image of the lawyer standing by helplessly, waiting for the jury to puzzle their way seriatim through the pictures while the trial judge scowls impatiently from the bench.

Relevant material in a documentary exhibit may be read aloud by a witness or by counsel. However, this method of publication is also likely to be slow and inefficient if the amount of material to be read is more than a sentence or two. It also undermines one of the primary virtues of the exhibit, the power of a visual presentation. It is counterproductive to diminish the authority of a written document by conveying it orally to the factfinders. Moreover, counsel is not permitted to publish a written document by reading a summary of it aloud. The complete text of the document must be read if it is published in this manner.

3. Publication by the Lawyer

The most effective means of publication of exhibits are generally those in which the lawyer or witness can play a role in showing the exhibit to the jury. Direct publication of exhibits by the lawyer usually saves time, retains control of the presentation, and better integrates the exhibit and its significance into the overall trial presentation.

For example, if the exhibits are photographs of an accident scene, the lawyer could have them enlarged to, say, 8 x 10, or even larger. The lawyer could then show the enlargements to the factfinders by holding them up in front of her one at a time and slowly moving a few inches from the jury box along the row of factfinders. As the lawyer displays the photographs to the factfinders, she can watch their eyes for flickers of recognition or satisfaction with what is shown them or observe their frowns of incomprehension. This feedback will cue the lawyer to pause longer or to move on to the next factfinder. In this way the lawyer is directly associated with and in control of this powerful and authoritative media.

In a case where the presentation includes a large number of photographs, slides can be made from the photographs and projected on a screen set up in front of the factfinders. These methods of publishing photographic exhibits ensure that the factfinders are all seeing substantially the same thing at the same time. The lawyer is in control of what the factfinders see and when they see it. The showing of the exhibit to the factfinders becomes a much more integrated part of the presentation.

Documents and other written materials can be also published to the factfinders in various ways other than by merely passing the exhibits among them or reading them aloud. One popular alternative is to provide sufficient copies of the document so that all the factfinders can look at their own copies. This method does save time. However, giving each factfinder a copy of a written document relinquishes control of the presentation to the factfinders during the time they are looking at their individual documents. Like a teacher giving a homework assignment, the lawyer has no particular control over what portions of the document are looked at and in what order. The interval of inspection will be determined by how long the most deliberate factfinder chooses to examine her document. The proceedings in the meantime are held in suspense. And unless the documents are passed out and collected frequently, there is nothing to prevent the factfinders from reinspecting them later on, while the lawyer would prefer that they be listening to testimony or looking at other evidence.

Present technology permits almost any document to be displayed on a screen with the aid of an overhead projector. For many trial lawyers this has become the method of choice for the publication of printed material and diagrams. While displaying the exhibit to the factfinders on the overhead projector, the lawyer or witness who is showing the document maintains the crucial role of teacher and can control what pages the factfinders see, how long they see them, and in what order.

When a lawyer publishes an exhibit to the factfinders during the testimonial phase of the trial, as opposed to its opening or closing, she is usually not permitted to comment on the exhibit or discuss its contents in any way. Sometimes the lawyer is not even permitted to point out the exhibit's relevant portions or features during publication without the express permission of the judge. The theory is that such comments or pointing would be a form of argument. Orderly court procedures require that argument by counsel be confined to the end of the trial.

4. Publication by the Witness

Frequently the most powerful means of publication of an exhibit is with the aid of a witness. A witness is permitted to point out features of an exhibit and discuss its contents as a part of the fact presentation. For instance, once a photograph has been admitted in evidence, it can be used to supplement and illustrate witness testimony.

> Q. Now, Ms. Farris, would you please take Exhibit 1 in evidence and show the members of the jury which is your house?
>
> A. (witness indicating). Here.
>
> Q. With the Court's permission, Ms. Farris, can you please come down from the witness stand and stand in front of the jury box so that all of the members of the jury can see where you are indicating?
>
> A. Yes [coming down]. Here.
>
> Q. You are indicating in the upper left-hand corner of Exhibit 1 what appears to be the front door of a house?
>
> A. Yes.

The last question, with which the lawyer "lays tracks" or makes a connection between the witness's indications and the transcript, is only necessary if (1) the point is important and (2) what the witness is indicating is not evident from the face of the exhibit itself in the context of the testimony given.

> Q.   Now, Ms. Farris, using Exhibit 1, can you show the members of the jury where you found the beer bottle that you just testified about?
>
> A.   Yes, it was right here.
>
> Q.   The point you are indicating is just below the window on your house?
>
> A.   Yes.

5.   Exhibits as Illustrative Aids

Exhibits in evidence can also be used as illustrative aids. An exhibit that conveys certain information in and of itself may also be used to illustrate the testimony of a witness.

> Q.   Will you mark an "X" on Exhibit 1 to indicate the location of the beer bottle you found?
>
> A.   Yes [marking].

The witness's marking on the exhibit is not the same kind of evidence as the photograph itself. The marks are illustrative of her testimony. They are subject to the same infirmities of inaccurate recollection and bias as any other testimony. However, they serve to convey the witness's information about the location of the bottle with a great deal of accuracy, far more accuracy than any oral description could have.

Strictly speaking, the visual witness testimony in the form of the marks in the photograph would be like any other illustrative aid and not admissible in evidence. In most cases, however, such marks are treated as incidental to the photograph and do not interfere with its continued status as an admitted exhibit.

Sometimes effective use of an exhibit during the presentation will require that it be enlarged considerably. Exhibits that are to be referred to frequently are sometimes enlarged and mounted on boards for easy portability and quick reference in opening, during presentation of evidence, and in closing.

The court retains the power to regulate the publication and use of exhibits throughout the presentation. The judge can restrict or forbid any activity with exhibits or any trial media if he is satisfied that the legitimate probative value is outweighed by the danger of unfair prejudice, confusion, or waste of time. The fact that a gory 8 x 10 photograph is admitted in evidence over a Rule 403 objection does not mean that counsel can necessarily enlarge the picture to lifesize or project it on a screen.

The use of exhibits as illustrative aids can raise the issue of whether any markings added to the exhibits by way of illustration should be permitted to go to the jury room as part of the exhibit for later scrutiny. The Federal Rules of Evidence and similar codifications offer little guidance on this issue. Their use is presently regulated by trial court discretion and common sense. Although practices may vary among jurisdictions, the court usually retains the discretion to permit an exhibit to go to the jury room even if it is marked to some degree to illustrate other testimony. This discretion might be exercised in favor of exclusion if the exhibit has been substantially altered or its character changed by its use as an illustrative aid.

There is also sometimes an issue of whether a lawyer may cause marks to be placed on an opponent's exhibits. It is certainly improper to deface the opponent's exhibits or alter their impact by marking on them as illustrative aids. Beyond the clear extremes, the issue here is usually a matter of court discretion. Rulings are case by case and are never appealed.

As is the case with pure illustrative aids, a lawyer who wants to mark her opponent's exhibits should be ready to protect the original exhibits with mylar overlays or in some other fashion. A lawyer who wants to be sure that his exhibits will not be marked on by his opponents should be ready to provide the exhibits with the same protection.

Chapter 12 Expert Witnesses

A. The Problem of Expert Testimony

1. The Importance of Common Knowledge and Experience

Common knowledge and experience are the primary tools that people use to communicate with each other. They are the primary tools trial lawyers and witnesses use to communicate with the factfinders and recreate an image in court. Common knowledge and experience are also the primary tools the factfinders use to understand and accredit the image presented.

When a witness describes an automobile accident, the words, illustrations, and other visual media used have similar meanings to the lawyer and witness making the presentation and to the factfinders hearing and seeing it. The lawyer, witness, and factfinders share basic knowledge and information about most of the elements involved in the presentation. The factfinders are able to assess and accredit the images proffered by the lawyers and witnesses based on their own experience with these and similar events. When trial lawyers argue the validity or authority of their images, they rely heavily on the common experience of the factfinders as the test for acceptability of a given fact picture or scenario. Does the image that is being proposed accord with the factfinders' common experience in the world with which they are familiar?

Analysis based on common experience is employed by everyone in making decisions. It is common experience that enables untrained factfinders and decision-makers such as juries to make reliable determinations in those many cases in which the issues involve the kinds of events or circumstances that people encounter in their daily lives.

2.   Issues Outside of Common Experience

Modern trials, however, frequently involve issues outside the factfinders' common knowledge and experience. How many jurors, or judges for that matter, have any knowledge about the design of immunological tests involved in a patent infringement case? How many factfinders have the knowledge or experience to assess the care used by the designer of an electrical power generating plant? What does the average person "know" about the effect of a head injury on psychoneurological function?

In bygone days, when life was simpler, most of the issues in litigation were within the experience of most people. However, in recent times specialized knowledge and technology have expanded far faster than has our ability to understand and absorb it. Many of today's activities are not within the common ken but are known only to a small number of scholars and practitioners. These specialists can talk to one another and can understand and evaluate what each other is talking about and doing. To the rest of us, however, their conversations and their activities are outside our language and experience and hence largely incomprehensible.

Legal disputes often involve areas of specialized knowledge and expertise. But without a base of knowledge or experience shared by the lawyers, witnesses, and factfinders, it is very difficult for a trial lawyer to make a meaningful presentation. How can the lawyer expect to generate the image of an immunological test procedure in the consciousnesses of the factfinders if they don't know what an immunological test is? And how will the factfinder be able to know which unfamiliar contentions about the test should be accepted? Somehow this gap between a specialized subject matter and the realm of common experience and understanding must be bridged if our trial process is to function in technical cases.

3.   Enter the Expert Witness

Ordinarily trial presentations are made in terms of basic facts. The factfinders are expected to evaluate the basic facts presented, accept those that they find credible, and then make the appropriate inferences to complete the picture. Whenever the subject matter of a trial presentation is not within the common understanding of the factfinders, they are simply not equipped to evaluate the facts, determine which ones to believe, and make inferences from them. Instead, resort must be had to expert witnesses. "Expert witnesses" are persons whose education or experience is such that they are presumably in a position to understand and assess relevant facts and circumstances that are outside the common knowledge of the other trial participants.

The expert witnesses are given the latitude to express their testimony in opinions and conclusions to be accepted or rejected by the factfinders, rather than to merely provide the basic facts from which the factfinders draw the conclusions. Of necessity, the experts are permitted not only to marshal the facts but also to perform at least part of the evaluation function themselves. For example, most lawyers, judges, and jurors would not be expected to assess the degree of impairment sustained by a person who has suffered a particular bodily injury. An orthopedic surgeon, however, is permitted to state his opinion, based on his specialized knowledge. He may provide testimony, for instance, that the patient can be expected to sustain a specific percentage of impairment to her bodily function over the remaining years of her working life.

Rare are the judge or jury who would know whether sound engineering practices require the addition of "soot-blowers" to the boilers in a generating plant. An expert engineer, however, may not only describe soot-blowers and their function but may also express her opinion, based on her specialized knowledge and experience, on whether these devices are required.

4.   Challenges in the Presentation of Expert Testimony

The presentation of an expert witness provides the lawyer with at least two challenges. The first is to communicate the ideas of the witness in such a way that the factfinders can understand those ideas, at least by analogy. How can the gobbledegook of the specialist be translated so that the factfinders can understand it and form an image from it?

The second challenge to the trial lawyer is to provide a means

whereby the factfinders can accept and accredit the presentation of
one expert in preference to the competing presentation offered by
the opposing expert witness. Why should the factfinders believe
this side's gibberish over that of the opponent?

Effective presentation, cross-examination, and argument of expert testimony calls for the trial lawyer's best talents and greatest
creativity. When a trial lawyer fails to make her expert witnesses
understood by the factfinders, the ultimate determination may be
based on entirely extraneous considerations. Or the factfinders
may simply go to sleep and ignore what the experts say in favor of
their own "common sense" assessment of what is being portrayed,
regardless of whether they are qualified to assess it.

5. Analogies and Visual Representations

Because the factfinders lack primary knowledge of the subject matter of the expert testimony, the trial lawyer often uses proxies from
common experience to assist in both understanding and accreditation of the unfamiliar testimony. The function of the presentation is to teach the expert's subject matter by analogy to things
and circumstances that are within the common knowledge and
experience of the factfinders. Thus a spinal column might be analogized to a pile of building blocks. The function of a steam boiler
might be described using the image of a tea kettle. Immunological
reactions might be shown as small magnets or as puzzle pieces
fitting together.

Choosing the analogies to be used is an important and creative
part of developing expert testimony. The goal is to find the right
analogy to generate an understanding of the expert's point. The
analogy might also contribute to acceptance of that point by the
jury. For instance, comparing the spine to a pile of building blocks
makes it easy to understand how the backbone may have become
misaligned in a traumatic accident.

Because of the strangeness of expert testimony in terms of most
people's common experience, visual aids often form an important
part of an expert presentation. If the terminology is unfamiliar and
the factfinders have never seen that which is to be depicted, it is
virtually impossible to get an understanding with a purely verbal
presentation. A picture avoids the problems of translation of lan-

guage. The picture can recreate a reliable image even in the absence
of experience with what is portrayed.

A verbal description of an air cooled condenser is meaningless
to factfinders because they don't know what a condenser is and
have never seen one. Even if they have been taught the function of
a condenser, a reliable image of one would not appear in their
consciousnesses from words alone. However, showing a picture
immediately teaches every factfinder what a condenser looks like.
And a simple diagram or schematic can better describe its function
than a torrent of technical jargon.

6. Risks and Dangers of Expert Testimony

With the challenges of expert presentation go serious risks and
dangers. Understanding and accreditation by analogy is risky at
best. Lack of direct experience makes it very hard to assess the
validity of analogies. Lawyers and witnesses can manipulate the
factfinders' assessment by the choice of analogy in a way that is
almost impossible to combat. If in fact the spine does not behave
the way a pile of building blocks does, the use of the block analogy,
however appealing to the untutored, may be seriously misleading.

It was once thought that an expert's fidelity to his specialized
discipline would prevent him from making contentions that were
not supportable according to that discipline. An expert would not
make erroneous assertions in court because he would be afraid
that his reputation would suffer. The expert would be accountable
to his peers. They would keep him honest.

Experience, however, has shown that the effectiveness of an
expert's reputation in the field to guarantee consistent expert testimony varies a good deal from field to field. In many fields of expertise there are partisan experts who are willing to make plausible
presentations of scientific propositions that are not necessarily well
accepted within the particular discipline. If an expert's opinion is
not shared by others in the field, opposing counsel may argue that
fact as a reason for the factfinders not to accept that opinion. However, the factfinders are rarely in a position to assess the significance
of a disagreement among experts. The lack of effective accountability among the experts and the limited ability of the factfinders to
assess expert testimony means that sometimes dubious opinions can

be persuasively asserted. Sometimes this "junk science" provides spurious bases for actual findings and verdicts. Efforts toward reform in trial advocacy are now focusing on better control of expert presentations.

B.   The Unique Role of the Expert Witness

1.   *Opinions and Conclusions in Lay Testimony*

Lay witnesses are supposed to confine their testimony to actual observations or experiences. They are not, as a rule, permitted to express conclusions, opinions, or inferences from the basic facts asserted. The theory is that the process of concluding and inferring is reserved to the factfinders, who are supposed to make those conclusions and inferences based on their experience in the real world.

Although the "opinion rule" forbidding lay opinion testimony is universal in American evidence law, it has many exceptions. Strictly speaking, it is almost impossible to describe any event without expressing some conclusions about what was going on. Even a rigorously factual recounting of an event will contain some inferences.

Under Federal Rule of Evidence 701 and similar rules in other jurisdictions, the "opinion rule" is applied pragmatically. A lay person may express opinions or inferences if they are

(1) rationally based on the perception of the witness, and

(2) helpful to a clear understanding of the witness's testimony or the determination of a fact in issue.

Another common formulation of the permissible scope of lay witness opinion testimony includes those opinions that are "shorthand renderings of the facts." However, once the inquiry goes beyond those facts that are in the general ken of the trial participants, the factfinders are much less well equipped to perform their function of analyzing the facts presented and drawing appropriate inferences and conclusions from them. They must rely on expert witnesses to draw the inferences and conclusions for them.

2. What Is an Expert Witness?

According to Federal Rule of Evidence 702, an expert witness is anyone who has "knowledge, skill, experience, training, or education" in "scientific, technical or other specialized knowledge" that will assist the factfinders to understand the evidence or determine a fact at issue. This definition presupposes that the issue on which the expert witness is to testify is one with which the factfinders need help. If the issue is within common understanding, the expert will not be helpful to the factfinders and will not be allowed to give an opinion.

Hand in hand with the definition of "expert witness" is the delineation of what an expert may do. Unlike the lay witness, the expert may assist the factfinder with testimony "in the form of an opinion or otherwise." [1] Because the factfinders lack the experience to draw the necessary inferences or conclusions, the expert is given the latitude to do that for them.

An expert witness may also be a fact witness. For example, a plaintiff's treating physician may testify as to facts about the injury observed and the treatment rendered. He may also testify as an expert witness about the cause of the injuries and their probable consequences over the plaintiff's lifetime. Similarly, an engineer who designed a generating plant may testify as a fact witness about the work done on the plant's design and also as an expert witness about the appropriate standard of care to be observed by engineers in the design of plants of this kind.

C. Accrediting the Expert Witness

Before a witness is allowed to assist the factfinders with opinions and conclusions about matters not within common experience, it must be shown that he has the appropriate skill, knowledge, or experience to give the expert testimony. This process is known as the "accreditation" of the expert witness. It is a foundation for the testimony the witness will deliver.

An expert witness is as broadly accredited as any other witness. Most trial lawyers will first want to show that the grey-bearded

[1] Fed. R. Evid. 702

bespectacled professor on the witness stand is a real human being, has a wife and children, and has lived in the nearby college town for a long time. In assessing what this expert says, the factfinders will first want to know how the witness is like them. Often the expert's human qualities will be as important to factfinder acceptance as his credentials of expertise in the specialized field in which he is testifying.

1. Display of Expert Credentials

A major part of the accreditation process for expert witnesses is the display of the expert's credentials. The purpose is two-fold: 1) to satisfy the judge, who will rule on the admissibility of any proffered expert testimony, that the expert is qualified to give the testimony sought; and 2) to accredit the expert as a source of information in the eyes of the factfinders.

The presentation attempts to show that the expert has recognition and accomplishments in his own field and therefore is sufficiently qualified so that his testimony will be of assistance to the factfinders. The argument is that if people in his own field accept the expert's opinion, the factfinders should do so as well.

A typical expert witness accreditation lays out in an orderly manner the expert's educational qualifications and experience, the depth and nature of his practical experience in his field, any recognition earned by the expert in that field, and any experience teaching, publishing, or testifying in court in those areas in which he will be asked opinion questions.

Q. Doctor, would you tell the members of the jury your educational background after high school?

A. I went to Harvard College and then on to Harvard Medical School.

Q. How long is medical school, Doctor?

A. That's a four-year course after college.

Q. What did you study at medical school?

A. I studied the basic medical course leading to the M.D. degree.

Q. After you received your M.D. degree, Doctor, did you go on to any further study?

A. Yes, I did. I did an internship and a residency.

Q. Doctor, what are an internship and residency?

A. An internship is a post-graduate training program in a hospital. Almost all doctors serve at least one year of internship.

Q. Doctor, would you tell us what a residency is?

A. Yes, a residency is a further period of hospital-based post-graduate training, usually within some specialty field.

Q. Doctor, did you have a specialty field in your residency?

A. Yes, I did.

Q. What was that specialty, Doctor?

A. Orthopedic surgery.

Note that the accreditation is a good time for the trial lawyer to introduce terminology and to make the doctor into a teacher of the factfinders. The lawyer acts as a translator or facilitator. The lawyer does not hesitate to ask for explanations to assist the factfinders. She increases her own credibility with the factfinders if she is seen as trying to help them understand the unfamiliar material being presented by the expert.

Q. Doctor, what do you mean by "orthopedic surgery"?

A. "Orthopedic surgery" is that branch of the science of medicine that deals with the musculo-skeletal system of the human body and certain nerves.

Q. What is the "musculo-skeletal system of the human body," Doctor?

A. That's the bones and muscles we all have.

Q. Does it include the backbone, Doctor?

A. Yes, it does.

In performing the function of guide or translator of the expert testimony, the trial lawyer should not appear to talk down to the factfinders. For this reason,

Q. Please tell us what you mean by "orthopedic surgery"?

or simply

Q. What do you mean by "orthopedic surgery"?

may seem less condescending than

Q. Doctor, please tell the members of the jury what you mean by "orthopedic surgery"?

The latter formulation implies that the lawyer and the expert know what is meant by "orthopedic surgery," and only the factfinders are ignorant. It also tends to distance the lawyer and the expert from the jury.

Because of the significance to most people of real life experience as a source of knowledge and expertise, it is important to stress this element in the expert's presentation.

Q. Doctor, following your residency, would you tell the members of the jury about your experience in the field of orthopedic surgery?

A. I have practiced for fifteen years here in Ames.

Q. Please tell us what kind of a practice have you had.

A. General orthopedic practice. I have tried to subspecialize in backs and back surgery.

Q. In your subspecialization in back surgery, about how many cases of back injury have you seen?

A. I would say several hundred, at least.

Publications, honorary and professional societies, and teaching appointments are usually disclosed during the course of accreditation of an expert.

> Q. Doctor, would you tell us about your publications in your field of expertise?
>
> A. Yes. I have published several articles and have contributed to some symposia.
>
> Q. Briefly, Doctor, could you tell us about the subject matters on which you have written articles?
>
> A. May I look at my list here?
>
> A. Yes, Doctor, if it is necessary to refresh your recollection.
>
> A. Yes. My publications are . . . [listing].

The more focused the accreditation is on the precise opinions to be offered by the expert the better.

> Q. Doctor, during the course of your professional practice, have you been asked to give opinions as to the percentage of permanent impairment and loss of patient function as a result of accident or injury?
>
> A. Yes, I have.
>
> Q. In what context have you given these opinions?
>
> A. I have given these opinions in worker's compensation claims and in court cases.
>
> Q. Doctor, is the determination of the cause of injuries also part of your area of expertise?
>
> A. Yes, it is.

Another area of qualification and accreditation that is seldom omitted is evidence of prior testimony as an expert witness.

> Q. Doctor, have you given expert testimony before?
>
> A. Yes, I have.

Q. Can you tell us where you have appeared as an expert witness?

A. Yes. I have appeared in this court, in the federal court, and before the workers' compensation board.

An important objective of the accreditation process is to make the expert appear as authoritative and impressive as possible. To a large extent, the factfinders will not be able to make a direct assessment of the validity of the expert's views. Therefore their overall impression as to the expert's authority is very important. Even more than with lay witnesses, the jurors' acceptance of the witness's expertise will depend on their acceptance of the expert himself as an authority in his field.

At the same time, the proponent of the expert must keep in mind the fact that the expert's qualifications are collateral to the vital issues of the case. Most people have little patience with having to listen to another person blow his own horn. A long, strictly verbal accreditation is likely to leave the factfinders bored and disengaged.

The scope, detail, and emphasis of the accreditation should be tailored to the overall image of the case. A physician, for instance, achieves an enhanced credibility merely by being the treating physician. A witness whose only role was to evaluate the patient may need greater explication of his credentials as an expert to gain acceptance of his opinion.

There is little that the opponent of an expert witness can do to control or blunt the witness's accreditation. Subject to objection for waste of time or excessive inquiry to collateral matters, the expert's proponent is usually given wide latitude to develop the factfinders' appreciation of the qualifications and credibility of the expert witness.

2. Stipulations as to Expert Credentials

At one time it was thought advisable for an opposing lawyer to offer to stipulate to the qualifications of the other party's expert witnesses. The purpose of the stipulation was to deprive the witness's proponent of the opportunity to build up the expert's authority and credibility during the accreditation process. By stipulating to the expert's qualifications in a particular field, the opponent would argue that development of the witness's expert credentials would be an unnecessary waste of time and should be limited or dispensed with entirely.

Further reflection and experience has shown this practice to be self-defeating. More often than not, counsel's generous stipulation does not win the sympathy of the jury. Instead, it is viewed as an admission of the obvious authority of the opponent's expert. Indeed, such a stipulation gives the opponent the ammunition to argue in final argument:

> *Opposing Counsel.* Ladies and Gentlemen, you remember the testimony of Dr. Swallow. As soon as he got on the stand, my opponent stipulated that Dr. Swallow is a qualified expert orthopedic surgeon. His qualifications are so exceptional that there was no way even my opponent could challenge them. This great expert testified that . . .

At the same time, such a stipulation usually does not actually shorten or eliminate the process of accreditation. The proponent might gracefully accept the stipulation, but the accreditation goes on. The opponent's objection that further accreditation is not necessary in light of the stipulation is usually overruled. While the accreditation may not be necessary to permit the witness to testify as an expert, it is still important to assist the factfinders in assessing the expert's credibility.

> Q. Doctor, what scholarly articles have you published in your field of expertise that relate to the issues on which you will be testifying today?
>
> *Opposing Counsel.* Objection! We have already stipulated that Dr. Swallow is a qualified expert orthopedic surgeon.
>
> Q. Your Honor, if our opponent will also stipulate that Dr. Swallow is the most qualified and credible expert available, we need go no further with this questioning. Otherwise, however, we suggest that these questions are important so that the jury can assess Dr. Swallow's credibility.

Stipulating to the expertise of the opponent's expert before the crucial questions are asked also makes it harder to object to a specific question on the ground that the witness lacks the expertise to answer it. Assume, for instance, that opposing counsel has already stipulated that a doctor is qualified as an expert in orthopedics and the doctor is asked a question on a subject matter that may not lie squarely within the field of orthopedics. Opposing counsel may have greater difficulty in objecting to such a question as one that the witness is not qualified to answer:

> *Opposing Counsel.*   Objection! Lack of expert qualifications.
>
> Q.   Your Honor, Opposing Counsel has stipulated to the expert qualifications of Dr. Swallow.
>
> *Opposing Counsel.*   Your Honor, we stipulated that Dr. Swallow is an expert orthopedic surgeon. However, this question is not within the bounds of orthopedic surgery.

Often the judge will have little patience for a discussion of the boundaries of an arbitrarily defined expertise.

> *The Court.*   How am I supposed to know whether this is within the bounds of orthopedic surgery? The witness may answer the question if he feels qualified to do so.

By withholding any kind of reaction at the time the expert's credentials are disclosed, opposing counsel preserves the option to object to particular questions on the ground that the expert witness, based on his particular training, education, and experience, is not qualified to answer the particular questions.

For these reasons, the practice of stipulating to an expert's qualifications is now rarely recommended. Opposing counsel is usually better off to remain silent and hope that the factfinders are as bored as they are impressed with the lengthy recital of an expert's qualifications.

The expert's accreditation is usually accomplished at the beginning of the examination so as not to interfere with the flow and tempo of the presentation. But the accreditation process need not take place at the beginning of the expert's testimony. The witness may also be on the stand to provide other relevant nonexpert testimony. If the witness has other relevant testimony, the expert accreditation can take place at a later point in the examination. In any event, the witness must be accredited as an expert before he is asked questions that depend on that expertise.

3. "Tendering" the Expert Witness

In some jurisdictions it is still customary to "tender" the expert to the court following the accreditation. According to this practice, before the expert witness is asked any opinion questions, the proponent of his testimony is expected to formally seek a ruling from the court that the witness is qualified to testify in a specified area of expertise.

> Q. Your Honor, we move that Dr. Swallow be certified as an expert in orthopedics.

or

> Q. Your Honor, I move that Dr. Swallow be permitted to testify as an expert in the field of orthopedics.

At this point the judge will determine whether the accreditation has demonstrated sufficient expertise on the part of the witness so that he should be considered an expert in the defined field.

When the expert is "tendered," the opponent is usually given the opportunity to voir dire on the expert's qualifications. The court's ruling that an expert is certified in a particular field would presumably permit the witness to testify as an expert on any subject matter within that field.

The practice of tendering and certifying an expert witness adds a new and unnecessary issue in the presentation of expert testimony. Ultimately, the issue is whether a particular witness possesses the expertise to answer a particular question. When the court has ruled in advance that a witness is qualified in a designated field of expertise and a potentially objectionable question is asked, the issue is not whether the witness who is on the stand has the expertise to answer the question; the issue is whether any expert of the discipline for which the witness has already been qualified would have the expertise to answer the question. There is the potential for a meaningless argument over what an expert in the designated subject matter should be expected to know. The issue should be "Does this witness have the expertise to answer the question?" regardless of how that question might be formally classified within any recognized field of expertise.

Another drawback to tendering an expert witness is that, by ruling that a witness is qualified as an expert, the court may be perceived by the factfinders as having approved the content or quality of the witness's testimony. The court in effect has been asked to "bless" the expert. However, in recent years this practice has been abandoned in many jurisdictions. It is not contemplated by the structure or orientation of the Federal Rules of Evidence and is not recommended unless local procedural rules or customs require it.

Under the more modern practice the lawyer elicits qualifications of the expert that in the lawyer's judgment should enable the witness to answer those questions that the lawyer plans to propound later on in the examination. At the conclusion of the accreditation there is no "tender." The lawyer merely goes on to introduce the subject matter of the examination.

Any issue of the witness's expert qualifications is first formally raised when the lawyer asks a question that calls for expert testimony. If the opponent does not dispute the expert's qualifications to answer that particular question, the opponent will raise no objection and the expert will give the answer. If the opponent does dispute the expert's qualifications to answer the question posed, the opponent may object on the ground of the expert's insufficient qualifications to answer that particular question.

Under this procedure the court has before it the actual question when assessing the expert's qualifications to answer it. The court can determine whether this particular witness has the expert qualifications to answer the particular question posed regardless of the subject matter classification of either the witness's expertise or of the question asked. The modern procedure also avoids any implication that the court has given a blanket preapproval to the testimony of any particular witness.

Because the procedure for addressing expert qualifications is in flux, there is presently considerable variation in practice from jurisdiction to jurisdiction and from judge to judge within the same jurisdiction. If an expert's qualifications to answer particular questions are likely to be an issue, opposing counsel can ascertain how the judge plans to proceed and interpose any objection or alternate proposal in advance, outside the presence of the factfinders. If unexpectedly confronted by a motion or request from the opponent that a witness be certified to testify as an expert, counsel may object to the motion and suggest that the expert's qualifications can be better assessed in the context of the questions actually put to the expert.

4. Voir Dire on Qualifications

A question that can be answered only by an expert puts the qualifications of the witness in issue. Is this witness qualified by education and experience to assist the factfinders with an answer to this question?

As indicated before, in jurisdictions where the expert is tendered for a ruling on qualifications in advance, the qualifications of the individual as an expert of the kind described in the tender are tested at the time the witness is tendered. In those jurisdictions, the issue of whether the particular witness is qualified to answer the particular question may be transmuted into the issue of whether an expert of the kind certified is qualified to answer the question.

> Q. Your Honor, we move that Dr. Swallow be allowed to testify as an expert in orthopedic surgery.

The inquiry at the point of tender is whether Dr. Swallow is an expert orthopedic surgeon. The assumption is that a person qualified as an orthopedic surgeon will be able to answer the questions ultimately put to Dr. Swallow.

Under both procedures, either at the time of the question calling for expertise or at the point of tender of the potential expert witness, the opponent is usually given the opportunity to voir dire on expert qualifications. The point of the voir dire is to demonstrate that the witness in fact lacks sufficient qualifications to be allowed to answer the question or to be allowed to testify as an expert.

    Q. Dr. Swallow, do you have an opinion, which you can
    state to a medical probability, as to the degree of perma-
    nent impairment suffered by Mr. Cluney as a result of
    the accident?

Although this is not the time for objection, many lawyers object
at this point for fear that if they do not, the witness will go ahead
and blurt out the opinion. Actually, though, the question calls for a
"yes" or "no" answer. If the answer is "no," there is no need for
objection. If the opposing lawyer is confident that the witness
knows the rules and will answer the question as posed, the opposing lawyer can hold her fire.

    A. Yes, I do.

    Q. What is that opinion?

    Opposing Counsel. Objection! Lack of qualifications.

    The Court. Would you like a brief voir dire on qualifications?

    Opposing Counsel. Yes, Your Honor.

    Opposing Counsel (on voir dire). Dr. Swallow, you are not
    holding yourself out as an expert in the assessment of per-
    centage of permanent impairment, are you?

    A. That's right, I'm not.

    Opposing Counsel. You have never testified in this court on
    degree of permanent impairment, have you?

    A. I don't believe I have.

    Opposing Counsel. Your Honor, we submit that although
    Dr. Swallow may be a competent treating physician, he
    should not be allowed to testify here as to degree of perma-
    nent impairment. He doesn't even hold himself out as an
    expert in that area.

This may not be the end of it. Before ruling on the objection
following voir dire, the judge will usually allow the proponent of

the witness to ask additional questions to fill in the holes made by the voir dire.

> *The Court.* Counsel, do you want to lay any more foundation?
>
> A. (by the proponent of the witness). Yes, Your Honor. Dr. Swallow, how frequently in the course of your orthopedic practice are you called upon to perform an assessment of degree of permanent impairment of one of your patients?
>
> A. Almost every day.
>
> Q. Where have you testified most frequently on degree of permanent impairment?
>
> A. The Ames Workers' Compensation Commission.

At this point the proponent of the witness believes that she has shown enough expert qualifications and has dealt with whatever was elicited on voir dire. A good way to pose the issue is by repeating the question calling for the expert testimony. In jurisdictions where the tendering process is followed, the proponent would repeat the motion that Dr. Swallow be allowed or certified to testify as an expert witness.

> Q. Dr. Swallow, what is your opinion as to Mr. Cluney's degree of permanent impairment from this crash?
>
> *Opposing Counsel.* Objection!
>
> *The Court.* Overruled. The witness may answer. Your objection goes to the weight, not the admissibility, of Dr. Swallow's opinion.

As with other kinds of voir dire, there is a temptation for opposing counsel to use voir dire of experts as a chance for some early cross-examination, even when there is no real hope of preventing the witness from testifying. As stated in Chapter 3, such a use of voir dire is an abuse of the prerogatives of a trial lawyer and should not be indulged in.

D.   The Factual Foundation for Expert Testimony

Once the qualifications of the witness to testify as an expert have been demonstrated, the expert must be introduced to the facts and issues of the case. Some witnesses, such as the treating physician or the designing engineer, already have some acquaintance with the facts of the case by virtue of their own participation. Some experts are retained by counsel or client solely to make an evaluation and provide expert testimony in the particular litigation. There are cases where the experts' prior personal knowledge of the facts is enhanced and enlarged to enable them to give additional opinions and expert testimony.

1.   Eliciting the Opinion First

Under Federal Rule of Evidence 705 and its state counterparts, it is now not always necessary to show the underlying factual basis before eliciting an expert opinion. Sometimes, for the sake of impact, the lawyer may want to get the opinion "up front," immediately following the expert's credentials.

> Q.   Doctor Z, do you have an opinion as to whether or not Dr. X's treatment of patient Y followed the standard of professional skill and care observed by specialists in internal medicine who were practicing in our state at the time the treatment was rendered?
>
> A.   Yes, I do.
>
> Q.   Doctor, what is that opinion?
>
> A.   His treatment was not up to the standard of skill and care.

That doesn't mean that proof that the doctor knows something about the facts of the case should be dispensed with altogether. Factfinders are not going to give much weight to an opinion that appears to have been given without knowing anything about the case. Regardless of the order of proof, it is usually important to show that the expert's opinion is based not only on the expert knowledge and experience of the witness but also on a careful examination and complete understanding of the underlying facts of the particular case.

Sometimes the factual basis for the opinion is disclosed when the expert gives the reasons for his opinion:

> Q. Doctor, what are the reasons for your opinion that the treatment by Doctor X of Patient Y was not up to the standard of professional skill and care exercised by specialists in internal medicine practicing in our state?

Note that this question repeats the "opinion" question, which has been answered affirmatively as the predicate for the "reasons" question. The difference between the terms "observed" and "exercised" in the two questions is probably not significant, but it indicates that the lawyer is a little sloppy and might make other more serious mistakes in the incorporation of previous questions or answers in the predicates of later inquiries.

> A. Well, in my opinion the standard of care observed by internists in this area would require that the patient be carefully followed for at least six hours after the bone marrow biopsy. In this case, Dr. X sent Patient Y home about 45 minutes after the biopsy, even though she complained of pain. . . .

Here the doctor goes on to summarize the reasons for his critical opinion of the other doctor's work. The summary should contain reference to the underlying facts of the case. In order safely to ask a question as wide open as this one, the lawyer must be confident that the expert is well enough versed in the case and skillful enough at testifying so as to respond with virtually no guidance from the lawyer. A more cautious approach might be

> Q. Doctor, in arriving at the opinion you just gave us, did you rely on a history of the patient?
>
> A. Yes, I did.
>
> Q. What was that history?

And so on.

2.   Developing the Factual Basis Before Eliciting the Opinion

Because of the importance of the factual foundation to most opinions, the expert's knowledge of the facts is usually shown before the opinion itself is elicited. Under Federal Rule of Evidence 703, this factual basis can be shown in a number of different ways.

a.   Personal Familiarity by the Witness

Where the expert witness has familiarity with the underlying facts, that personal knowledge can be shown by his testimony.

Q.   Doctor Swallow, is Raymond Cluney a patient of yours?

A.   Yes, he is.

Q.   Would you tell us how Mr. Cluney came to be a patient of yours?

A.   May I look at my record?

Q.   Yes, Doctor, to refresh your recollection.

A.   Yes; here it is. I first met Mr. Cluney at the emergency room at St. Mary's Hospital. . . .

b.   Other Information Relied on by Experts in the Field

Sometimes it is necessary to supplement the personal experience of the expert with other information that the expert may have had access to. This may even be information supplied or made available by the lawyer.

Under Federal Rule of Evidence 703, an expert opinion can be based on facts that are not in evidence and are not even admissible in evidence "so long as they are the type and kind usually relied upon by experts in the field." At one time it was thought that an expert opinion could be based only on facts actually admitted in evidence or at least admissible in evidence. Now both the Federal Rules of Evidence and corresponding evidence law in most jurisdictions allow greater latitude for the factual basis of an expert opinion.

If, for example, the medical record of a plaintiff's earlier hospitalization is for some reason not authenticated or otherwise admissible in the case on trial, the expert witness can nonetheless rely on it in giving her opinion if this is the kind of record she would ordinarily rely on in the course of her practice.

If there is any doubt about any particular component of the factual record, the issue can be addressed by asking the expert,

> *Q.* Doctor, in your profession, is it customary for doctors in diagnosing and treating their patients to rely on records requested and received from hospitals at which the patient has been hospitalized?
>
> *A.* Yes.
>
> *Q.* In evaluating Mr. Cluney's condition, did you rely on a record from a prior hospitalization?
>
> *A.* Yes, I did.
>
> *Q.* Is the record you relied on for your opinion in this case the kind of record that doctors rely on in diagnosing and treating their patients?
>
> *A.* Yes, it is.

This latitude should not be overstretched, however. If factual material on which an expert relies for her opinion is not admissible in evidence, it should at least be the kind of material that the factfinders would consider reliable based on their own common sense.

Often an expert witness is a busy professional who may have difficulty remembering details of a particular case. Counsel should be ready to prompt him to refresh his recollection with questions and documents to show thoroughness and completeness in the expert's investigation and analysis.

> *Q.* Was there anything else you had upon which to base your analysis and opinion?
>
> *A.* I think so, but I can't remember without looking at my file.

Q. Doctor, did you also review the records of the Massachusetts General Hospital in Boston concerning Mr. Cluney's
prior hospitalization?

A. Yes, that's right, I did.

c. In-Court Testimony and Evidence

Sometimes the expert's testimony is based on prior testimony of
witnesses in court:

Q. Dr. Swallow, have you heard the testimony of Mr.
Cluney and his wife, Mrs. Cluney, here in court yesterday afternoon and this morning?

A. Yes, I have.

Q. Based on your professional education and experience,
based on your treatment of Mr. Cluney since September
14, 1990, based on your review of the prior medical
records of Mr. Cluney, and based on the testimony of
Mr. Cluney and Mrs. Cluney as you have heard it here in
the courtroom today, do you have an opinion as to the
degree of permanent impairment to physical function
that has been sustained by Mr. Cluney as a result of the
back injuries for which you treated him?

A. Yes, I do.

Q. And would you please tell us, Doctor, what is that
opinion?

A. In my opinion, Mr. Cluney has a 35 percent physical
disability to the whole person.

d. Hypothetical Questions

A time-honored means of establishing the factual basis for an
expert opinion has been the hypothetical question. According to
this procedure, the proponent of the expert marshals the facts from
the evidentiary record that are relevant to the expert's opinion and
presents them to the expert in the form of a hypothetical question,
which the expert is then permitted to answer.

Q. Doctor Swallow, assuming that on September 14, 1989, the plaintiff, Mr. Cluney, was a passenger in an automobile driven by one Mr. Clark, and that the car in which Mr. Cluney was riding was struck in the left side by an automobile driven by the defendant, Ms. Borak, and further assuming that at the time of the impact Mr. Cluney was violently thrown about in the car and felt a sharp pain in the mid-section of his back, and further assuming that the plaintiff was brought to St. Mary's Hospital, where he was x-rayed and found to have sustained a comminuted compression fracture of L-2 vertebrae, and further assuming that Mr. Cluney was treated at St. Mary's Hospital via immobilization in a circlelectric bed, and received a prescription of Darvon for pain, and further assuming that Mr. Cluney remained immobilized for a period in excess of two weeks and was discharged on September 29, 1989, with a hyper-extension brace, and further assuming that Mr. Cluney wore the brace for the next month, after which time he was examined and found to have flexion of 70 degrees and normal extension, and further assuming that three years after the accident the patient relates a history of back pain upon sustained sitting or lying on a soft surface or in connection with any physical labor, and further assuming, [etc., etc.], do you have an opinion as to the degree of permanent impairment sustained by Mr. Cluney as a result of the injuries sustained in the September 14th automobile accident?

A. Yes, I do.

Q. What is that opinion, Doctor?

A. In my opinion, he has sustained 10 percent permanent impairment to his overall function as a result of the back injury.

Many trial advocates use the hypothetical question to organize and marshal their evidence and, in effect, give a mini-summation in the middle of the trial. On the other hand, hypothetical questions often have the sound of artificiality. And, unless they faithfully follow the actual evidence, they are subject to objection for irrelevance.

> *Opposing Counsel.* Objection! Irrelevant. There is no evidence that Mr. Cluney was "violently thrown about" in the car.

If the basis on which the expert opinion is sought does not accurately reflect the facts of the case, the opinion is irrelevant. If the testimony is that Mr. Cluney was "thrown forward and then back again in the back seat," a strict judge might sustain the objection and force the lawyer to go back and revise the hypothetical, or even repeat it.

> *The Court.* The Court will see Counsel at sidebar.

Objections in which the lawyers discuss the facts are almost always heard by the judge out of the hearing of the factfinders.

> *Opposing Counsel.* Your Honor, Counsel's hypothetical question does not accurately reflect the evidence. The testimony was that Mr. Cluney was "thrown forward and then back again in the back seat," not "thrown violently around in the car."
>
> Q.   Your Honor, may we rephrase the hypothetical question?
>
> *The Court.* You may.
>
> Q.   (back in the presence of the factfinders). Doctor, assuming the hypothetical question that I just posed for you, but assuming at the time of the crash that Mr. Cluney was not "thrown violently around in the car" but, instead, that he was "thrown forward and then back again in the back seat," do you have an opinion as to the degree of permanent impairment sustained by Mr. Cluney as a result of this crash?

Sometimes, by judiciously retreating and regrouping, the examining lawyer can keep the presentation under better and smoother control than by forcing the issue to a ruling.

The hypothetical question may be the best way to show the factual basis for an expert opinion where the facts are complex and where there is no other way in which it can be developed. However, now that the rules allow greater latitude in how and when the factual basis for the expert opinion must be established, the hypothetical question is often bypassed in favor of a more natural and understandable factual development.

E.   Eliciting the Expert's Opinion

The opinions of experts can be elicited in many forms. The classic formulation of the opinion question was generally a two-step process:

> *Q.* Doctor, based on your education and experience, and based on your treatment of Mr. X as you have outlined it to us today, do you have an opinion as to the degree of permanent impairment sustained by Mr. X as a result of the September 15th automobile accident?
>
> *A.* Yes, I do.
>
> *Q.* Then would you tell us, Doctor, what is that opinion?
>
> *A.* My opinion is . . .

This formulation alerts the opponent that an opinion is coming and permits opportunity for objection. Usually the objection is posed to the second question. An objection to the first question would be premature, because until the witness answers that question, no one knows whether he has an opinion on the subject matter. If he does not, then there is no reason to object.

> *Q.* What is that opinion?
>
> *Opposing Counsel.* Objection! Lack of expert qualifications [lack of adequate factual basis].

At this point the judge makes the determination required by Federal Rule of Evidence 702. Are the witness's qualifications such that her answer would be helpful to the factfinders? As suggested above, if the opponent has some questions that might address the qualifications for the opinion, she can request a voir dire in support of her objection.

An objection that the expert lacks sufficient factual basis for the requested opinion may also be made at this point. If it is obvious that the witness has no factual basis, the objection may be sustained. Or the court may use its discretion under Federal Rule of Evidence 705 to require that the proponent of the opinion question lay a foundation before ruling on the sufficiency of the factual basis. Or if satisfied that there probably is a basis for the opinion, the court may overrule the objection. Such a ruling would leave the issue for later development by the proponent or attack by the opponent on cross-examination.

Opinions of experts may also be elicited more informally.

Q. Mr. Fields, as a part of your investigation, did you make
     a determination of the cause of the turbine failure?

A. Yes, we did.

Q. And what was that cause?

A. In my opinion, the turbine failed because . . .

The rules do not require that the opinion question even use the word "opinion." Under Rule 702, the expert can testify in the "form of an opinion or otherwise." Often the informal methods of presenting expert opinion sound more natural and more in accord with the methods employed by experts in real life. Testimony clothed in the terminology of the real world may have greater authority than a pronouncement that is obviously artificial. By the same token, counsel opposing an expert witness should be alert to potential opinion testimony coming in without the warning associated with traditional expert opinion questions. Any question that can be answered with some kind of expert opinion presents the potential for an objection based on lack of either expert qualifications, factual basis, or both.

F. Explaining Expert Testimony

From a trial presentation standpoint, the biggest challenge to the proponent of expert testimony is to make the expert's opinion understandable and credible. The function of the trial lawyer is not only to elicit the opinion but also to get the expert to explain it so the factfinders can understand it, properly assess its significance, and incorporate the expert opinion in their ultimate image of the case. An expert opinion is no better than the degree of understanding and acceptance that it carries to the factfinders. A doctor's expert opinion that an injured plaintiff has sustained 10 percent permanent impairment as a result of an automobile accident does not carry much meaning unless it is explained.

Q. Doctor, would you tell us what you mean when you say that the plaintiff has suffered a 10 percent impairment to the physical function of the whole body?

A. Well, this percentage estimate is arrived at as a result of a process that we orthopedic surgeons are often called upon to carry out. Over the years we have tried to estimate the totality of the physical functions of the human body. When a member of the body is injured and permanently disabled to some extent, that overall physical function is reduced. The degree of percentage of impairment is an estimate of the degree by which that overall physical function is reduced by virtue of the permanent disability suffered as a result of the accident.

Q. Doctor, so what does that mean to Ray Cluney's ability to function in his daily life?

A. Well, it means that he will be able to do only about 90 percent of all of the things that he could have done in the absence of the impairment.

Q. Doctor, can you associate that 10 percent permanent impairment with particular activities that Ray Cluney might do?

A. Well, the 10 percent figure relates to overall bodily function. However, when one looks at the nature of the injury to his back, it is likely that the activities that would be directly affected would be activities involving bending, lifting, running, hard physical work, as well as those activities involving sitting or lying for periods

       of time on an unstable surface such as a soft bed or
       chair.

Q. And how would Mr. Cluney be affected in these activities?

A. Well, some of them he just couldn't do or shouldn't do if
      he wants to avoid further injury. Others, such as sitting
      on a soft bed or chair, he could perhaps do for a while,
      but would feel some pain or discomfort.

The object is to have the expert explain the opinion and its
significance in terms understandable to the factfinders. Usually this
requires concretizing the opinion as much as possible and trying to
relate it to matters within the common experience of the participants. Often this requires the lawyer to ask the expert to translate
unfamiliar or technical terms.

Q. Doctor, would you tell us your diagnosis of Mr. Cluney's
      injury?

A. Mr. Cluney has a comminuted compression fracture of
      the L-2 vertebra with a split in the spinous process.

Q. Doctor, would you tell us what you mean by a "compres-
      sion fracture?"

A. That is a fracture produced by compression or squeezing
      of the bone.

Q. And what does "comminuted" mean?

A. That means that the bone was broken in several pieces.

Q. Doctor, which bone is the L-2 vertebra?

A. That is the second vertebra in the lower, or lumbar
      spine. The spine is divided into three sections for pur-
      poses of medical description. The lowest section is
      called the lumbar spine. The L-2 vertebra is the second
      from the top of the five vertebrae in the lumbar spine.
      It is about here [pointing to the middle of his own
      back].

Q. Doctor, are you indicating a spot on your back at about
      the level of your belt?

A. Yes.

Q. So was it your diagnosis that Mr. Cluney had broken the second from the top of the five bones in the lower back, and the bone was broken in several pieces?

A. That's it in laymen's terms.

Note that the last question is a soft leading question. Such questions are permissible for the purpose of pulling complicated testimony together in a factual and nonargumentative manner. However, it is important that the summarizing question be completely faithful to the preceding testimony and that nothing be added.

Once the expert opinion has been explained and understood, the trial lawyer still has the task of supporting the opinion and making it credible in the eyes of the jury. As discussed above, one of the ways in which this is accomplished is to make the source of that opinion, the expert, authoritative and credible in terms of his qualifications, his personal appearance, in the courtroom and the form in which his testimony is given. In addition, if the opinion can be explained and supported by common-sense reasoning and understandable analogies, it is more likely to be accepted by the factfinders.

Q. Doctor, can you tell us the reasons for your opinion that Mr. Cluney will have a 10 percent impairment to his overall physical function?

A. Yes, I can.

Q. What are those reasons, Doctor?

A. Well, as you can see from the X ray here [indicating], Mr. Cluney has a permanent deformity in his back as it healed from the accident. The L-2 vertebra that healed is not like the others in the spinal column. It is squashed a little bit along the anterior edge here and is uneven on the top. This means that Mr. Cluney is a little out of alignment with his spine. The structural integrity of this part of his body has been impaired. And the musculature of his back has to try and compensate for that misalignment. The added strain put on his body by the

misalignment and his attempts to compensate for the
misalignment are what cause the disability.

Successful expert presentations make the witnesses into teachers. Using visual aids, the experts enlarge the knowledge of the
factfinders. Because the factfinders are usually unfamiliar with the
subject matter of the expertise, language alone is often inadequate
to generate much understanding. Simplifying and visualizing media are important here.

Q. Doctor, would this medical model of the spine assist you
in illustrating your testimony?

A. Yes. As you can see here [indicating], the vertebral bodies
look a little like blocks. The rubbery disc between the
vertebral bodies acts like a buffer that enables the back
to bear the weight of the body and to bend at the same
time [bending the model]. Now, in Mr. Cluney's case,
one of these vertebral bodies was crushed when the spine
flexed, or bent forward suddenly and with great force
[demonstrating]. . . .

G.   Cross-Examination of
the Expert Witness

In a sense, the cross-examination of an expert witness is very much
like that of any other witness. The same considerations of selectiv-
ity, precision, and control apply. However, the fact that the expert
is usually fighting in his own territory can make the control of the
expert on cross more difficult and risky than with a lay witness.
Usually when a lawyer cross-examines an expert she can take
fewer risks and must exert more control than when she cross-
examines a lay witness. When a lawyer takes on an expert witness
in a head-to-head battle, the expert usually wins.

1.   Controlling the Expert with the Expert's Own Discipline

With many expert witnesses, an important control device available
to the cross-examiner is the expert's own discipline, which con-

trols the expert the same way common experience controls lay testimony. A lay witness is aware that testimony that does not ring true will not be accepted and will damage that witness's credibility. By the same token, a reputable expert is ordinarily reluctant to give testimony that contravenes the essential teachings of the expert's field. The expert has a stake in the recognition of his expertise by other members of his disciplinary group. He does not want to be recorded as saying something that other respected experts in his field would instantly recognize as "bunk." His reputation is worth more to him than the outcome of a single case.

In such situations one can use the teachings of the discipline as a control device.

Q. Doctor, isn't it true that you cannot say that any of these possible consequences will actually occur?

A. That's right.

Q. You cannot say that it is probable that any of them will occur, can you?

A. That is right; I can't.

Q. And as a matter of orthopedics, it is possible that none of them will occur, isn't that right?

A. Yes, it is.

Q. When you say that something "is a possibility," you mean just that — that it is possible, not that it is likely in fact to occur?

A. That's right.

Q. Doctor, isn't it true that in life anything is possible? Isn't that right?

A. Yes, I guess so.

In this example, although the party sponsoring the doctor's testimony might have wished the doctor to say that traumatic arthritis and a spinal fusion were likely to occur in his case in the future, the prevailing state of knowledge in the orthopedic field supports these consequences only as "possibilities," and not to be anticipated in any particular case. If a doctor testifies that such possibilities are in fact probabilities, the doctor could be out of line with the authority in his field. Quite apart from the trial, the doctor would be subject to disapprobation or lack of status within his profession.

It should be noted that when a lay witness testifies contrary to common experience, the factfinders can evaluate that testimony and draw appropriate conclusions from their own common experience. When an expert testifies contrary to the teachings of a specialized discipline, however, the factfinders are not usually in a position to make that determination on their own. Disreputable experts can bring a lot of "junk science" into the courtroom. If a lawyer is seeking to control an unknown expert with the teachings of the expert's own discipline, she will have to be in a position to confront the expert with those teachings and to convince the factfinders that the expert is departing from them.

2. Controlling the Expert with Learned Treatises

The accepted knowledge within an expert's field may be more or less accessible and useful to the cross-examining lawyer. Treatises by other experts in the field can be used by the lawyer to control or even impeach an expert witness.

Q. Doctor, I show you a book, which has been marked as Exhibit 12 for identification. Exhibit 12 is a copy of *Jones on Bones,* by George Jones, M.D., 8th Edition, published in Boston in 1989, is it not?

A. Yes, it is.

Q. Well, Doctor, isn't it true that *Jones on Bones* is an authoritative treatise in your field?

A. I suppose it could be considered authoritative.

Q. In fact, *Jones on Bones* is one of the standard medical school text books in orthopedics, isn't it?

A. Yes, it is.

Q. We offer Exhibit 12 in evidence as a learned treatise, Your Honor.

The Court.   Admitted.

Q.   Doctor, isn't it true that on page 53 of *Jones on Bones* Dr. Jones states, "In cases of mild to moderate compression fractures to the lumbar spine, sequelae such as traumatic arthritis are possible, but cannot be associated with any degree of probability."?

A.   That is what it says.

Q.   And you, Doctor, would agree with that statement by Dr. Jones, wouldn't you?

A.   I suppose so.

3.   Controlling the Expert with Other Expert Testimony

In other contexts, the predominant expert opinion in the field may be less defined and less accessible. Sometimes the only form in which it is available is the testimony of the opponent's own expert witness.

Q.   (by the opponent during direct examination of his own expert). Dr. Cox, if Dr. Swallow testified earlier in this trial that he thinks that the plaintiff is likely to suffer traumatic arthritis at some point in the future as a result of these injuries, would such testimony, in your opinion, be in accord with the prevailing state of medical knowledge in the field of orthopedics as you know it?

A.   No, it would not be.

Q.   What do you mean by that, Sir?

A.   The research in our field has shown that no doctor can say in a case like that of Mr. Cluney whether or not there is any likelihood of future complications. In some cases, there are such complications, which may or may not be traceable to the original injury. In a great many of other cases there are none. It is impossible to say in any one particular case. There are possibilities, but no more than that.

If the expert who contradicts the opposing expert is more authoritative, if his opinion makes more sense to the factfinders, the testimony of the opposing expert can be neutralized. The prospect of such adverse testimony can also be used to control the opposing expert even before the testimony is given.

> Q. (on cross-examination). Dr. Swallow, you are acquainted with Dr. Cox, aren't you?
>
> A. Yes, slightly.
>
> Q. You are aware of his reputation as an expert in degenerative diseases of the spine, are you not?
>
> A. I am aware that Dr. Cox has done quite a lot of work in that area.
>
> Q. And if Dr. Cox testified that in fact it is impossible for any orthopedic surgeon to predict whether a twenty-three-year-old man will eventually develop traumatic arthritis from a compression fracture of the spine, you would not contradict him, would you?
>
> A. Well, no.

Such cross-examination must be based on a good-faith representation that Dr. Cox will appear and will testify as represented. Misrepresentation of the other expert's anticipated opinion, or bluffing, are ethical violations that will not be countenanced by opposing counsel or the court.

4. Cross-Examining as to Factual Basis

Experts are frequently cross-examined with reference to the factual basis on which their opinions are based. If it can be shown that the expert is relying on a fact that is not true, or if the expert has failed to take into account some fact that is in the case, the validity of the opinion can be undermined.

> Q. Doctor, when you gave us your opinion as to the degree of impairment sustained by Mr. Cluney as a result of this

accident, you were assuming, were you not, that Mr. Cluney did not have any prior injury to his back?

A. Yes, I was.

Q. If you learned that Mr. Cluney had a prior injury to his lumbar spine, that would affect your opinion as to the degree of impairment he may have sustained from this particular accident, wouldn't it?

A. Well, I suppose it would.

Q. Doctor, you did not review the records from Massachusetts General Hospital of Mr. Cluney's hospitalization in March of 1987, did you?

A. No, I did not.

Q. And if that hospitalization were for treatment of Mr. Cluney's lumbar spine, that record would be important to your opinion, wouldn't it?

A. It certainly would be.

Again, the lawyer must have a good-faith belief that the changed elements of the factual record with which the witness is confronted are already in evidence or will be offered and admitted during the trial. Attempts to drag in "red herrings" that never materialize in the hopes of raising vague doubts are unethical and improper and can backfire in summation.

> *Plaintiff's lawyer (in summation).* Members of the Jury, you heard Opposing Counsel attempt to cast doubt on Dr. Swallow's expert opinion that Mr. Cluney will develop further complications such as traumatic arthritis in the future. You heard him refer to some Dr. Cox and some claimed record of a hospitalization in Massachusetts. Did Dr. Cox ever testify? No. Was any hospital record ever produced? No. All that was just an effort by the defense to smear Dr. Swallow by baseless innuendo. Right now, Members of the Jury, as this case is being given to you, Dr. Swallow's expert prognosis of Mr. Cluney's future, including the pain, the traumatic arthritis,

and the possibility of a spinal fusion is unchallenged and unimpeached!

5.   Cross-Examining for Bias and Interest

Unlike lay witnesses, expert witnesses usually give their testimony for compensation. This raises the potential for cross-examination on the ground of bias or interest.

The traditional formulation

Q.   Doctor, you are being paid to testify here today, aren't you?

A.   Yes, I am being compensated for my time in investigating this matter and giving my testimony.

is not always effective. Although it may support the argument that the expert is just a "hired gun," a more effective line of cross-examination might seek to support an inference that the content of the expert's testimony is materially distorted by financial or other interest. The lawyer should be prepared to show that the compensation is large compared to the factfinders' expectations, that the compensation is contingent in some way, or that the witness has some other interest in the outcome of the case that might give him the motive to shape his testimony.

Q.   Doctor, you expect to be compensated for giving your expert testimony in this case, don't you?

A.   Yes, I do.

Q.   And, in fact, you have not yet received your compensation for testifying in this case, have you?

A.   That's right, I haven't.

Q.   You haven't even billed the plaintiff or the plaintiff's lawyer for any compensation yet, have you, Sir?

A.   No, I haven't.

Q.   You aren't going to bill for that compensation until this case has actually been decided, are you?

A.   That's right.

Q.   After the case has been decided, then is when you are going to send the bill for your testimony in this case, right?

A.   Yes.

At this point, the cross-examiner might be tempted to ask the payoff question,

Q.   And the amount of your compensation is going to depend on the amount the plaintiff recovers in this case, isn't it?

Such a question would likely be met with the answer,

A.   Of course not. I will charge the same hourly rate I always charge when I have to appear in court to testify about an injury I have treated. That will be $250 per hour. As soon as I know how many hours you lawyers will be keeping me away from treating my patients, I will send the bill.

This last question extends the escalation too far. The previous questions have laid the groundwork for an implication or actual argument that the doctor has some direct financial interest in the outcome of the case that might affect his testimony. The lawyer should leave this line of cross-examination and save it for summation.

Similar restraint should be exercised with most cross-examination designed to show bias or interest on the part of the witness. It is unrealistic to expect that a witness will admit the bias on the stand.

A treating physician or other expert witness who has a professional connection with the events in the case apart from the litigation is usually less subject to impeachment on this basis. Like any other witness, however, all expert witnesses can be impeached by the usual types of evidence of bias, interest, and the like.

Q. Dr. Swallow, you have been the family doctor for the
Cluney family for the last 20 years, haven't you?

A. Yes, that's right.

Q. And you and Mr. Cluney's father, Arthur Cluney, were
classmates in high school, weren't you?

A. Yes.

6. Using the Expert's Report in Cross-Examination

Another control device that is frequently useful in expert witness
cross-examination is the expert's report or pretrial disclosure. Under pretrial procedures in force in most jurisdictions, a proposed
expert witness is required to make advance written disclosure of
the expert opinions to be given at trial and the grounds for the
opinions. These pretrial disclosures can be effective control devices
for cross-examining expert witnesses.

For witness control purposes the best of these control devices is
a written report signed by the witness. Ordinarily such a report
would be inadmissible hearsay if offered by the proponent of the
expert. However, it may be used by the opponent on cross-
examination and may be admitted for impeachment if inconsistent
with the witness's in-court testimony.

The bottom line of the expert's report usually favors the proponent of the testimony, but the report will often contain qualifications and limiting terminology that can be used effectively in
cross-examination. One common line of cross-examination of an
expert witness is simply to extract from the witness's report every
statement that qualifies his opinion or helps the other side. These
then are formulated into strong leading questions.

Assume that an office note in the report of the plaintiff's treating physician reads as follows:

I saw Raymond Cluney again on November 15th. At that time he
told me he was doing well. No pain. He said that he had felt pain
occasionally since the last visit. Neurological examination was normal. X rays indicated that the fracture had stabilized but without

bony bridging. I told him he was making good progress and that he should continue to wear the brace and come back in a month.

The cross-examination could go something like:

Q. Doctor, you saw Mr. Cluney again on November 15th, didn't you?

A. Yes, I think I did.

Q. He told you then he was doing well, didn't he?

A. Well, I don't know.

Q. Doctor, why don't you look in your file there and see if that office note dated November 15th refreshes your recollection. [Pause] Isn't it true that on November 15th he told you he was doing well?

A. Yes, he did.

Q. At that time he didn't have any pain, did he?

A. (checking). That's right.

Q. And you saw on the X rays that the fracture had stabilized, didn't you?

A. Yes.

Q. You told him he was making good progress, didn't you?

A. Yes, I did.

Q. You told him to come back in a month, right?

A. Yes, I did.

By using phraseology right from the report in a strong leading fashion, the cross examiner can marshal those facts that will tend to minimize the injury. If the witness is reluctant, the report can be used to refresh the witness's recollection on cross-examination.

Q. He was having no pain at the time, was he?

A. Well, I don't know about that.

Q. Please look at the bottom of your note, Doctor. Doesn't that refresh your recollection that he was having no pain at the time?

A. Ah, yes, that's right.

If the witness still refuses to acknowledge the facts asserted by the lawyer in the leading question, the lawyer may cross-examine the witness more directly about the report.

Q. Doctor, you wrote in your office note of November 15 "No pain," didn't you?

A. Yes, that's right.

As a matter of evidence, this formulation can be used only as a prior inconsistent statement to impeach the witness unless the witness acknowledges the truth of the fact in current testimony.

Q. And so on November 15, Doctor, Mr. Cluney was having no pain, isn't that right?

A. Yes, I guess that's right.

As a last alternative, the opponent can offer the doctor's report in evidence as a prior inconsistent statement. This should be done only if counsel is satisfied that the benefit to be obtained from the impeachment outweighs the adverse effect of making the rest of the expert's report into an exhibit that can be taken into the jury room. A small glitch between report and testimony will generally not counteract the adverse effect of making available in specie a report that is overwhelmingly favorable to the other side and allowing the factfinders to read and reread the expert's report as they deliberate on the merits of the case.

Chapter 13 Summation

A. Purpose and Role of Summation

The traditional image of the trial lawyer in summation is that of an orator weaving a spell over the factfinders by the eloquence of her language, the power of her delivery, and the drama of her persona. Anecdotal trial advocacy literature cites, summarizes, and quotes great summations that have been claimed to sway the outcomes of famous trials. All too often the reaction of the student to this image of the trial lawyer in summation is "How could I ever do that?!"

The fact is that in most cases the role of the lawyer is both more pedestrian and more achievable. The summation is the opportunity for the lawyer to explain to the factfinders why they should accept counsel's presentation in preference to that proposed by the other side. It is the time during which the trial lawyer uses the credibility she has built up during the trial to teach the key facts and inferences to the factfinders.

The emphasis on summation is on the word "why." Presumably, in the opening statement the trial lawyer has laid out for the factfinders the image that will be recreated by the overall presentation. During the body of the trial, the lawyer has given substance to that image. Witness testimony has provided the facts in such a form and sequence that the picture provided in the opening statement has emerged and been strengthened in the consciousnesses of the factfinders. The lawyer has tried to give to the presentation as much precision, authority, and acceptability as possible. The summation is the lawyer's opportunity to explain to the jury why the picture in their consciousness should be the same as that which the lawyer described in the opening statement.

B. Planning the Summation

It has been said that the lawyer should be able to give the summation before the case is even put on. This means that the lawyer should prepare not only the evidence she proposes to introduce to support the fact picture but also know why the factfinders should assimilate that evidence into the fact image desired.

The lawyer plans the summation by thinking about the issues, the picture to be presented, and the problems to be faced in the trial over and over again in the months, weeks, days, and hours before the actual presentation. The lawyer may rehearse the lessons of the summation in advance of the trial by explaining her theory of the case to others, preferably lay people, and seeking their reactions. Does this picture make sense? Is this explanation sufficient, based on one's knowledge of human nature? What do you think of this image? Sometimes it is helpful for the lawyer to imagine that she is describing her case to a friend or relative who is a nonlawyer and who is inclined to be skeptical. How would this person react to her presentation?

There is no question that even before the trial starts, the lawyer must be able to present every element of the fact picture of her case, and she must also be ready to explain to the factfinders every important inference, favorable or unfavorable, and to tell them why her version of the story is the one to accept.

A trial rarely runs exactly as planned. Particular elements of the picture might turn out differently from what was originally anticipated. Fuzzy areas may need to be clarified. Shaky matters may need to be shored up. Unexpected sallies of the opponent may need to be dealt with. Thus, while the major part of the summation can indeed be planned before the case is even put on, part of the summation must be reserved to deal with the issues that have come up during the trial.

Some texts recommend a particular structure for summation in each case. While there are certain elements that commonly appear, the basic rule is that the form of the summation should be adapted to the overall presentation. For instance, if the issue most difficult to understand is damages, the closing might be planned to start, end, and focus largely on damages. If the major issue is the credibility of a single witness, that should be the focus of the summation. There may be a unifying theme that acts as a structure of the summation. The thrust should be on why the fact-finders should accept the lawyer's contention and base their decision on it.

C. Feelings and Motivation in Summation

The factfinders' feelings toward a party, its counsel, and the case's overall presentation significantly affect the factfinders' willingness to accept the picture propounded by that party. If the factfinders like a particular party and want to help him, they will be more disposed to accept that party's version of the case.

By the same token, if the factfinders do not like a party, it will be more difficult for them to identify with that person and accept that party's version of the events or circumstances in question. Throughout the trial, it is the lawyer's job to motivate the factfinders to want to help the lawyer's client.

In summation, as well as throughout the trial, it is important for the lawyer to increase the factfinders' identification with her client and her overall presentation. One way this can be accomplished is by using language of inclusion. In summation, as well as during the examination of the witnesses, the lawyer places herself in the jury box.

> *Counsel.* Members of the Jury, we all know, based on our common sense, that when a person tells us one story one day and another story a few days later, and then yet another story on the witness stand, there must be something wrong with one of those stories.

Another way the lawyer increases the factfinders' identification with the client or case is by stressing facts that are likely to relate to the factfinders' own experience.

> *Counsel.* And what kind of a person is Mr. Maxfield? We all heard what kind of a man he is. He has lived here in the City of Springfield all his life. He is a father — a father who loves and cares for his children. He has served his country in our armed forces. He is the kind of person whom we are all glad to know and have as a friend.

Like the people involved in the case, the factfinders are real
people. A lawyer who can understand and address human needs
and emotions at several levels is likely to be particularly effective in
presenting her case.

D.   Arguing the Facts

The essential purpose of the summation is to argue the facts. This
is when the lawyer can fill in the blanks and explain the inferences
that should be drawn from the fragmented presentations of the
witnesses. This is when the lawyer articulates the reasons why the
facts presented should add up to the image described by the lawyer
in the opening. It is the time when the lawyer can explain why the
factfinders should accept her fact picture in preference to the picture her opponent attempted to portray.

1.   *Dramatic Recitation*

Many trial lawyers' summations consist largely of dramatic recita-
tions of the pictures described during their openings.

> *Counsel.*   So Mr. Maxfield wants to make sure that the men
> would not escape into the darkness. He drives out of his
> driveway and heads east on Jackson Street. After a moment
> he catches a glimpse of a figure silhouetted against one of
> the buildings further down the street. He continues down
> the street trying to get his headlights focused on the figure
> up on the lawn. Suddenly he sees in front of him a large
> maple tree! Instinctively he swerves — to the right — up on
> the sidewalk and between the tree and the nearby porch of
> Number 37. It is all over in a moment and he's back on the
> street. Then the lights of the police car — and he stops.

In a "dramatic recitation" summation, the lawyer often speaks
in the present tense to increase the sense of immediacy. The lawyer
will also use his tone of voice and the volume and pace of delivery
to add drama to give the presentation color.

Such narrative summations may be appropriate in cases where

the fact picture presented by the trial evidence is so fragmented that the factfinders need a reminder to get the overall view, but in most cases the overall view has been imparted at the opening. The role of the testimony has been to fill in, support, and accredit the picture described initially by the lawyer's opening statement. In such cases a dramatic re-recitation in summation of much of the story that is not controverted or is unimportant is likely to be superfluous.

The dramatic recitation summation relies largely on the drama in the lawyer's narrative and tone of voice to suggest why the picture being described should be accepted. Usually it is more helpful to the factfinders, and hence more helpful to the lawyer's case, if the lawyer uses the summation to articulate and explain particular reasons why the picture already described and accredited should now be accepted by the factfinders.

> Counsel. How do we know that Mr. Maxfield did not have any intention of running over anyone on the night of October 10th? Well, just moments before we know that he had been in the house with Imogene. She was calling the police! And he knew that she was calling the police. We remember that out on the porch she told him, "I'm going to call the police!" An he said, "Yeah, go call the police." Even Jerry Ralston heard that.
>
> Now, does it make sense for anyone, no matter how he feels, to go out and try to run someone down when he knows that the police are on the way to witness the whole thing? We all know that human beings just don't behave that way.
>
> Mr. Maxfield's explanation of what did happen is perfectly in accord with our understanding and common sense. We have all had experiences when we were driving a car and watching something intently. When we are watching something intently, we often don't see other things come up right in front of our eyes. Then suddenly it is almost too late.
>
> That's what happened to Mr. Maxfield. He was watching Jerry Ralston's silhouette here in front of Number 39 [indicating on diagram] and was trying to get his headlights on him. He didn't notice the fact that he was angled

toward the sidewalk and the big maple tree in front of Number 37 was practically right in front of him. It wasn't until it was almost too late that the bulk of the tree came into his view. Of course, he swerved to avoid it.

The fact that he swerved between the tree and Number 37 and didn't hit either one speaks more to the fact that he was a pretty good driver, rather than that he tried to hit anything.

A variation on the dramatic recitation summation is the "witness-by-witness" summation, in which the lawyer uses her argument to re-recite the testimony of all the witnesses, usually in the order in which they appeared. While there may be the rare case in which such an organization is effective, usually such a summation does nothing more than remind the factfinders of what they have already heard and seen. This kind of summation does not take advantage of the opportunity to knit the whole picture together, to persuade the factfinders as to why they should make a particular inference or accept the lawyer's picture as true rather than that of her opponent.

2. Arguing the Inferences

The closing is the time to argue the inferences. Not all of the facts necessary to make up the complete picture can be proved directly. Sometimes evidence cannot be made available. For instance, it is not always possible to obtain testimony concerning a person's state of mind. And when it is, the testimony is so subjective as to be of questionable reliability. Thus the factfinders' images of relevant states of mind must be established by inference.

Was the defendant's act intentional? Summation is the time when the inferences that answer that question should be discussed:

> Counsel. Ladies and Gentlemen, you will remember that the defendant said to Officer Groves, "I did something foolish, I know I did, but those bastards shouldn't have been throwing beer bottles at the house."
> That was the first thing he said to the police officer. If, as the defendant says, he had merely been trying to find the

> two men and had foolishly driven up on the sidewalk look-
> ing for them, don't you think he would have said some-
> thing like, "I did something foolish, I know I did, but those
> men were getting away."? Instead he said, "*but those bas-*
> *tards shouldn't have been throwing beer bottles at the*
> *house.*" He knew he had done something to "those bas-
> tards," something more than drive up on the sidewalk look-
> ing for them. He wanted to try and justify what he did! But
> throwing beer bottles at a house is never justification for a
> murder.

Arguable inferences are not limited to issues of state of mind or
intent. They may relate to almost any issue of proof for which
direct evidence is not available.

> *Counsel.* If Mrs. Mercer, some ninety-four feet away looking
> out through the windows of her house, could see Roscoe
> Savage lying there on the sidewalk, isn't it fair to conclude
> that the defendant, driving that car, peering intently out,
> looking ahead, with the aid of powerful headlights not only
> could but *did* see that body and aimed his car right at it?

The common ingredient in most inferences is overall common
knowledge and experience. People use their experience of how
things are to infer facts that have not been directly proved but that
experience allows them to associate with the facts that have been
proven. Thus experience teaches that visibility depends on light
and distance. If someone some distance away can see something, a
person who is closer is likely to see it better. That experience
shared by the factfinders is referred to by the lawyer to support the
inference that Mr. Maxfield did in fact see the body of the decedent before striking it with his car.

E. Arguing Witness Credibility

Summation is also the opportunity for the lawyer to address with
the factfinders the credibility of the various witnesses for both
sides. Witness credibility can be argued both ways. The lawyer can
point out reasons why the factfinders should believe her witness

and why they should not believe the opponent's witness. A witness's credibility can be argued based on that person's ability to observe and recount as well as on his bias and other factors affecting his integrity.

> Counsel.   Certainly, we have to take Jerry Ralston's testimony with a grain of salt. After all, he was the decedent's brother-in-law. Moreover, at the time of the accident, he was drunk. During the three or four hours before he and his brother-in-law accosted Bob Maxfield and Imogene Farris, he had eight drinks and smoked marijuana. There are a lot of reasons why we shouldn't place much faith in what he has tried to tell us.

Summation is the point where certain witness impeachments that have been set up during the testimony can be safely carried out.

> Counsel.   Officer Groves claims that Mr. Maxfield said something about "bastards getting what they deserved" when he saw the body lying under the tree. But Mr. Maxfield has no memory of that. Nor does Ms. Farris. And you will remember that during his cross-examination Officer Groves admitted that when he made out his report, he didn't say anything about these statements either. Surely if Mr. Maxfield had said anything like this at the time of the accident, Officer Groves would have written it down in his report. Under the circumstances, is there any way we can believe that these statements were made beyond any reasonable doubt?

Summation is also an opportunity for the lawyer to discuss how well a particular witness's testimony squares with the testimony of other witnesses or other evidence in the case. An important test for the reliability of any image asserted is how consistent the image is with all of the evidence and how well it comports with the factfinders' experience with real life. Some evidence, such as photographs, is likely to be of very high credibility. Such evidence is often used as the touchstone for witness testimony. Is the image the witness is asserting consistent with the credible images generated by the photographs?

Other evidence, such as testimony of credible disinterested witnesses, is also used to evaluate images from sources that may be inherently less reliable. During summation the trial lawyer can analyze her own image or the image projected by the opponent for consistency with credible evidence or with the factfinders' experience with real life.

> *Counsel.* You remember, Ladies and Gentlemen, that Jerry Ralston tried to tell us that the decedent was standing up when he was struck by the car. But that just simply can't be true! Charlotte Mercer, the totally disinterested eyewitness, saw the decedent falling down out of sight under the maple tree just before the accident.
> The best evidence, however, is the car itself. Exhibit 5 is a photograph of the car exactly as it looked just after the accident. You will have this picture to look at yourselves during your deliberations [showing picture]. As you can see, there is not a scratch on Mr. Maxfield's car. If the decedent had been standing, certainly there would have been some mark left on the car. As the policeman testified, the only marks on the car are on the undercarriage. How can we believe Mr. Ralston under these circumstances?

A lawyer in summation is a teacher. She is teaching a particular image and complexion of the facts. The resources to be used, the text, are the testimony and other evidence presented at the trial. But the lesson to be taught is how that testimony and evidence add up to the ultimate picture to be understood and accepted by the factfinders.

F. Exhibits and Illustrative Aids

As in all teaching, the visual or mixed-media approach is usually the most effective. The lawyer teaching in summation should use the actual exhibits in evidence as well as the illustrative aids to make the summation visual. There is nothing wrong, and a great deal right, with the lawyer drawing her own illustrations on a tablet or blackboard during summation. Pre-prepared aids, such as "featherboard" enlargements of key exhibits or diagrams, may also be incorporated in the final presentation.

The media used to illustrate the summation can be objects or pictures that were referred to by the lawyer in opening statement or by a witness during testimony. They can range from the blackboard to elaborate charts and simulations. Sometimes a lawyer can make effective use of the opponent's illustrative aids in her own summation!

> *Counsel.*   Members of the Jury, do you remember that when Mr. Borak testified he used this drawing of the intersection of Wood and Vale Street? He tried to tell us that he came up to the stop sign here [indicating], that he stopped, that he looked, that he saw nothing, and that he then drove into the intersection.
>
> But his own drawing proves that he couldn't have done what he said he did! Look here. Wood Street is a straight street for some blocks to the south of the intersection [indicating]. Mr. Borak had an unobstructed view for at least several hundred yards down Wood Street. No matter how fast the Clark car was travelling, if Mr. Borak had really stopped and looked, as he claimed he did, he would have seen that car. There is no way that the Clark car could have moved from a position of out of sight several hundred yards down Wood Street to the intersection of Wood and Vale in the time it took Mr. Borak to enter the intersection.
>
> Either Mr. Borak didn't stop, or he didn't look. If he had done what he said he did, this terrible crash simply would not have happened.

The exhibits admitted in evidence should be integrated to the extent that they assist in the teaching function. During the evidentiary part of the trial, the lawyer is not permitted to discuss the significance of the exhibits with the factfinders or to suggest what inferences may be drawn. However, in summation the lawyer may and should take the exhibits in hand and use them to teach the factfinders.

> *Counsel.*   If we look again at Exhibit 4 [holding and pointing to a photograph of the scene of the incident], we can

see how difficult it must have been to steer that car between the twenty-four inch maple tree here and the porch there. We can also see where the body was. It was right between the tree and the steps, right within the area that was illuminated by the defendant's headlights. He couldn't miss.

G. Quoting Witness Testimony

Often it is helpful in summation to quote to the factfinders a witness's exact words and then discuss their significance.

> *Counsel.* Members of the Jury, you will remember that Ms. Mercer said, "He fell out of sight in the darkness. ..." "Out of sight in the darkness." He fell out of sight of Ms. Mercer, who was looking right at him and trying to see him. She couldn't see him from her window about six feet above the ground and facing the place where he disappeared. "Out of sight in the darkness." It was dark there under that tree. So dark that she couldn't see him, even though she was trying to. ...

Modern stenographic technology will frequently permit counsel to obtain daily — or even simultaneous — transcriptions of the oral proceedings during a trial. However, that does not mean that counsel may overtly use that transcript during summation as if it were a trial exhibit.

Although court rules on the practice are not uniform, in most courts it is considered improper for counsel to read from an identified transcript of the trial in process. Phraseology such as

> *Counsel.* Ladies and Gentlemen, I am reading from the official transcript of Mrs. Mercer's testimony as she gave it to us yesterday. She testified, "He fell out of my sight into the darkness."

gives an undue aura of reliability to the testimony as it is being read because it is contained in the official transcript. Under this rationale, it would also be improper for counsel to quote the witness's testimony while reading from something that obviously looks like a transcript.

On the other hand, there is nothing wrong with consulting the trial transcript for the witness's exact words and then quoting them to the factfinders without mentioning or implying that they have come from the transcript.

> *Counsel.*   Ladies and Gentlemen, we can all recall Mrs. Mer-
> cer's testimony. She told us under oath that, as she was
> watching him, the decedent, and I quote, "fell out of my
> sight into the darkness."

It is also permissible to look at notes to get the exact words as long as neither the notes nor the ultimate source of the quotation is identified as a trial transcript.

H.   Body Language

The lawyer's own gestures and body language are important resources to be used in presenting an effective summation. By tone of voice, gestures, and changes of position, the lawyer can give emphasis to particular points or illustrate the picture being presented. The lawyer can even act out parts of a scene to show how she believes an incident took place.

> *Counsel.*   And so we have Officer Levy, with his back
> against the car and his hand on the wrist of the man with
> the knife . . . [demonstrating a man grappling with a knife-
> wielding assailant] holding that wrist with the best grip he
> could have, trying to hold that knife off from stabbing him
> again.

Tone of voice and body language tell the factfinders a lot about how the trial participants feel about the case and the people involved in it. If a lawyer's manner is removed and aloof or, worse, apparently condescending, the factfinders are likely to "turn off" to the lawyer and to the picture she is trying to present. If the lawyer appears to like the factfinders, identify with them, and trust them, it is often easier for the factfinders to accept the position the lawyer is advancing. Summation gives the lawyer the opportunity to relate directly with the factfinders. This opportunity should be used to build up trust and confidence.

One way in which the lawyer tries to foster factfinder trust and confidence is to adopt an open and accessible manner. The lawyer is talking to the factfinders about an important matter. She is not lecturing them or reading a speech. As she speaks to them she implicitly seeks their feedback through eye contact and body language. If the lawyer appears friendly and down-to-earth, it is likely that the factfinders will get a favorable impression. There are no prizes to be won for "highfalutin airs" in the courtroom.

At the same time, the lawyer must be very careful not to appear to be talking down to the factfinders. Folksy approaches that appear instead to be insincere, inappropriate, or condescending are likely to alienate those whom the lawyer is trying to persuade.

By including the factfinders in the argument, the lawyer reinforces the image of the helpful fellow investigator. This feeling of inclusion often involves the use of the words "we" and "us."

> Counsel. And what do we know for sure? We know that Raymond Cluney was riding in a car that was going too fast. Much too fast. We heard Officer Anderson tell us that the driver of the car admitted he was going 50. Fifty in a residential area where the posted speed limit was 25.

Many lawyers believe that it is important that there be no barrier between the lawyer and factfinder during final argument. Although a podium may give the lawyer a feeling of security and a convenient place to set the script, the lawyer speaking to the factfinders from behind a podium conveys a more formal and remote image than one who is talking right out in front of them.

Notes also can detract from the spontaneity and directness of a final argument. If a lawyer appears to be reading from a script, the impact of the argument can be greatly compromised. Excessive reliance on notes tends to inhibit the lawyer from really "living" the argument and making it her own. The yellow pad in the hand makes effective gesturing impossible. Part of the factfinders' attention will be distracted by speculation about what is on the pad. As suggested in Chapter 4, the final argument is important enough so that the lawyer should maximize directness of presentation and personal contact with the factfinders. In most cases this means no reading from notes.

It is said that "the eyes are the windows of the soul." Effective presentations rely heavily on eye contact. Final argument is no exception. A lawyer's aura of sincerity and straightforwardness are enhanced if she can look at the factfinders as she talks to them. And often a person's eyes can convey nuances of meaning more effectively than can the voice or gestures.

"Eye contact" means literally that. Looking in the general direction of an unseen audience is not effective eye contact. For eye contact to contribute to a presentation, each individual factfinder should have the feeling that the lawyer is looking at him, and that it is very important to the lawyer that the factfinder understand what the lawyer is saying. The lawyer must see each member of the jury as a person.

I. Rhetoric in Final Argument

Final argument is the time for the rhetorical question. A trial presentation is a one-way conversation in which the lawyer does all of the talking. Nonetheless, it is often effective to make a particular argument not in the form of a positive assertion but as a question to the factfinders. The strength of the rhetorical question is that it brings the factfinders into the analysis. Because the factfinders supply the answers, they are more likely to accept them as correct than if the lawyer simply asserts the same propositions as positive statements.

Rhetorical questions are an effective way to submit desired fact inferences to the factfinders. The lawyer points out the bases for the inference and asks the factfinders to make the inference themselves.

> *Counsel.* There are some things we do know. Imogene
> Farris had called the police. Robert Maxfield knew the
> police were coming. They would be there any minute. Un-
> der these circumstances, can we believe that Robert

> Maxfield would decide to get into his car and commit a murder right under the nose of the police?

Or,

> *Counsel.* Jerry Ralston stood there on the witness stand and told us that he had seen Roscoe Savage standing up when he was hit by the car. Yet we know that there was not a mark, not even a scratch, on the front of the car after the accident. Can what Jerry Ralston told us be true?

Both of these questions are structured so that the factfinders will themselves come to the right answer — "No."

Arguments that address the honesty and integrity of a trial participant are often best understated by the lawyer. Ordinary politeness and civility recoil at direct accusations of dishonesty in the presence of others. In extreme cases an accusation by counsel that "He lied!" might be considered an ethical breach. When someone's credibility is in issue, it is usually better to underplay any argument based on dishonesty and let the factfinders come to the conclusion themselves. Sometimes a rhetorical question can guide the way.

> *Counsel.* One of the things you will have to do, Ladies and Gentlemen, is to assess the credibility, or believability of the witnesses. When there is a dispute in the testimony, you will have to decide which version to accept. In assessing the credibility of the testimony, you will consider whether the testimony in question accords with the physical evidence and with the testimony of disinterested observers.
>
> For instance, you all remember the testimony of Jerry Ralston. He said that the decedent was standing up when he was struck by the car. We also know that the car was totally unmarked after the accident. And Charlotte Mercer saw the decedent fall out of sight on the ground before the car even left the driveway. What do these facts tell us about the testimony of Jerry Ralston?

It is far better for the factfinders to think to themselves, "He's a liar!" than for the lawyer to declare it to them.

J. Human Nature and
Common Experience

Factfinders assess whatever is put before them based on their knowledge of human nature and their common experience. It is often effective in final argument to invoke human nature or common experience as touchstones. If some aspect of the lawyer's presentation involves a well-known trait of human nature or if some part of the case concerns matters with which the factfinders are likely to share common experience, it is often helpful to remind the factfinders.

> *Counsel.*   You remember the testimony of Officer Groves and Mrs. Mercer. Neither of them saw any brake lights on the defendant's car as he left the roadway and sped over the body of Roscoe Savage. Yet the defendant is trying to tell us that he swerved to the right in order to avoid a maple tree that had jumped into his view. Ladies and Gentlemen, if a driver suddenly sees an obstacle, isn't the natural reaction to put on the brakes? —maybe to swerve, yes, but to put on the brakes. If a car is out of control and threatened by an onrushing tree, doesn't the driver put on the brakes? From our own experience as drivers we all know that if the defendant's version were true, those brake lights would have come on.

On the other hand, it is usually not proper to ask the factfinders to put themselves in the place of a participant in the case and to compare his action to how the factfinder would have acted under similar circumstances.

> *Counsel.*   Ladies and Gentlemen, ask yourselves, if you were in Mr. Cluney's place, would you have crammed yourself in that Camaro with a driver who had been drinking?

> *Opposing Counsel.*   Objection, Your Honor. That is not the right standard. He is asking the jury what *they* would do. . . .

> *The Court.*   Sustained. Members of the Jury, the issue in this case is not whether any of you would have done what Mr.

Cluney did, but whether a reasonable person would have done what he did. The last two sentences of the argument will be stricken. Counsel, you may continue.

Counsel. Thank you, Your Honor.

The Court. Counsel, approach the bench. [at the bench]: Counsel, I told you earlier that if you tried to thank the Court for an unfavorable ruling one more time you would be in contempt. I know this is a habit, but it is a bad habit. You are in contempt. Your sanction is to serve for five days as Lawyer of the Day at the Volunteer Lawyers' Project within the next six months and advise the Court by letter that you have done so. [1]

Counsel. Yes, Your Honor.

The Court. You may proceed.

Counsel. Members of the Jury, would a reasonable person have crammed himself into that Camaro with a driver who had been drinking?

K.   Dealing with the Opponent's Presentation

In closing argument the trial advocate usually cannot satisfy herself with trying to complete the inferences and paint her own picture. She must also deal with the presentation of the other side. The inferences and arguments asserted by the opponent must be dealt with.

Counsel should not be afraid to concede an adverse point if contesting the point will damage her own credibility. In an ideal world the trial lawyer would be able to refute or explain away every one of the opponent's points. In the real world, the lawyer does the best she can.

Defendant's Counsel. Ms. Mercer has told us that she saw the body of the man in the hat illuminated in the head-

---

[1] Bad habits can be unconsciously perpetuated and can cause real irritation to a judge.

lights of the car for a split second as the car went up on
the sidewalk just before it went to the right of the tree.
We do not contest that. But that also does not mean that
Mr. Maxfield, who was down behind the wheel of that
car as it lurched up on the sidewalk, could see that body.
After all, Ms. Mercer knew the body was there, where it
had fallen in the darkness before Mr. Maxfield even left
the driveway. . . .

By refraining from arguing implausible positions, the trial lawyer gives the remainder of her argument added credibility.

> *Counsel for the state.*   We are not going to argue to you that
> Mr. Savage was standing when the defendant ran him
> down with his car. Even though that is the way Jerry Ral-
> ston thinks it happened, we suggest that the testimony of
> Ms. Mercer and the condition of the front of the car make
> it plain that Mr. Savage was lying on the sidewalk when
> Mr. Maxfield ran over him. We suggest that Ms. Mercer
> was also right when she told us that the body of Mr. Sav-
> age, lying there on the sidewalk, was perfectly illuminated
> by Mr. Maxfield's headlights as he drove down the street
> and up on the sidewalk.

Note that the prosecutor has slightly overstated the witness's
testimony. The witness testified that the body was illuminated
for "a few seconds" as the car left the street and mounted
the sidewalk. Is it fair comment in summation to suggest that
she testified that the body was illuminated "as he drove down
the street"? When referring to witness testimony, it is improper
to go beyond what the witness actually said and "improve"
upon it.

> *Opposing Counsel.*   Objection, Your Honor. Ms. Mercer
> never said that anybody was visible as Mr. Maxfield
> "drove down the street."

Unfortunately, policing such lapses is often impossible. The
judge herself does not always recall the precise words of the witness that were the subject of the misquotation.

> *The Court.*   Overruled. The jury will recall what the witness
> said. Members of the jury, it is your recollections of what
> the witnesses said and not what counsel says in summation
> that govern in this case.

It is also important when arguing against the opponent's image
that the trial lawyer not subconsciously "buy into" the opponent's
image. Sometimes by disputing a detail of the opponent's argument a lawyer can appear to have accepted the greater premise. It
is even possible to make Freudian slips that cause much greater
harm than good.

> *Counsel* (arguing for the prosecution in a murder case).   Mr.
> Maxfield has told us that he does not remember what he
> told Officer Groves right after the accident. But doesn't it
> make sense that he must have said something? And who
> knows better what he said than the man he said it to?

The prosecutor may not even notice that he referred to the alleged
murder as "the accident." Although there may be no visible reaction to such a slip, the subconscious message can be devastating to
the sender.

Sometimes final argument can be used to suggest that evidence
offered for a particular inference by the other side can also be
considered in an entirely different sense.

> *Counsel.* The prosecution has mentioned some statements
> that the Officer Groves says Mr. Maxfield made when he
> was stopped. If you find that Mr. Maxfield actually made
> those statements, were they some kind of acknowledgment
> of guilt? Ladies and Gentlemen, wouldn't these statements
> be the kind of thing that any motorist would really in fact
> say if he had done something foolish like running up on the
> curb?
>
> If Mr. Maxfield had really just run over someone and
> killed them, do you think he would have called it "some-
> thing foolish"?
>
> If Mr. Maxfield really said those things, don't they
> sound more like the kind of a justification that any motor-
> ist would give if he was about to be given a ticket for a

driving violation? "Something foolish" is not the confession of a murderer conscious of his guilt.

Sometimes the opponent will fail to point out a weak point in the other lawyer's case. This does not mean that the lawyer should sit back and assume that the weak point will not be noticed by the factfinders. In planning final argument the trial lawyer should try to anticipate every question that a skeptical factfinder would ask about the image the lawyer is presenting. The argument should then be structured to meet those potential questions, regardless of whether the opponent raises them. There is no opportunity to address these questions or shore up weak points in the case once the factfinders have retired.

> Counsel.   You may recall that some of the witnesses said that they did not see any brake lights when Mr. Maxfield jerked his car to the right to avoid the tree. But is that all that unusual? Sometimes things happen so fast that the driver doesn't have the chance to put on the brakes. All he can do is jerk the wheel, as Mr. Maxfield did in this case.

L.   Discussing the Law in Summation

Another use of final argument is to discuss with the factfinders the manner in which they are to apply to the facts the law that they will receive from the court in its instructions. The law itself, its policy and construction, are not appropriate for argument. What is appropriate is to discuss how the law applies to the fact pictures to be created.

In discussing the law, however, counsel should make it clear that the source of the law is the court, not counsel's argument.

> Counsel.   As the Court will tell you in a few minutes in the instructions, Mr. Maxfield is not guilty of murder in this case, unless and until each and every one of you believes beyond any reasonable doubt that he intentionally or willfully caused the death of Roscoe Savage.
> Now there is no question in this case that Mr. Max-

field's car caused the death of Roscoe Savage and that Robert Maxfield was driving at the time. The issue, however, is whether Mr. Maxfield intended to hit the decedent with his car, or whether he even saw the decedent before his car hit him.

When the rules of law that the court will be explaining to the factfinders in its charge seem to favor one side or the other, the lawyer favored by the law can argue the law to good effect. Also, if the trial lawyer correctly teaches the factfinders the law that the judge ultimately discloses to them, the lawyer's credibility will likely be enhanced in the factfinders' eyes. One legal standard that is frequently argued in summation in criminal cases is the requirement that proof of guilt be beyond any reasonable doubt.

M.   Themes, Patterns, and Symbols

An effective case presentation involves not only a persuasive theory or outline of the main picture. It also includes subsidiary themes or motifs that illuminate the presentation or motivate the factfinders to accept it. Patterns of physical objects, events, or behavior are also powerful elements in the presentation process. People recognize recurring themes that tend to mutually reinforce themselves with repetition. Simple visual symbols of complex images and ideas are quickly recognized by the factfinders and affect their perceptions both consciously and subconsciously. The effectiveness of themes, patterns, and symbols often lies in their recurrence at various times during the trial. When planning final argument, counsel should weave in any themes, patterns, or symbols that have been used during the presentation. The trial lawyer who sees the light of recognition in the factfinders' eyes at repetition of the thematic phrase will become a strong convert to the use of thematic material in presenting cases.

An apt term or descriptive phrase used during opening statement and repeated during testimony by a witness, during cross-examination of opposition witnesses, and once again during the summation can become thematic in the case. Or the theme may be more complex:

Counsel. . . . he took the law into his own hands and made himself into the judge, the jury, and the executioner.

The theme may be merely an orientation of the presentation. For instance, a murder case tried in a blue-collar community might center around the theme of a hapless lower-class victim run down by a privileged defendant.

While sometimes the themes are part of the oral presentation, often they can also be reflected by visual aids or exhibits. If the lawyer uses the same visual aid in opening, during the testimony of witnesses on both direct and cross-examination, and again in closing, that visual aid becomes thematic in the case. Carefully chosen themes that point to the desired result can be powerful tools in trial advocacy.

N. Expressions of the Lawyer's Personal Beliefs

In closing argument, as in every other part of the trial, the trial lawyer should demonstrate a commitment to the rightness of her cause and the accuracy of her fact presentation. If she does not appear to be convinced of the truth of what she is presenting, it is very unlikely that she can convince the factfinders. This conviction can be expressed by directness of glance, tone of voice, forceful argument of favorable inferences, and overall demeanor in conducting the trial. However, the lawyer is not permitted to express her own belief as to any issue to the factfinders directly in words:

Counsel. I believe that Mr. Maxfield is not guilty.

and

Counsel. I think you will come to the same conclusion that I have that Mr. Maxfield should not be permitted to get away with this . . .

are both improper.

Opposing Counsel.   Objection. Counsel is expressing personal belief.

The Court.   Sustained. Members of the jury, you are to disregard the prosecutor's last remarks. Counsel is not permitted to express to you her belief in the guilt or innocence of
the defendant. That is for you to decide, based on all the
evidence.

Nor may the lawyer express a personal belief in the credibility of
any witness:

Counsel.   You won't believe Jerry Ralston any more than I do.

The rationale behind this prohibition is to avoid putting the
personal credibility of the lawyer on trial. In that sense it is a little
artificial. Factfinders do not leave their common sense at home
when they come to court. There is no question that the lawyer's
evident belief in the strength of her own position can be an important element to the factfinders as they appraise the strength or
weakness of that position themselves.

O.   Order of Summation

The order of final argument is frequently important to the structure of the presentation. In most jurisdictions the party with the
burden of proof has the right to the last word with the factfinders. Traditionally, in both civil and criminal cases, the defense
argued first, followed by the prosecution. There would be no
rebuttal. More recently it has become customary in many courts
for the prosecution to give the first summation, with the defense
to follow. The prosecution then has the final word via a brief
rebuttal.

The modern method is preferred by many because the argument
is usually better structured to follow the pattern of effort at trial.
The party with the burden of proof (usually plaintiff or prosecution) will do most of the affirmative work of creating the trial
image. The defense often is focused on destroying or undermining
what the prosecution or plaintiff have tried to create. If the defense

is required to go first, it is put in the position of trying to attack an image before the finishing touches have been put on it. This may result in argument that is unnecessary or that misses the point. If the party having the burden of proof goes first, the defense argument can be directed at the actual image on which the initial party is relying, rather than on a prediction of it.

The party with the opportunity for the last word has a slight advantage in terms of being able to rebut the arguments of the other side without having to undergo further rebuttal. Sometimes the opposing counsel may try to enlist the factfinders to rebut arguments that she will not be permitted to do:

> *Defense Counsel.*   Ladies and Gentlemen, this is my last opportunity to talk with you. But my opponent, as the prosecution, will have the opportunity of rebuttal. He will be able to make arguments to you that I will not be allowed to get up and rebut.
>
> All that I can tell you is that for each and every argument that he may present in his rebuttal there is an answer. But you will have to find that answer for yourselves. Bob Maxfield and I can only ask you, as you listen to the prosecution's argument, to stand in my place and think to yourselves, "What would Mr. Hartwell have said to that argument?"

P.   Anecdotes and Analogies

Sometimes anecdotes and analogies from history, literature, current culture, or folklore are good ways to illustrate points on summation. They are also entertaining and can engender good feeling between factfinders and lawyer. On the other hand, anecdotes can backfire if they are seen as attempts to evade the issues on trial or to condescend to the jury.

The rules of court procedure give broad latitude to the trial lawyer as storyteller as long as the story or analogy has something to do with the issues in the case.

> Listening to the state's evidence in this case reminds me of a time when I was a little boy living in the country. My mother used to

make wonderful sugar cookies—you know, the kind that are big and white and round and all covered with white sugar. In those days she would make them and put them away for supper in the cookie jar. And whenever she would make them, at some point when she wasn't around or wasn't looking, you know, I would go in there, ever so quietly, tip toe, tip toe,—and snitch one of those sugar cookies. I would sneak in and grab it out of the jar and run off with it. Boy, would it taste good!

But you know, my mother would always find out. I never knew how she found out. But somehow she always knew! And she would always punish me.

Years later, after I had moved away from home and became a lawyer, I asked my mother one day, "Mother," I said, "when I was a little boy and used to snitch those sugar cookies, how did you always know that I done it?"

And I remember how my mother smiled and said "Oh, yes, my son, I always did know when you had snitched one of my sugar cookies. I knew when you had snitched one of my sugar cookies because of the sugar on the floor.—I could feel it crunching under my feet when I came back into the kitchen."

That's what you will find, as you listen to the prosecution's case, as you talk in the jury room—sugar on the floor![2]

The foregoing story calls the factfinders' attention to potential clues or inconsistencies in the opposing case and suggests that these inconsistencies mean that the case is not all that it seems to be.

Another anecdote might appeal more to the factfinders' fundamental sense of justice and remind them of their direct responsibility for the outcome of the case:

Members of the jury, this case reminds me of a story I heard many years ago, about a wise old man who lived in the forest. And this wise old man who lived in the forest, he loved all living things, the animals, the birds, even the insects and the snakes.

One day, my friends, there came to the forest a smart-alecky young man. And he said to himself, "I'll show this old man. . . . We'll see if he is so wise." He caught a small bird and cupped it in

[2] This story is attributed to Eugene Pincham, of Chicago, one of America's great trial lawyers and teachers of trial lawyers, who used it to great effect with juries during his career as a defense lawyer and with students and lawyers during countless demonstrations at the National Institute of Trial Advocacy and at law school trial advocacy programs.

his hand. And the little bird was there in his hand, trembling, frightened [demonstrating cupped closed hands].

And the young man went to the wise old man with the bird in his hand and said, "Old man, old man, if you are so wise, you tell me. . . . I have a bird in my hand. You tell me if it is alive . . . or if it is dead." And the smart-alecky young man thought he would win in any case. If the old man said, "It is dead," he would open his hands [demonstrating], and the bird would fly away. And if the old man said "It is alive," he would squeeze his hands together [demonstrating] and drop the bird dead at his feet. He couldn't lose!

But the old man shook his head sadly and said, "Oh, my son, oh, my son. . . . The bird is neither alive nor dead. The life of the bird is in your hands." [3]

Members of the Jury, the life of Bob Maxfield is in your hands.

---

[3] This story was used by Gerry Spence, of Jackson Hole, Wyoming, another great American trial lawyer, both in actual trials and in trial advocacy demonstrations.

Index

References are to page numbers.